EVELYN WAUGH

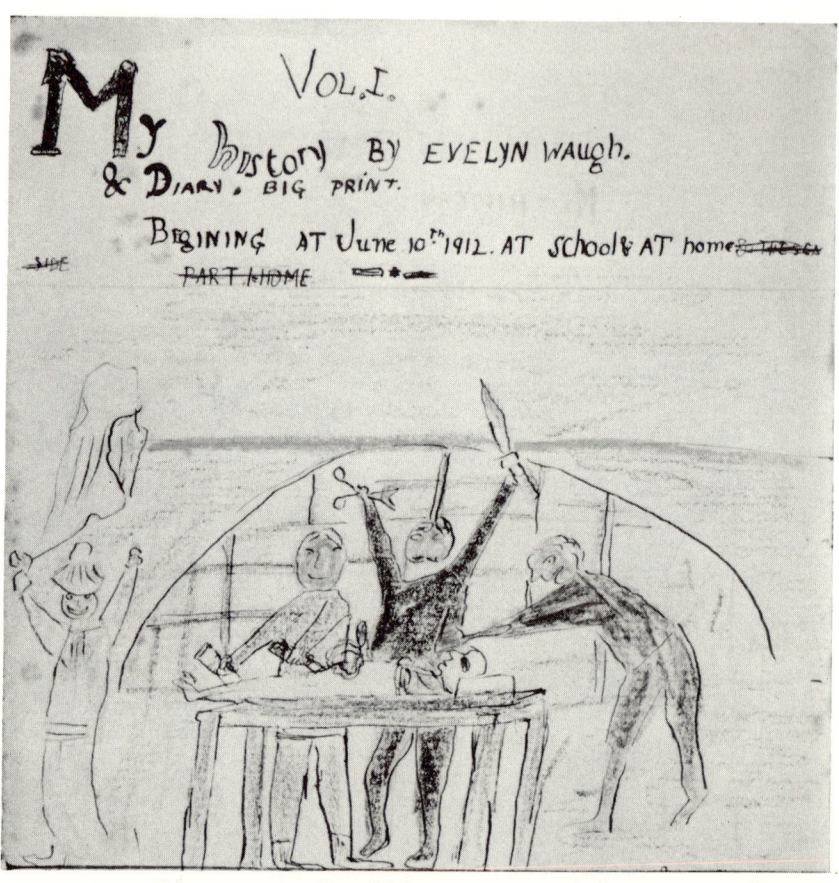

Cover of the second installment in the diaries of Evelyn Waugh. Depicting his appendectomy at age eight, the drawing is an early example of Waugh's tendency to portray himself as a victim. The figure on the far left seems to have been on the wall of Waugh's nursery; in Waugh's picture, the clown mocks the surgeon. The identity of the other two figures is uncertain, though they resemble Waugh's parents, father on the left, mother on the right. It looks as if the boy is about to be castrated. Courtesy of the Harry Ransom Humanities Research Center, The University of Texas at Austin.

EVELYN WAUGH

A Literary Biography,
1903–1924

John Howard Wilson

Madison • Teaneck
Fairleigh Dickinson University Press
London: Associated University Presses

© 1996 by Associated University Presses, Inc.

All rights reserved. Authorization to photocopy items for internal or personal use, or the internal or personal use of specific clients, is granted by the copyright owner, provided that a base fee of $10.00, plus eight cents per page, per copy is paid directly to the Copyright Clearance Center, 222 Rosewood Drive, Danvers, Massachusetts 01923. [0-8386-3670-5/96 $10.00+8¢ pp, pc.]

Associated University Presses
440 Forsgate Drive
Cranbury, NJ 08512

Associated University Presses
16 Barter Street
London WC1A 2AH, England

Associated University Presses
P.O. Box 338, Port Credit
Mississauga, Ontario
Canada L5G 4L8

The paper used in this publication meets the requirements of the American National Standard for Permanence of Paper for Printed Library Materials Z39.48–1984.

Library of Congress Cataloging-in-Publication Data

Wilson, John Howard, 1961–
    Evelyn Waugh : a literary biography, 1903–1924 / John Howard Wilson.
      p. cm.
    Includes bibliographical references (p.   ) and index.
    ISBN 0-8386-3670-5 (alk. paper)
    1. Waugh, Evelyn, 1903–1966. 2. Authors, English—20th century—Biography. I. Title.
PR6045.A97Z498   1996
823'.912—dc20
[B]
                                                               96-5275
                                                                 CIP

PRINTED IN THE UNITED STATES OF AMERICA

*In memory of my father,
Jack Wilson
1920–1993*

Contents

List of Abbreviations	9
Preface	11
Acknowledgments	13
1. Not at Home in Hampstead, 1903–1916	17
2. A Less Important Place than Eton, 1917–1920	43
3. Limited Bolshevist, 1920–1921 and After	71
4. *Et in Arcadia Ego,* 1922–1924	105
5. Oxford Revisited, 1924 and After	141
6. Spirals of Self-Discovery	176
Notes	180
Bibliography	186
Index	191

Abbreviations

ALL	*A Little Learning*, 1964
ALO	*A Little Order*, 1977
BM	*Black Mischief*, 1932
BR	*Brideshead Revisited*, 1945
CRS	*Charles Ryder's Schooldays and Other Stories*, 1982
DEW	*The Diaries of Evelyn Waugh*, 1976
DF	*Decline and Fall*, 1928
DIM	"Dominus Illuminatio Mea," MS, HRHRC
EAR	*The Essays, Articles and Reviews of Evelyn Waugh*, 1983
EWA	*Evelyn Waugh, Apprentice*, 1985
FS	"Father and Son," MS, HRHRC
HRHRC	The Harry Ransom Humanities Research Center, The University of Texas at Austin
L	*Labels*, 1930
LEW	*The Letters of Evelyn Waugh*, 1980
R	*Rossetti*, 1928
RK	*The Life of the Right Reverend Ronald Knox*, 1959
TB	"The Balance," 1927
US	*Unconditional Surrender*, 1961

Preface

THIS is a literary biography focusing on the first third of Evelyn Waugh's life; I hope to devote two more volumes to the other two-thirds. More conventional biographies have already been written by Christopher Sykes, Martin Stannard, and Selina Hastings, and I have not tried to reproduce the enormous detail of their imposing books. I have, instead, concentrated on the delicate relationship between Waugh's life and his writing, reviewing childhood and education with one eye on the works that came out of them, and trying to describe circumstances that inspired juvenilia. Most stories I have attributed to the influence of some person, event, or attitude, but I have also suggested thematic continuity between early efforts and later work. Though some lasting interests appear very early, Waugh's writing developed as he grew, and I have tried to show how change and experience impelled him to introduce new themes as he modified old ones. I have thus used literature as a kind of evidence for biography, avoiding strictly literary interpretations in order to portray Waugh's writing as a direct response to life. "Oxford Revisited" goes past the biographical limits I have had to set, examining Waugh's use of experience at Oxford in later writing. The book combines literature and biography, charting reverberations of early experience in the writings of a lifetime.

Waugh used much experience in his fiction, but he also distorted experience in certain ways. I have tried to explain why. I have also asked how and why Waugh represents himself in his heroes. To indicate the difference between representation and real life, I have compared Waugh's fiction to his autobiography, diaries, and letters, recollections of friends and family, and findings of biographers. I have not been deterred by the notion that it is intellectually unsound to compare literature and life. The two are obviously connected, and the more clearly we understand the connection, the more fully we can appreciate both the work and the writer. In Waugh's case, an abundance of biographical material complements and elucidates the finished fiction. Waugh's youth yielded relatively few documents—a schoolboy diary, a handful of letters, and an assortment of poems, plays, and stories—but they nevertheless bring to life an extraordinarily clever, calculating boy, who grew up as he grew apart, isolating himself in order to create, but also articulating different sides of a complicated personality. Different sides animated many characters in Waugh's early work, as he began to discover and to project conflicts within himself. Inner conflicts generated fiction throughout Waugh's life, and his mature work reached remarkable depth largely because initial descents had started so early and had gone so far, years before he finished his first novel.

Acknowledgments

THIS book owes much to others' encouragement. Enoch Brater awarded the fellowship that started the research and writing. James A. Winn supported work in the summer and created the C. A. Patrides Memorial Fellowships, one of which minimized distractions during winter term 1988. The Horace H. Rackham School of Graduate Studies at the University of Michigan extended a dissertation grant to study manuscripts at the Harry Ransom Humanities Research Center, the University of Texas at Austin. There I was hosted by George Zemlicka and helped by Cathy Henderson, Ken Craven, and Mary Ellen McNamara. Cynthia Farar microfilmed and mailed stories and diaries. Janet Pennington sent information and photographs from Lancing College. Mark Amory, Michael Davie, Robert Murray Davis, and Donat Gallagher edited reams of material I would not have otherwise seen. Critical work by Jeffrey Heath has been illuminating.

Quotations from the works of Evelyn Waugh are reprinted by permission of the Peters Fraser & Dunlop Group Ltd. Quotations from *The Diaries of Evelyn Waugh,* copyright © 1976 by the Estate of Evelyn Waugh, are reprinted by permission of Little, Brown and Company. Quotations from *Brideshead Revisited* by Evelyn Waugh, copyright © 1944, 1945 by Evelyn Waugh, renewed 1972, 1973 by Mrs. Laura Waugh, are also reprinted by permission of Little, Brown and Company. Quotations from *Oxford in the Twenties* by Christopher Hollis, published by William Heinemann Ltd., are reprinted by permission of Reed Consumer Books. Paul Doyle allowed me to use parts of essays that appeared in *Evelyn Waugh Newsletter and Studies.* Paul Neumarkt allowed me to use an essay that appeared in the *Journal of Evolutionary Psychology.* Joseph Blotner, Hubert English, and Raymond Grew read early versions and made many valuable suggestions. The late James Gindin read my work several times in various forms and posed questions that led past my reading and preoccupations. The preoccupation of scholarship stems from my parents, who have supported me in many ways through life. My mother will have to settle for an expression of love and thanks seldom given to my father. Guides have saved me from many mistakes; any that remain are entirely my own.

EVELYN WAUGH

1
Not at Home in Hampstead, 1903–1916

LOOKING back on his life at age sixty, Evelyn Waugh remembered childhood love of his aunts' house at Midsomer Norton, near Bath. He was "instinctively drawn to the ethos" he saw as "mid-Victorian," an ethos belonging to an age that he "instinctively, even then, recognised as superior" to his own.[1] Waugh's emphasis on instinctive love of the past obscures instinctive distaste for the present. The Victorian age was not much better than the modern period, replete with its own problems, inconsistencies, and uncertainties. It could seem superior only to a sensibility like Waugh's, deeply alienated from his own world. Alienation is obvious in Waugh's later life, when he retreated to the country, grew despondent over changes in the Roman Catholic Church, and took small comfort in how he offended friends and visitors. Alienation is evident even in childhood, a happy time according to the autobiography, where Waugh asserts that it is the "common fate" of all exiles to "have been born into a world of beauty, to die amid ugliness" (*ALL* 33). Fifty years separated the author from the experience he described, and evidence indicates that Waugh did not regard childhood as beautiful when he was going through it. Even then he had been drawn to a past perceived as superior, and he was also eager to criticize the present. These inclinations became characteristic of his life's work, which often satirizes present foibles, implicitly or explicitly pointing to the superiority of the past. The same attitudes are evident in Waugh's juvenilia, indicating both the extent of his alienation at an early age and the importance of writing in dealing with it. Writing enabled Waugh to articulate what was wrong with a world he found hard to accept, leading to self-assurance that proved indispensable in maintaining his balance against recurring onslaughts of insecurity and paranoia. These defenses were formed in Waugh's childhood and adolescence, when he overcame a number of physical, emotional, and intellectual difficulties, and in doing so developed ways of thinking that shaped the art of his maturity.

The chief disturbance in Waugh's infancy was his brother Alec, five years old when Evelyn was born on 28 October 1903. The family lived in a small house in West Hampstead, northwest of central London, and Alec was the only other child. Boisterous and demanding, Alec was obsessed with cricket to the point of playing in the nursery, pretending that chairs were fielders and bouncing tennis balls all over the room. Often they landed in his brother's crib, which had to be protected with a net. Alec had hoped that his new brother might grow up to be a wicket-keeper,[2] but Evelyn never showed any interest in living up to this expectation. Alec was always Arthur Waugh's favorite son, and Evelyn soon noticed his father's preference. According to Martin Stannard, "Evelyn apparently felt, from first becoming conscious of the situation, that there was something of a conspiracy between his father and Alec to make him appear foolish,"[3] though Alec and Arthur's intentions are less clear than Evelyn's emerging sense of himself as a victim of discrimination. Sometimes he felt persecuted, running to a favorite chair of his mother's and shouting "Sanctuary!" whenever he felt threatened by Arthur or Alec. Sometimes he questioned the fairness of his parents. Once he noted that his father preferred Alec and asked his mother if she, in turn, preferred him. When his mother said that she loved both sons the same, Evelyn observed that he was "lacking in love." Alec remembered returning from prep school when Evelyn was six. Arthur displayed a large sign welcoming "the heir of Underhill" back to the family's house in North End Village, still part of Hampstead, where they had moved in 1907, seeking more space. Evelyn wondered "When Alec has Underhill and all this in it, what will be left for me?" Arthur "never put up the notice again."[4]

Sometimes Evelyn's grievance against father and brother led to open hostility. A mother in the neighborhood thought Evelyn was an only child, but she soon learned from her own child that Evelyn had a "brother at school whom he hates" (*ALL* 60). At age four or five, Evelyn became angry with his father when, after a "long and fully indulged morning at Hampstead Heath Fair," Arthur tried to take Evelyn home to lunch. Evelyn "rolled in the sandy path abusing him as: 'You brute, you beast, you hideous ass'" (*ALL* 29). Evelyn compensated for estrangement from Arthur and Alec by attaching himself to his nurse, Lucy, and his mother, Catherine. Evelyn's first memories of his father are of an "interloper" who sent his son to the nursery and separated him from his mother.[5] Family life was already beginning to disappoint him, and at an early age he began to develop interests other than his father, mother, and brother.

These interests were diverse and apparently ordinary, but they anticipate traits more obvious in Waugh's mature personality. He was, like most boys of his age, fascinated by stories of sensational crimes. More unusual is Waugh's lamenting the absence of connection to such crime, which might have made his family, and himself, more interesting. Another boy had had an "enviable experience," when his nanny had been murdered in his nursery in India. Though he agreed never to mention the murder for fear of upsetting the boy, Waugh thought he would have been proud of such an experience (*ALL* 51). His father's work as a publisher, and thus his own background, seemed pedestrian by contrast, and even at age seven he thought the offices of Chapman and Hall looked like an "offely dull plase." Perhaps contrasting the publishing house with a place of greater appeal, Evelyn noted that he was going to church.[6] Evelyn decided later that Arthur's "sedentary and cerebral occupations" had seemed "ignominious" during his childhood. He would have "better respected a soldier or sailor" like his uncles. Arthur's dullness became a handicap, which Evelyn felt impelled to overcome through self-conscious brilliance. After a lifetime of consideration, he changed his opinion, no longer regarding Arthur as "somewhat humdrum," feeling grateful for the "warm stability he created" (*ALL* 63, 79). Stability did not interest Evelyn as a child, and, conscious of appearance even then, he saw his father as a social liability that might detract from his own appeal.

Evelyn's distaste for his father extended to his father's friends. He remembered meeting Edmund Gosse at age eight or nine. Gosse asked where Evelyn carried his "bare knees." Waugh said, "*They* carry *me* wherever I want to go." Gosse envied the "confidence of youth" and the ability to "envisage an attainable destination," while Waugh found him "absurd and offensive." Waugh was already being critical when he might have made relations easier by being deferential, perhaps because he disliked Gosse for reasons other than his patronizing manner. Gosse seemed to embody everything "ignoble in the profession of letters," especially in his "sedulous pursuit of the eminent." Gosse was also "drab," whereas Waugh was "drawn to panache." He compared Gosse to Mr. Tulkinghorn, the "soft-footed, inconspicuous, ill-natured habitue of the great world" in *Bleak House,* and Waugh "longed for a demented lady's-maid to make an end of him" (*ALL* 65–66). Literary imagination is evident here, along with the cruelty of early novels, though Waugh described this relationship at the end of his career.

More suggestive in the interpretation of youthful character is his apparent awareness of social climbing. Like many socially insecure people, Waugh tried to climb himself, but he disliked anyone who seemed to be doing the same thing.

Uncomfortable at home with immediate family, Waugh soon became interested in other, more congenial surroundings, especially his aunts' house at Midsomer Norton. As an example of the mid-Victorian ethos, the house was largely a vestige of the past. It had deteriorated by the time Waugh visited, but he "relished" the "decay" (*ALL* 53). The present's inability to sustain accomplishments of the past may well have stimulated lifelong interest in entropy and the fragility of civilization, explored in many novels and travel books. Inexorable movement from past to present seemed to be part of the house, partly because, he noticed as a child, "people had died there." The house also offered the ballad of Lord Randal, sung by Aunt Connie, and Waugh "repeatedly demanded it." Her version introduced him to betrayal, a preoccupation in his fiction, as Aunt Connie made it clear that Lord Randal had died at the hands of his "true love." Suffering of innocents is another recurring theme in Waugh's fiction: in "Lord Randal" he was moved by the death of the dogs. After the ballad he would go to bed, "genuinely but delightfully frightened," already recognizing some of the emotions that would propel much of his writing (*ALL* 44, 46).

Midsomer Norton was also attractive because Waugh found at least one resident more worthy of emulation than either his father or brother. Of Arthur's three sisters, Aunt Elsie was his favorite, perhaps because she was, like him, "selfish, capricious and sharp tongued"; perhaps because she became an invalid, presenting herself as a martyr, as her nephew often presented himself. Waugh also realized that Elsie was least conventional of the three, the only one to show "tolerance for very slightly indelicate fiction." Each sister led a Bible class on Sunday afternoons, beginning and ending with a hymn. Waugh noticed that the "singing always began last and finished first in the drawing-room," where Elsie was in charge. After a few years Elsie's group merged with Aunt Connie's, and Elsie went back to her novels (*ALL* 49–50).

Midsomer Norton was above all a refuge from Arthur's more modern house in North End Village. His sisters' house offered "dark and musty seclusions" where Evelyn could hide like an "animal preparing to whelp." He sought the same seclusions at his father's house, attracted to an overgrown garden behind the greenhouses. Waugh thought his time there had made him vulnerable to the "common English confusion of the antiquated with the sublime," which had "remained with [him]." Once he got into a cupboard and dug a hole, so that he could crawl under the floor (*ALL* 44). Waugh found it hard to accept the world and the people in it, and at an early age, probably before he even knew what he was doing, he began to withdraw, preferring privacy and fantasy. In later years he considered withdrawal an essential part of writing, isolating himself at the quiet hotel at Chagford or, more simply, in his own library, after insisting that the children be kept quiet.

Midsomer Norton remained an alternative. During the Second World War, when he was with the British Military Mission in Yugoslavia, Waugh thought he might keep his aunts' house as a "working studio" (*DEW* 583). Though the plan never materialized, Waugh explained it in a letter to his wife, imagining a "secret house to which no guests would come." He hoped to restore the rooms to the "splendid state" of 1870, perhaps leaving the house as a "public museum & memorial" to himself.[7] A month earlier he had been "rejoicing in the mass of vine" outside his bedroom window, enjoying the "light coming through the leaves." After thinking about it, Waugh realized that it reminded him of the "light through the vine that used to hang round the smoking-room verandah" at Midsomer Norton (*DEW* 581). The last of the sisters, Aunt Elsie, died in 1953, and the house was to be sold shortly thereafter. Waugh paid his "final visit . . . without emotion," gathering a "few objects and papers" (*DEW* 718).

Even as he withdrew, Waugh wanted to make his mark on the world, to show that he had been there. At Ivy House, near Underhill, Waugh wrote his initials in wet cement and went back to find them fifty years later, unfortunately "somewhat eroded, so that they read 'FW.'" Urge to document his presence also surfaced at Midsomer Norton, where, in the stable-loft, Waugh recorded his visits in scratches on the beams. Sometimes he demonstrated his presence more directly, through magic shows that were "very tedious" to those he was "constantly attempting to mystify," especially since he "composed a facetious patter in imitation of . . . professionals." Perhaps Waugh was attracted to magic's defiance of conventional explanation; certainly he was ready to show off, to exhibit competence and intelligence in front of others. Performances forced him to confront fear of being belittled, a fear he seems never to have lost. A show at Midsomer Norton was devastating. Waugh borrowed a hat for part of his act and asked the owner if there were any holes in it. The answer was yes, the hole he put his head in (*ALL* 39, 53, 61). Embarrassment was acutely painful to Waugh, who liked to imagine himself in control of every social crisis. It often drove him into seclusion, but sense of his own importance was always enough to lead him back out again. He consistently felt impelled to attract others' notice, through magic shows, through leaving initials, or, later, through novels and autobiography.

Successful public presentation depends on the good will of the audience and the absence of malice. Even in childhood, Waugh suspected that others were somehow intent on injuring his feelings and reputation. In *A Little Learning* he remembered a neighbor, an "aged misanthrope" with whom his family had "no communication except by letters of complaint about trespasses" of Evelyn's. Waugh sometimes intruded on her meadow, "usually with the innocent purpose of retrieving a ball" (*ALL* 36), her objections seeming ill-natured and unreasonable. He also remembered pain caused by others' incompetence. A pet rabbit with cancer went to the veterinarian "to be killed," and Waugh was "reconciled to its loss." The doctor tried surgery and thought he had solved the problem. Waugh was overjoyed when the rabbit reappeared, but the animal died that night (*ALL* 29). Waugh's cousin Claud Cockburn remembered his first meeting with Evelyn, when he noticed an "eager, challenging, yet bewildered stare," seeming to belong to a boy who had just been told that his "pet rabbit has been lost, but that . . . there is a pirate's cave full of treasure somewhere in the garden if one can only find it."[8] This mixture of despair and hope, this disappointment in one thing offset by enthusiasm for another, recurs throughout Waugh's life and fiction. He deeply resented people like the incompetent vet, who seemed to destroy his hope deliberately, but he was usually willing to trust someone else, only to be disillusioned again.

As a child, Waugh was misled in other ways, sometimes intentionally. One of the autobiography's recurring themes is the difference between the truth and what Waugh was told. He repeatedly corrects childish misapprehensions, as if he resented deception because ignorance might have exposed him to ridicule. He remembered that he could not buy ice cream during Hampstead's Fair Days. With the suggestion of "something very obnoxious," he was told that the "Italians kept the mixture under their beds." Waugh had "a pot" under his bed, and he concluded that ice cream consisted of urine (*ALL* 42). He also remembered walking past a "fallen tree named 'the gibbet elm'. Highwaymen had been hanged on it," he was told; "falsely," he had since learned. Instead, the tree was only the marker of an execution that had taken place in

1: Not at Home in Hampstead, 1903–1916   23

1673. Even at Midsomer Norton, Waugh fell victim to misrepresentation. His aunts had a silver bowl, supposedly one of a kind, yet Waugh later learned that a local silversmith had made a large number of copies (*ALL* 40, 48). Waugh's insecurity and high standards impelled him to strive for perfection, and he held a grudge against anyone who, innocently or otherwise, blocked his way. Heroes in the novels are hindered in various ways, vulnerable to lies, malice, and incompetence, and throughout life Waugh pondered how innocence had made him vulnerable to the same things.

Other early interests included writing and drawing. The earliest of Waugh's drawings date from 1908. Though they look like any other four-year-old's pictures, someone, probably a parent, has attributed them to Evelyn and has supplied the ages of four years, nine months and four years, eleven months (HRHRC). Precise ages show how serious the Waughs were about the development of their children; presumably they encouraged Evelyn to keep a diary and preserve juvenilia. Another survivor is "The Curse of the Horse Race," his first story, written in 1910. Waugh thought it the only one of his early stories to show "imagination." He very violently depicts the undoing of a gambler and enjoins the reader "never to bet." In later years Waugh thought the moral must have come from his pious nurse, dismissing the plot as "imitative of the worst" of his reading (*ALL* 62). The story is, however, more than just a derivation of her lessons and boys' magazines. Its overt didacticism stems from the author's conviction that, even at a very young age, he had something worth saying to his audience. "The Curse of the Horse Race" includes four drawings of the action, as Waugh combined two interests in one of the experiments that led to *Decline and Fall: An Illustrated Novellette* (1928).

A more complicated story, "Fidon's Confetion," seems to have been written sometime between 1910 and 1914. Like "The Curse of the Horse Race," "Fidon's Confetion" conveys a moral lesson, as an older son named Ralfe is "in debt to a villainous money lender." Ralfe tries "gambling in a great efort to 'raise the wind,'" but he keeps losing to a man named Baycraw. Ralfe's brother Tom tells him to give up, but Ralfe says, "Get off to bed youngster," and Tom leaves with "despair in his heart." The characters are clearly based on Alec and Evelyn Waugh. Gambling doesn't seem to have been one of Alec's vices, but Evelyn used it to explain his brother's impatience and his own inability to understand Alec's concerns. Baycraw (sometimes "Braycaw") and an accomplice named Fidon murder the brothers' father with Ralfe's knife, avenging earlier identification of them as bank robbers. Baycraw blames the murder on Ralfe, who is "heir to all his father's property and money." These seem to be considerable: Waugh refers to the "spaceous hall of Cantonville Chase," the first of the grand houses that became a feature of his fiction. He also seems to have been remembering Arthur's sign for the heir of Underhill. Fidon confesses to Tom, but Baycraw kills Fidon and steals the transcript. Through superhuman effort, Tom retrieves the confession and hurries to Ralfe's trial: "suddenly there staggered into the room a young man his colar undone his tie twisted and blood on his face a bandage round his head."[9] Tom's intervention saves Ralfe and prevents miscarriage of justice, but more personally Evelyn was suggesting how valuable he could be to Alec. "Fidon's Confetion" also presents three illustrations of scenes described in the text.

Clearly Waugh was still looking for more effective ways to express moral views through fiction, and he was beginning to express his views through other means as well. About 1912 Arthur gave a garden party, and after most guests had left the lawn, "he traced them to the day-nursery. Evelyn was holding their attention with an impassioned speech about the injustices of what is now called male chauvinism and the need to secure votes for women before the next General Election."[10] The speech shows surprising self-confidence and, along with the stories, suggests that Evelyn was trying to prove he was worth listening to, even if Arthur and Alec seemed indifferent to his existence. The speech is also an early example of Evelyn's attraction to the less popular side of a question, a tendency to oppose general or received opinion on any social or intellectual issue. In youth it is especially evident in arguments before the Lancing College Debating Society and the Oxford Union.

More childhood energy went into writing than debating, and in 1911, just before his eighth birthday, Waugh started a project that would occupy him irregularly for the rest of his life. He wrote "My History" on a piece of paper, drawing "Mr Coopers Classroom" underneath and commenting briefly on school and family. Already disenchanted with teachers, Waugh noted that they all hated Mr. Cooper, their teacher in arithmetic. The picture shows a clownish figure waving a cane over boys at their desks. For many years Waugh illustrated his history, another combination of writing and drawing. Creative impulses behind the novels are clearly evident, but it is at least equally remarkable that a seven-year-old child should think his life already interesting enough to write about. The diary appears to be another assertion of importance in spite of Arthur and Alec's indifference. He did not make another entry until June 1912, when he added "Diary" to the title of "History" and identified the installment as "Vol. I."[11] Stannard thinks Evelyn's attention to volumes and chapters reflects his father's work as a publisher,[12] but it may well reflect something else. Even as a child, Waugh imagined that the diary might be a long project, a life's work, requiring many volumes for completion, as it eventually did. Volume two did not appear until June 1913; Waugh had not intended to start "another number," but he found the old one, and it encouraged him to try again. Early in life Waugh sensed the value of his writing, preserved it, and drew inspiration from it. Fifty years later, he still had his juvenilia, and they refreshed his memory as he wrote his autobiography. After Waugh's death, his manuscripts became available for study at the University of Texas, and large parts of the diaries have been published in a version edited by Michael Davie.

Waugh's other major interest outside family was Heath Mount School, which he first attended in September 1910. Alec had gone to a boarding school, Fernden, in Surrey, but Catherine Waugh thought the place too rough for her younger son, preferring to keep him home as a day-boy. The new regimen began to improve relations between father and son, as Arthur walked Evelyn to school each morning before taking the tube to London. Alec was at Fernden most of the year, and Evelyn began to enjoy his father's stories of criminals and rebellions. Gradually Evelyn overcame early estrangement from Arthur, largely by reconsidering the relationship in several novels and other works, many of them written long after Arthur's death. Studies never excited Waugh, and a few weekly reports from Heath Mount place him in the middle of the pack, occasionally higher. His performance cannot have been helped by relations with the masters, who met resistance typical of Waugh's response to authority. Some rebelliousness was only the self-assertion of a boy who had never been "shouted at or threatened" (*ALL* 82), refusal to submit to verbal and physical abuse common in schools of that time. Sometimes he went beyond self-assertion, deliberately irritating masters in the same way he irritated masters at Lancing, dons at Oxford, and superiors in the military. By 1914 Waugh was feeling sorry about the departure of Mr. Vernon because he "used to rag him so." In 1915 a master called "Dumpy" was wondering if his form's books had been lost or stolen, because Waugh had somehow hidden all the books in the room, and in 1916 Waugh and his friends had the "most gorgeous rags" with a master they called "Water Rat." Waugh found him "almost as funny as Mr Vernon" (*DEW* 8–9).

Waugh could afford to be disruptive partly because he was a day-boy, near parents who could be called upon to intimidate the masters (*ALL* 85). But Waugh was not disruptive just because he was spoiled. He questioned the competence of masters, and he wondered if another school might put his ability to better use. In 1914, though he was settling down at the beginning of the term, his lessons were "awful." The master, Mr. Hynchcliffe, was "obnoxious," partly because he was "slobbering over the unfortunate Spenser who has the bad luck to be the favorite of a man like Hynchcliffe" (Diary HRHRC). Waugh continued to lament the "miseries of school," concluding that Heath Mount was the "worst managed school in England." In 1916 he resented having to change their boots "like a kindergarten" (*DEW* 7–8). Waugh began to regret the time he spent at Heath Mount, and later developments only intensified that feeling. In his autobiography he suggested that he might have won a scholarship to Eton or Winchester, if he had gone to a school that prepared students for the examinations. He also felt that if he had been introduced to the "violence and hardships of school-life," he might have been "less forlorn" when he left home for Lancing (*ALL* 86). He still questioned Heath Mount's reputation, noting that it was supposed to be the best school in the neighborhood, though he never knew why it appealed to parents outside the district since Heath Mount did nothing that was not "being done better in fifty other schools" (*ALL* 80–81).

Choice of the school became another complaint against his parents, especially his father, who had been through the school system and, at least in Evelyn's view, should have known better. Waugh's frustration found expression in cruelty toward both masters and other boys. Cecil Beaton remembered his "first morning at Heath Mount," probably in 1911, when the "bullies, led by a tiny, but fierce Evelyn Waugh, at once spotted their quarry," as a "terrified" Beaton "crept around the outer periphery of the asphalt playground."[13] Waugh explained that tears on Beaton's "long eyelashes used to provoke the sadism of youth," and Beaton was "tormented . . . on the excuse that he was reputed to enjoy his music lessons and to hold in sentimental regard the lady who taught him." Beaton published a volume of diaries in 1961, claiming that Waugh and friends had twisted his arms. Waugh reviewed the book for the *Spectator*, pointing out, as he did in his autobiography, that they had stopped at "sticking pins into him" and had been "soundly beaten for doing so" (*ALL* 90).

Waugh was more than just a bully, however. He never backed away from a fight with someone his own age or even older. The early diaries are in part a record of fights with other boys: in 1913 he fought Geogan, in 1914 he attacked Fletcher, and in 1915 he boxed against Pappenheimer (HRHRC). Belligerence was both an outlet for frustration and a means of protecting himself. He disliked his often feminine Christian name, regarding it as only a "whim" of his mother's. At school he had to "silence ridicule by quoting the precedent of Field-Marshal Sir Evelyn Wood" (*ALL* 27). Almost all secondary sources give his name as Evelyn Arthur St. John Waugh, but the autobiography says he was christened Arthur Evelyn St. John Waugh. Humphrey Carpenter claims that Waugh discovered the correct order only when "he came to write his memoirs, and looked at family papers." By then, even Waugh could not remember how he had come to be known as "Evelyn." Carpenter says that the name prevented "confusion with his father," but if this was the parents' intent, it is hard to see why they chose "Arthur" in the first place. Carpenter also asks if "Evelyn" contains a "hint that Mrs Waugh, already blessed with a son, really wanted a girl."[14] Perhaps she did, but she must have realized that a sexually ambiguous name could not change a biological fact. In 1903, moreover, Arthur and Catherine Waugh were young enough to try having another child, though Catherine was ill and depressed for six weeks after Evelyn's birth.[15] Whatever his parents thought, Waugh never used "Arthur," not even as a substitute for the embarrassing "Evelyn." Did he, even then, wish to dissociate himself from his father by refusing to use Arthur's name? Or did he invite ridicule and contention by insisting on the unconventional "Evelyn"? Hard to tell, especially since the parents' preference often determines the familiar form of a child's name. He never tried St. John either, considering it "more absurd" than Evelyn, the contribution of a "High Church godfather" who wanted his godson to have the name of a saint. Waugh would have preferred "plain John," but he was given the "prefix of sanctity, thus seeming to claim a spurious family connection" (*ALL* 27). He had come to see his name as another kind of disadvantage created by shortsighted parents.

Even "Waugh" was a problem. In 1916 another boy at Heath Mount called him "Wuffles." Waugh threatened "to chastise him" if he did not desist from using the "corrupted form." The other boy was bigger and "continued in the name," Waugh fulfilling his "promise one hundredfold." At Lancing in 1920, Waugh was glad when the debate committee "decided to take Minutes in alphabetical order. Some advantage in Ws after all" (*DEW* 9, 57).

Heath Mount also made Waugh more conscious of difference

between social classes. Whenever it rained, a few boys arrived in automobiles, attended by drivers. Though he "plodded up in goloshes," Waugh said that others' wealth generated neither "respect" nor "resentment," taking his reaction as evidence of "genuine 'good tone'" at Heath Mount (*ALL* 88–89). The scene nevertheless stuck in his memory; it does not appear in his diaries. Waugh enjoyed meeting the upper class, which seemed to raise his own social standing, and he seized every chance to affirm highness of station. In 1913 he started a "ripping row," claiming that his nose was bleeding, then telling the other boy that it is "rude to look up peoples noses." By 1916 Waugh was distinguishing schoolmates from "Street cads." He and a friend were leaving school when a ten-year-old scoffed at the caps they were wearing. Waugh chased the boy until an older brother came out with the "usual 'Ere d'you want a fight?'" Waugh said yes, and a "mixture of wrestling and boxing" resulted in "victory." That summer, on holiday at the seashore, Waugh noticed "vile Southend trippers" and complained about a revue in which "ladies," or rather "females," were "so aged and so cockney and so dreadfully painted that they simply spoilt the whole show." Mrs. Freeman ruined his introduction to badminton when she arrived with an "atrocity of about seven" and disrupted the game: "Whenever he 'no-served' she used to say, 'Never mind darling try again'" (*DEW* 7, 9, 10, 11). Waugh's distaste for others gave him a sense of superiority, and he repeatedly attributed others' inferiority to youth, social class, or social ineptitude.

Waugh knew he didn't really belong to the upper class, and while still a child he became interested in the reasons. Cockburn noticed a "peculiar social insecurity . . . at an early age." This insecurity derived, in part, from the idea that Evelyn's mother, a "connection of the Cockburn family," had "married beneath" herself when she had accepted Arthur Waugh, who was only a publisher, a "man in trade." Cockburn dismisses this "absurd report" of "*mesalliance*," but he believes it "really did affect Evelyn as a boy," contributing to "snobbery" that was "evident at Oxford" and "obsessive in his later life."[16] Waugh may have preferred his mother's side of the family, including two great-great-grandfathers, one "appointed a Lord of Justiciary" in 1837, the other belonging to an Irish family "briefly ennobled at the Union (the second and last peer died insane and childless)" (*ALL* 3). It is not clear when Evelyn learned of this marginally noble background, but it may have contributed to distaste for his father. A passage in the diaries indicates that Arthur may have been the source of Evelyn's snobbery, though it also

1: Not at Home in Hampstead, 1903–1916

indicates that Evelyn accepted his father's prejudices instead of reacting against him. At Bath in 1914, he and his father tried to avoid an "ass of a guide" with a "repulsive look" (*DEW* 7). It is hard to imagine a ten-year-old making these comments without encouragement. Perhaps Evelyn adopted his father's views only to question them later, as he became more sensitive to the origins of prejudice. Perhaps questioning and family lore led to a conception of social class different from his father's, more appreciative of the aristocracy. Influences on Waugh's early conceptions of class remain obscure, but he certainly had recognized his place in the middle of the social spectrum, finding it necessary to denigrate others in order to secure that place.

Just as he started to notice threats to his status, Waugh survived a serious threat to his health. In the summer of 1912 he developed appendicitis. The second attempt at his history refers to "something wrong" with his stomach, and Waugh had to stay in bed for a week. He found it "awful not to be able to get up," but still he was able to compose a little rhyme:

> I hate so much to stay in bed
> They seem to think I'm almost dead
> I want to sing, and dance, and leap
> And not to have to go to sleep.
>
> (HRHRC)

Not bad for an eight-year-old with appendicitis: the second line conveys real alienation from "them," presumably his family. A doctor decided surgery was necessary, and, according to the practice of the time, Waugh was "chloroformed and cut open on the kitchen table."[17] The operation appears in a picture at the start of the second entry in the diaries. In a frightening scene, a doctor brandishes scissors and a large knife over a cadaverous boy, who is being restrained by two assistants, one looking slightly sadistic, the other slightly alarmed. The boy's abdomen seems to have been opened, and something, perhaps an inflamed appendix, seems to protrude. Recovery was slow: Waugh describes the operation as having happened six days before, not having been "able to write this till now" (Diary HRHRC). He was strapped down for a week so he wouldn't rip out the stitches, and when he finally tried to stand up, his legs collapsed. Signs of his resilient humor were evident—he named his nurse the Scoundrel—but jokes alone could not effect his recovery. Arthur decided to send his son to a girls' school that was on vacation (*ALL* 56), where electrical treatments and swimming in the Thames were supposed to restore Evelyn's use of his legs.

The boy was miserable, feeling "abandoned" in an "empty, ugly house." Waugh's only consolation was a woman who came three times a week to tend to his legs. To her he expressed his sense of desolation, and, with his parents' permission, she took the boy to her home. The house was "extraordinarily Dickensian," and Waugh was happy there in a way reminiscent of feelings for his aunts' house. He had his first sexual encounter there; the therapist's daughter, "Muriel," occasionally exposed her genitals and Waugh reciprocated. He recovered use of his legs but failed to write to his parents. His father sent a "letter of rebuke," emphasizing Evelyn's insensitivity. Instead of feeling sorry, Evelyn reacted with "intense resentment" (*ALL* 56–58). Mutual irritation soured relations that had only just begun to improve, and Waugh distanced himself from his family, preferring retreat into a refuge associated with the past.

Commenting on this episode, Robert J. Kloss makes many connections between Evelyn's childhood and later writing, but he goes too far in interpreting "the boy's inability to walk" as "a hysterical paralysis." Retrospective diagnoses are unreliable, especially when only literary evidence is available. It seems too simple to say that Waugh was "cured" (Kloss's quotation marks) by going to live with his therapist's family, finding himself "loved once more and no longer a victim."[18] The problem had started before he had even left home, immobility apparently debilitating his developing muscles. Waugh had never seen himself as a special object of his family's love anyway. The Dickensian world of his therapist's family had, moreover, stimulated fantasies of escape into the past, just as his aunts' house had already. Kloss is perceptive to see that Waugh's "'persecution mania' . . . life-long insomnia, unrelenting depression, hallucinations, tendencies toward cruelty, and homosexuality" form "part of a larger pattern that would today be recognized as paranoia."[19] The same paranoia is evident in youthful sensitivity about Alec's preeminence and his own social status, but Evelyn was also intelligent and orderly enough to write more than twenty-five books. We can be skeptical when Kloss asserts that "Waugh's pre-oedipal conflicts dominated his creative urge," or that "he is impelled to re-enact in his fiction the significant ordeals of his childhood in an attempt to undo their traumata."[20] Waugh was interested in much more than his childhood, but early experience did suggest ways of responding to trouble, ways he found useful for the rest of his life. He consistently saw himself as a victim of others' indifference or incompetence, as he had at the girls' school in 1912, and he often sought refuge from a graceless present by revelling in the idealized virtues of the past. His fiction is filled with heroes who suffer in the same way and seek the same consolation.

When Evelyn was nine years old, probably late in 1912, Arthur gave him a book called *The Story of Rome,* dedicating his gift with a poem.

> *All roads, they tell us, lead to Rome;*
> *Yet, Evelyn, stay awhile at home!*
> *Or, if the Roman road invites*
> *To doughty deeds and fearful fights,*
> *Remember, England still is best—*
> *Her heart, her soul, her Faith, her Rest!*

The inscription may be only a series of easy rhymes, but Evelyn reproduced it in his autobiography and still wondered about its meaning. He focused on the capital letter in "Rest," interpreting it as a reference to death. As a Roman Catholic, Evelyn could not help noting that the book's account of Rome ended with the Battle of Actium in 31 B.C. Arthur seems to have anticipated his son's taking the "Roman road," and his references to "doughty deeds" and "fearful fights" can hardly be coincidental. Arthur had certainly noticed Evelyn's quest for notoriety and attraction to conflict; perhaps he sensed similarity between his son's personality and those of other English converts to Roman Catholicism. Thus, as Evelyn observed, the "profession of Englishry is plain enough" (*ALL* 68). Perhaps adverting to "England," "Faith," and "Rest" was Arthur's way of recommending, as gently as possible, conformity and patience to a son seemingly bent on disruption. Whatever Arthur may have meant, his inscription strongly suggests that difficulty between father and son stemmed not from failure to understand each other, but from natural antipathy, perceived by both early in their relationship. By giving Evelyn the book, Arthur may have intended to make up for mistakes of the previous summer, but his inscription does not seem very optimistic about the prospect of reconciliation.

Other childhood occupations reflect the peculiarity of Waugh's mature personality, and writing continued to be prominent among them, then as later. He helped to form the Pistol Troop in 1912, building a fort and hiding provisions in the builders' rubbish of Hampstead. The troop was supposed to defend England against invasion by Germans or Jews, a manifestation of Waugh's defensive, slightly paranoid personality and his conviction that he could be valuable to his country in a crisis. German invasion preoccupied English boys at the time, but the idea that Jews somehow threatened England is rather odd. Waugh did not mention the idea in his autobiography, but it probably derived from the growth of Golders Green, adjacent to Hampstead and already stigmatized as a suburb of middle-class Jews. The Pistol Troop saw some action in "scuffles with roving bands" who tried to get into their fort. Waugh insisted that he and his friends were "not provocative" (*ALL* 59). The diary describes one such conflict, when Waugh "fought wildly" in the "longest and fiercest" of his "many wars" (HRHRC). Pseudo-military bands and street fighting are common among male children, but in retrospect Waugh preferred to see the Pistol Troop as an exception. Dismissing while still respecting the standards of his past, Waugh noted that the troop was "rather priggishly high-minded." Their favorite word was "honor," and "dishonesty, impurity or cruelty would have been inconceivable." Waugh also stressed a social distinction, supposing that he and his friends had found their own "innocent, imaginative version of the street gangs of the slums" (*ALL* 59).

The Pistol Troop occupied Waugh until summer 1914, and it produced a magazine that printed one of his stories, "Multa Pecunia." Waugh later thought it uninteresting (*ALL* 60), but the story is reminiscent of "The Curse of the Horse Race" in its simple morality, redeeming a neglected boy who discovers Elizabethan treasure in his own house. He also foils the butler's attempt to steal it, thereby exposing the "worst thief that ever puzzled Scotland Yard."[21] As in "Fidon's Confetion," Waugh seems to have seen himself in the role of hero, saving people who fail to recognize his quality. He took to writing plays for performance by family and friends, still emphasizing eventual dispensation of justice and frustration of villains' schemes. "The Sheriff's Daughter or In Parker's Ranch" probably dates from 1913. In a "Comic Operor," a rival suitor tries to thwart the approaching marriage of hero and heroine. They discover the plot, however, and their wedding takes place along with two others at the end. Waugh had certainly become conscious of social considerations in marriage. His hero, Jack, sings that

> though a common cowboy
> I can love
> As much [as] all the haughty earls
> Who say that common men should
> marry common girls.[22]

1: Not at Home in Hampstead, 1903-1916

Apparently sympathizing with this commoner, Waugh allows Jack to marry Celia after he captures the notorious El Maduff.

In 1914 Waugh wrote another play, "A Woman's Curse." A Chinese villain named Tse Fing kidnaps the heroine and suddenly dies when she curses him. Waugh played Tse Fing in the only recorded performance, suggesting that he was for the first time projecting the wicked side of himself. Foreigners also appear in two cartoons, in which Waugh seemed to sympathize with their English prisoners. "The Slaves of Hurre Len. A Revised Rajah Shoo" is not dated, but it may have been finished just before the more elaborate "In Quest of Thomas Lee," dated 1914. Both stories are a series of drawings with captions. In the first, a character named Flashfire Dick falls into the hands of Hurre Len, an Indian slaveholder. Though threatened with execution, Dick is rescued by his friend Tom Barnell. The revision of "Rajah Shoo" perhaps confirms Waugh's judgment that early stories were only imitations of boys' magazines, but it is interesting that he felt impelled to revise something, to tell it another way. In the second story, the Kio tribe captures Thomas Lee while he is exploring in the Amazon. Lee's brother "Cristopher" and his friend "Lenard" come to the rescue, and all three manage to escape from a battle between the Kio and "the cults."[23] Lee's imprisonment in the Amazon anticipates Tony Last's imprisonment there in *A Handful of Dust* (1934). Both juvenile stories seem to show, if anything, fascination with vulnerability, characteristic of Waugh's novels. Certainly Waugh sensed his own vulnerability, and perhaps he was already using writing to explore the problem. Deliverance of the characters reflects, no doubt, a child's idea of poetic justice and dramatic resolution, evident also in "Fidon's Confetion" and "Multa Pecunia." In early novels, there is no chance of rescue, though curiously enough, in later ones, beginning with *Brideshead Revisited* (1945), salvation of the heroes is quite literally miraculous.

Outbreak of war in 1914 affected Waugh's life in several ways. He seems to have imitated his father's response and to have followed Arthur's lead in this as in other respects. For a few weeks Arthur supported the war and encouraged enlistment by speaking at Midsomer Norton. Evelyn also found war "at first a keen excitement" (*ALL* 87–88). Explaining "Why Britain is at War," he made the usual references to Britain's having "kept her word" and having sworn "to protect Belgium's neutrality." He also thought that declaration of war had saved Britain from being "envaded."[24] Arthur was also writing, denouncing aggression against countries that were familiar to him and promising retribution (*ALL* 88). Perhaps inspired by his father, Evelyn wrote "Told by the Refuggee," a story about Monsieur Lebouge and his wife. The man is killed and their cottage is destroyed as the "Vandal Hun reeks his awful vengeance on this brave nation." Economically, Evelyn claims that the "sequel to this small sketch is even worse than the first," giving a brief portrait of a woman left alone and heartbroken, asserting that "on the morro . . . soon to dawn for every one such case will treble toll be taken."[25] Certainly the war attracted Evelyn's attention, but the self-conscious summary and brevity of the pieces suggest that he wasn't really committed to writing about it, as Arthur apparently was.

Waugh also spent some time drawing popular conceptions of the war. One shows the "9th Lancers at Mons," cavalry attacking German infantry in a way that was no longer possible. Many concentrate on German treachery and cowardice. A dirigible over the channel is labeled "Aerial Spies." A concealed machine gun firing on British wounded exemplifies "German use of Red Cross waggons." Waugh's contempt applied to American diplomacy as well: when "America's Note Arrives," the Kaiser says "What a joke," but he falls over when he reads "Britain's Ultimatum" (HRHRC). Propaganda encouraged such narrow patriotism, and Arthur Waugh apparently endorsed it. The drawings, even more than the stories, indicate how eagerly Evelyn supported his country's declaration of war. Both drawings and stories contrast with the understanding of the war he would develop within two years.

Effects of war were evident at school, though Evelyn thought the changes at Heath Mount were "less dramatic" than those described by Alec at Sherborne, his public school. Mr. Vernon joined the army. On his last day, the boys presented him with a watch. The headmaster asked for three cheers, and "many chaps . . . hid behind each other so as not to be caught blubbing" (Diary HRHRC). Later Waugh remembered a few boys with "names suddenly anglicized," one changing from Kaiser to Kingsley. Waugh and friends refrained from harassment, and Heath Mount was "admirably free of the kind of malice which . . . seems to have been rampant elsewhere" (*ALL* 88). A Dutch master named Coetz did become known as the "Dashed Dutch Devil" and was suspected of being a spy. Waugh was no more patient with Pappenheimer's irregular play in football, attributed to his "being a subject of that miserable Germans nation (?)." Englishmen were also questioned: at Dulwich Waugh played cricket against "two giants (who ought to have taken comissions the funks [?])" (Diary HRHRC). Concerned as always with propriety and status, Waugh found that the war presented endless opportunities to ridicule friend and enemy alike. In *Work Suspended* (1942), John Plant remembers a schoolmate with whom he

> enjoyed a week of unrestrained confidence; one afternoon . . . I revealed my greatest secret, that my father was an artist and not, as I had given it out, an officer in the Navy; by tea-time the story was all over the school, that Plant's pater had long hair and did not wash. (Revenge came sooner than I could have hoped, for this was the summer term, 1914, and my betrayer had an aunt married to an Austrian nobleman; he had boasted at length of staying in their castle; when school reassembled in September I was at the head of the mob which hounded him in tears to the matron's room with cries of 'German spy'.)[26]

The story may well be an invention, but it does at least seem to stem, if not from actual events, then from Waugh's uneasiness about friends' impressions of his father and his father's vocation. Though he makes the hero's father an artist rather than a publisher, Waugh does have Plant represent his father as a naval officer, one of the vocations Waugh said he would have better respected as a child.

Despite his enthusiasm, Arthur realized that the war could ruin his income. He had often published in the *Daily Telegraph,* but when war broke out, the newspaper stopped taking the work of freelance writers. Arthur wrote to the headmaster of Heath Mount, explaining that he might be unable to pay for his son's tuition. The headmaster expressed willingness to educate Evelyn free of charge. Perhaps seeking some means of steadying his son, Arthur read the headmaster's letter with "some solemnity," encouraging Evelyn to be an "exemplary pupil." Evelyn understates his rebelliousness, unable to say that the headmaster's generosity made him "any more industrious or orderly." He did become industrious in the war effort, gathering empty jars to raise money for the Red Cross and cutting out soles of slippers for the wounded (*ALL* 87–88). Schoolmates seemed to have "gone cracked on the war funds," and many made models of boats or Zeppelins, selling them to other boys in order to raise money for refugees (Diary HRHRC). Evelyn's mother may have served as an inspiration, as she worked in a hospital as a voluntary aid. In 1915 Waugh even became a messenger at the War Office, and he had begun to collect "war relics," including shrapnel, spent shells, and a German helmet (*ALL* 94–95).

By then, Arthur's understanding of the war had changed, and

Evelyn's seems to have changed with it. Arthur's initial enthusiasm was, Evelyn decided, an "uncharacteristic phase," and the casualties "sickened him early" (*ALL* 88). Though Arthur had been in the habit of praying with his family each morning, he gave up in August 1914, on what seemed to Evelyn "very curious grounds": prayer was "no longer any good" (*ALL* 68). Arthur also stopped subscribing to *Punch,* unable to appreciate the magazine's "lighthearted patriotism." Though older men were working as special constables or "packing parcels for prisoners of war," Arthur withdrew from the national effort and "watched with foreboding the *impasse* on the Western Front" (*ALL* 95), where Alec seemed to be headed. In 1915 Alec enlisted in the Inns of Court Officers' Training Corps, then entered Sandhurst, the British military academy. Arthur often read poetry aloud to the family, and these readings developed into a ritual on Sunday, when Alec had to go back to camp, Arthur always taking him to the train station. Among Arthur's favorites were the English lyric poets of the 1890s. For the rest of his life, whenever he read their works, Evelyn remembered a "sturdy young soldier with a cup of cocoa under the rosy lights of the book-room at home" (*ALL* 95–96). Though only eleven years old, Evelyn sensed his father's depression and started to grasp the great cost of the war. His enthusiasm waned, as his father's had, and after a few months he had "little interest" in the war. He came to see it as a "condition of life" (*ALL* 94).

If he tried to ignore the war in France, Waugh could hardly ignore it in Hampstead. The Germans raided London several times, Waugh finding them "agreeable occasions" when he was treated to an "uncovenanted picnic." He was "quite unconscious of danger," dismissing it as "negligible," though he sometimes saw the "thin silver rod of the enemy caught in converging search-lights." Once he saw a Zeppelin destroyed, and as it sank "very slowly in brilliant flame," a crowd gathered, and Waugh joined in their cheers (*ALL* 94–95). The entry in Waugh's diary which probably inspired this passage is a somewhat different response to the Zeppelins. Sometime in 1915 there was a "Zeplin Raid." Alec woke Evelyn at 11:00 P.M., the special constable "rushing about yelling 'Lights Out'" and warning people that the Zeppelin was "right overhead." Two bombs fell, anti-aircraft guns opened fire, and the "Zep went away in their smoke cloud to do some baby-killing elswear" (*DEW* 8). That last comment is consistent with earlier writing, full of contempt for the "Vandal Hun" and his indifference to the suffering of innocents. It seems, nevertheless, more deeply cynical than even "Told by the Refuggee," with Waugh becoming more contemptuous as the war moved closer to home or, possibly, just listening to his father. The incident seems to have inspired another play, "Come to the Coach-house Door, Boys," another attempt to express his sense of the war's significance. A boy escapes his music lesson by telling his parents that a Zeppelin is overhead. After damaging the coach-house while trying to take cover, the parents realize that they have been deceived. They persuade a warden that a bomb has hit the coach-house, qualifying for damages paid by the government. The play is the first literary evidence that Waugh was beginning to question popular understanding of the war, seeing self-aggrandizement as more sensible than sacrifice. The play also suggests increasing interest in his personality's devious side, the side he named Basil Seal in his fiction.

After he had finished the play, Waugh wrote little about the war, perhaps because his father was ignoring it, perhaps because Alec, never a favorite, was by then involved. Even if his family did help to cool his enthusiasm, Evelyn developed other interests and devoted more and more of his diary to them in 1915 and 1916. On vacations especially he started to collect all kinds of specimens. Early in 1915 he mounted some examples of seaweed. Another interest may be suggested by his giving some to a girl whose family happened to sit at the same table as the Waughs. A holiday enabled him to find some "ripping pieces of strata," and the acquisition made him want to reorganize his "musseum." Waugh doesn't mention giving tours of his museum, but he was self-conscious about it anyway. He thought he was lacking exhibits in natural history, and he tried to build up his collection. Since birds' eggs were not in season, he settled for butterflies. About the same time, summer 1915, he invested his "total fortune in the world (2/) in a microscope," a "beauty." That autumn he started chemical experiments, and all "people who hope for life" had to "keep clear of the laboritory," where Waugh was trying to make "clorine." Chlorine gas had already been introduced on the Western Front, and perhaps it had piqued Waugh's curiosity about chemistry. Most of his hobbies had nothing to do with the war, however. The following year, 1916, he was gathering flowers to earn a merit badge. A few flowers and some seaweed are preserved in Waugh's diaries at the University of Texas (HRHRC). Waugh remained something of a collector all his life, though in later years he delighted in bizarre objets d'art. Certainly he remembered early efforts in *A Handful of Dust,* where Tony Last keeps a "cabinet called 'the Museum,' filled with a dozen desultory collections, eggs, butterflies, fossils, coins."[27]

Waugh's pursuits were not entirely private matters, as he also helped to organize several groups in 1915. Though all were versions of the Pistol Troop, none seems to have noticed the war or the prospect of invasion. That summer Waugh started the "noble society of Limits." He didn't explain the name, but perhaps it had to do with the limits of endurance, one passage suggesting that initiates had to sign their names in blood (Diary HRHRC). Back at school in the fall, boys became excited by the study of medieval history and separated themselves into Scottish and English sides. Combative as usual, Waugh joined what was probably the smaller, less conventional group. He was "only a quarter Scotch" but "ardently of their party" (*ALL* 88). Waugh had started using language to make fun of himself as well as others, his diary referring to a "small country called england which we are given to understand carries on its small existance somewhere South of Scotland." The English were "too bumpstious," and it was the Scots' "duty to squash them." That fall also saw the appearance of Wuffles and Company, a private detective agency intended to foil a gang reputed to be thieves (Diary HRHRC). Forming such groups became habitual for Waugh, enabling him to indulge his imagination, exert control over others, and generate the conflicts he enjoyed.

Writing was another way to generate conflict. In 1916 Waugh started *The Cynic,* a magazine supposed to undercut the school's official publication and another way to antagonize the authorities. In 1914 Waugh had been old enough to go to Alec's prep school (*ALL* 87). Worried about money, his parents had kept him home, but by 1916 it was clear that Evelyn was outgrowing Heath Mount. In his diary he resolved that at the beginning of the term, the school would "hum." It was supposed to be his last term, and he wanted "to raise Hell." His "first shell to smash the ramparts of convention" was *The Cynic,* the "most gorgeous paper out," with "smacks at every chap and master who 'cuts ice' at all" (HRHRC). Years later Waugh considered the magazine "flippant rather than cynical; the few jokes that are now intelligible seem very feeble" (*ALL* 94). Mr. Hynchcliffe, Waugh's form master, found the paper objectionable, forbidding sales of *The Cynic,* though Waugh had "already sold out." After paying for printing, Waugh was left with half a crown. He gave it to the war fund, perhaps trying to justify the magazine's existence, though obviously he was more interested in speaking his mind. In spite of opposition, *The Cynic* ran for five issues. Among many pieces by Waugh were the contentiously titled "Things We'd Like to Know," "Our Contemporary: 'The Heath Mount Magazine',' and "Sufficient unto the Day or the Importance of Being Lazy."[28] Waugh was always determined to assert the importance of his views, especially if people tried to prevent him from doing so.

Despite his cynicism, possibly because of it, Waugh became increasingly religious in 1915 and 1916. At first his interest seems to have been architectural. On holiday at Watchet in the summer of 1915, he went to an attractive church with a "dreadfuly plain service." He also visited the abbey at Cleve, finding it "beautiful" and lamenting its "bad state" (Diary HRHRC). The buildings helped rouse some sort of spirituality, which in turn affected Waugh's artwork. In 1914 he had drawn "countless pictures of German cavalry plunging among English infantry," relishing his country's role as the underdog, just as he would in 1939. By 1916 the war had settled into stalemate, and Waugh's "drawings were no longer of battles but of saints and angels inspired by mediaeval illuminations" (*ALL* 88, 93). He gave up "War Work," finding that it cut into his holidays "so frightfully" (*DEW* 9). He also began to feel pleasure serving at the altar of an Anglican church at Midsomer Norton, though he was "always embarrassed" when he had to lead the confession in front of a "sparse congregation." The Waughs had started attending St. Jude's in Hampstead Garden Suburb, partly because of the "highly flamboyant clergyman," Basil Bourchier (*ALL* 91–93). Carpenter suggests that Bourchier's personality may have drawn Evelyn to church,[29] but Waugh himself called Bourchier a "totally preposterous parson," who once introduced a salt shaker into the service: "'My people,' he announced, 'you are the salt of the earth', and scattered a spoonful on the carpet." Waugh seems to have been more attracted to another clergyman, who taught him how to participate in services at Midsomer Norton. Back home, in the nursery, he made a shrine by his bed, "three brackets of diminishing size, each hung with a kind of little frontal." There he "arranged brass candlesticks and flower vases and statues of saints" and burned "incense on a brass ashtray" (*ALL* 92–93). Waugh's aunts encouraged this behavior, for whatever reasons, giving him at least one frontal, a crucifix, and two brass bowls (*DEW* 9). He said that he wanted to become a parson, and he used evening prayers as an opportunity to "recite long devotions from a pious book." Waugh's mother was "unsympathetic . . . to all this phase of churchiness," perhaps because she had been exposed to the "drearier side of clerical life" in childhood (*ALL* 94), perhaps because she did not care for Midsomer Norton's influence on her son.

Waugh continued to study churches and became conscious of Anglican hierarchy. In 1915 he went to church in Brighton, happening upon a "horrible low one." He was the only person who crossed himself and "bowed to the altar" (*DEW* 8). He seldom enjoyed communion with other Christians, ignoring advice to show humility and insisting on social distinctions separating him from the rest of the flock. High Church approaches Roman Catholicism, and Waugh started to notice the differences. A "most lovely old church" at Prittlewell still had a "staircase in the wall," going up to where the rood screen used to be. When he went to Leigh, he found a church that was "very spikey," with some "very Roman candles on sort of rings standing on the ground but without the image in the centre" (Diary HRHRC). Long after he had become a Roman Catholic, Waugh wondered if early piety represented "faint contact with an objective reality" (*ALL* 94). It certainly did meet many of his own needs. Even then he was capable of using religion to defend himself and criticize others. When his mother observed that he had the "besetting sin" of a "quick and spiteful tongue," Waugh asked if she knew what her own besetting sin was. Catherine didn't know what to say, but Evelyn informed her that it was "lack of faith in Catholic doctrine."[30]

It is not clear why Waugh would have been committed to Catholic doctrine. Arthur had gone through an Anglo-Catholic phase at the time of Evelyn's birth, but he was not very serious about religious matters (*ALL* 68), and he regarded Bourchier as a "rollicking joke" (*ALL* 92). Arthur objected to Catholicism's "clarity of dogma" (*ALL* 68), and he was not anxious about his sons' religious education. Evelyn disliked his father's bemused indifference, but he rebuked his mother for ignoring doctrine he expected her to follow. His mother's grandmother, Theodosia, had converted to Roman Catholicism, an extraordinary decision in an "Anglo-Irish Protestant family." She was the only one of Waugh's ancestors known to have done so. Her son, Waugh's grandfather, had been born by the time her husband died. Theodosia remarried and converted, and her sisters-in-law adopted her son. Waugh's mother remembered her great-aunts dwelling on the "insidious character of popery," evident in the boy's retention of a rosary, undiscovered for years. Waugh guessed that the rosary may have been only a "memento of his lost mother." Theodosia had more children, but Waugh's grandfather was "never allowed to meet his popish half-brothers and -sisters" (*ALL* 3-4). Waugh sympathized with the bereaved little boy, beginning to see Catholicism as a religion more ancient and more legitimate than that practiced by his father. On his mother's side, he had found slight connections with Roman Catholicism and aristocracy, forebears more romantic than middle-class Protestants on his father's side. Later Waugh would create the Flytes and the Crouchbacks, Catholic aristocrats in England, in *Brideshead Revisited* and the war trilogy. At age twelve he lacked only the understanding of history and, perhaps, the trauma of divorce, which would lead him to formal acceptance of Roman Catholicism.

Sometime in 1916 Waugh wrote *The World to Come,* a "deplorable poem" privately printed by a friend of his father's. Composed in emulation of Newman's *Dream of Gerontius* and in the meter of Longfellow's *Hiawatha,* the poem describes the "experiences of the soul immediately after death" (*ALL* 93). A strange subject for a boy of twelve or thirteen, and one that might be taken, along with the beginning of his religious phase, as further evidence of extreme alienation from the world as he found it. *The World to Come* draws on imagery of the First World War, referring to bayonets, shells, and machine guns, but Waugh's attitude is clearly detached and ironic. By this time, he saw the war not as a conflict between England and Germany, but as a conflict between two sides equally estranged from Christian sensibility. After the sacking of an enemy oratory, "friendly" priests and servers give thanks to God for the "soldiers' outrage" (*EWA* 49). Having seen through the way of the world, the narrator enters heaven; the poem indicates why Waugh never really lost the spirituality he had shown as an adolescent. Christianity promised another world, better than the one he had found so difficult. Christianity gave him the responsibility and privilege of instructing others, confirming importance that Waugh sensed but often doubted. His religion also extended the comfort of faith in his own immortality.

Waugh needed all the comfort Christianity could give him when he entered the next phase of life at Lancing College. Heath Mount had, as he said, done little to prepare him for the "endurances of adolescence" at public school (*ALL* 86). Waugh was extremely self-conscious and socially insecure, accustomed to the privacy and comfort of a house he took for granted. Nevertheless, he had already developed several qualities that would help him get through the Lancing years and the rest of his life, among them a strong sense of his own importance, a desire to make himself heard, a delight in confrontation, and, perhaps most important of all, an interest in writing. His first thirteen years had been hard, he thought, but the next five would be even harder, strengthening sense of himself as a victim of neglect and discrimination. Once he had gone to Lancing, childhood started to look good, but by then he resented his father's choice of the school too much to feel any gratitude for past favors. Waugh's childhood also started to look good to him at age sixty, when he realized that the world of his youth had long since passed away. Fifty years earlier, he had been drawn to the mid-Victorian ethos of his aunts' house, itself fifty years out of date.

2
A Less Important Place than Eton, 1917–1920

WAUGH's weariness with the First World War increased after he had been sent to Lancing College in May 1917. As early as 1914 Arthur had considered sending Evelyn to a preparatory school, probably Fernden, before entering him in public school, but the war reduced income and kept his younger son home, still going to Heath Mount. The school could do no more for Evelyn in the fall of 1916, and Arthur had hoped to send him to Sherborne, where he and Alec had gone. Authorities there had already asked Alec to leave, however, after they had discovered a homosexual relationship. Alec felt he had been treated unfairly, had been made an example, and he threatened to write a novel exposing the school's hypocrisy, published in 1917 as *The Loom of Youth*. Arthur realized that Evelyn would not be welcome at Sherborne, but he resisted his wife's advice to send their son to a London day school. The most prestigious, most selective public schools were out of the question, because Evelyn had not competed for a place or a scholarship. Arthur didn't know what to do, and after a "minimum of deliberation," he chose Lancing, though he was unfamiliar with it. On the South Downs between Brighton and Worthing, Lancing dates from 1848, founded by Nathaniel Woodard, who wished to educate the middle class in affordable public schools affiliated with the Church of England. Arthur thought Lancing appropriate for Evelyn, who was still in his religious phase and still had some notion of becoming a parson. Waugh himself said he would have been "ashamed to remain a day-boy" (*ALL* 96), indicating why Lancing, much as he hated it, was nevertheless well-suited to his temperament. He thrived on adversity, and going to Lancing encouraged him to contrast the hardship of his life with the ease of everyone else's. Though stimulating, adversity also gave him reason to resent his father and brother, the one for having chosen Lancing, the other for having forced the choice. From Evelyn's point of view, Alec had, as usual, been given the best opportunities and had made the least of them, not only embarrassing himself, but also spoiling the prospects of a brother who considered himself brighter and more deserving.

Waugh was obviously ready to leave Heath Mount, but to go to Lancing, he needed to pass the Common Entrance examination. He took it early in 1917 and passed with low marks. With "no misgivings" (*ALL* 96), Waugh went to Lancing on 9 May. Arthur went with him, returning to London before the other boys were due to arrive. Evelyn wrote that separation presented no difficulty, as he anticipated a "new and exciting phase of life" (*ALL* 100). One of the masters, Dick Harris, gave Waugh a book, but it failed to interest him. Harris also led him into the empty House Room, with a table set aside for "new men." After Waugh had sat alone for an hour, two boys showed up and muttered "'O God. Same old House Room'; 'Same old smell.'" They looked at Waugh with "cold disdain." The rest of the house followed in a "noisy incursion" of about forty-five boys, all ignoring Waugh until he was joined by another new man, Roger Fulford. Later Fulford and Waugh became "cronies," but in 1917 Waugh would not have "chosen him as a friend . . . had any choice been possible" (*ALL* 101–2). Lancing code of conduct outlawed association with new men until they had finished their second term. Except for an "underschool" appointed to take charge of a new man during his first three weeks, no older boy could seek Waugh's company until January 1918. Not until the following May, a year after he had started, could Waugh himself approach the large class of boys who arrived in September 1917. Waugh was just beginning to realize that he had become the "unconscious victim" of his father's desire to "push every affair on to completion." His first day was marked in black on his calendar, used to check off each day of the term. Some days were darker than others, depending on the extent of his unhappiness, Waugh "surrounding the page with a border of chains" (*ALL* 97).

He and Fulford were left to themselves, though Fulford's family was at least familiar with the school's observation of Ascension Day. It occurred a little more than a week after Waugh's arrival, a holiday for the entire school. After chapel in the morning, both boys and masters disappeared. Some went to nearby towns with family or friends; others walked to attractions including teagardens, an old castle, and a display of stuffed animals. Waugh "knew no one and had nowhere to go." He learned that dinner would not be served, though the steward gave him some bread and a "ghastly kind of sausage meat." It started to rain, but his House

2: A Less Important Place than Eton, 1917–1920   45

Room was locked, and he was not allowed in the library. Waugh finally sought "shelter among the trees called Lancing Ring, ate a little and, for the first and last time for many years, wept." Late in the afternoon he was comforted by the "noisy return of the holiday-makers." The effect of the experience lasted long after Waugh had left Lancing. He taught his children to "make a special intention at the Ascension Mass for all desolate little boys" (*ALL* 110). In a letter in 1960, Waugh wrote that every year on Ascension Day, he "felt that things can never be as bad as that" (*LEW* 542).

Things did not improve very quickly. Lancing was in many ways strange and depressing. There were blackouts along the coast, and after sunset the school was completely dark. Waugh missed his mother, and the school seemed "chilling" compared to home. Other boys' contempt was new to him. In childhood he had met only those who were inclined to like him (*ALL* 103–4, 107). As he would find out, Waugh was ill-suited to public-school values. Fulford recalled that "regimentation was the thing. Scholarship, skill in athletics and good looks made regimentation possible to bear and opened the door to popularity." Fulford considered Waugh "clever but not a scholarship-boy, courageous but no games-player, pleasant-featured but not good-looking." Because other boys considered him useless, Waugh immediately "sank to a low place in the esteem of the House and school." Fulford thought he was "too independent, too prone to notice oddities and comment on them, to be popular." Fulford often heard "those ominous words 'that awful little tick Waugh.'"[1] Small consolation in Waugh's first term came from being beaten along with the rest of his dormitory after an attack on a senior boy. He and Fulford had had nothing to do with it, but Dick Harris refused to make exceptions, giving Waugh a "slight sense of kinship" instead of leaving him "totally alien" (*ALL* 107).

Arrangements at Lancing discouraged development of kinship. Meals were repulsive, partly because the food was bad enough to cause "mutiny in a mid-Victorian poor-house," and it got worse until the war ended. Meat and other luxuries were scarce, and boys subsisted on bread and stew made from potatoes and rutabagas. The boys' manners seemed to have been an "unconscious protest against this prison diet," and they spilled as much as they ate. As a "fastidious little boy," Waugh was also uncomfortable whenever he was physically close to other boys. He found the latrines so embarrassing that he was reluctant to use them. At Lancing they were called "The Groves," and Waugh judged them "both inadequate in number and . . . appallingly exposed." Because boys had little time to use the latrines, there were lines and arrangements about who should be next. There were no doors, and Waugh was too shy to relieve himself under these conditions. Usually he went to the latrine during school hours in exchange for a composition of twenty-five lines. Boys had a bath once a week in the evening, which Waugh remembered as "bliss," but they also had to bathe in the afternoon. Hot water was in short supply, and it was not often changed after tubs had been filled. After football matches, the water quickly turned into "tepid mud." Loathing the communal nature of these baths, Waugh "boggled at the contact of all these naked bodies," and his "repugnance communicated itself" (*ALL* 107-9).

Alienated from other boys, Waugh deliberately isolated himself, eschewing the easiest means of making friends. Though younger boys often did lessons for older ones, Waugh declined to do so, regarding the practice as "dishonest" (*ALL* 109). He seems, understandably, to have devoted himself to studies and to Dick Harris, his house-tutor and first instructor. Waugh discovered to his dismay that he was in the wrong form. His work was superior to that of the other boys, and after half a term he was promoted to the Upper Fourth Form. Typically, Waugh imagined that his Common Entrance examination had been given "cursory attention." Perhaps he was studying harder than he had at Heath Mount. Too bright for Harris's classroom, Waugh sought another sanctuary in the library, where he spent most of his time looking at books on art. His favorite was a series called *The Bible in Art*. Waugh's interest in religion meant that he also enjoyed chapel, twice each day and thrice on Sunday. Some found this schedule "excessive," but Waugh appreciated the language of the service and the King James Version. Chapel became a "refuge from the surrounding loneliness; contact with home and with Midsomer Norton rather than with Heaven" (*ALL* 112-13). Waugh and Lancing may have been compatible in this respect, if in few others, but still he was using religion as an imaginative escape to a more desirable place, just as in Hampstead he had dreamed of Midsomer Norton.

Waugh's only contact with other places during his first term was imaginative, since he could not leave school. Boys could get leave for excursions with family or friends, but Waugh did not know anyone in the area, and Lancing was a long trip for his parents to make from London, especially since the war was on. Selina Hastings has shown that his parents did visit Lancing several times in 1917, but Waugh chose not to mention these visits in his autobiography.[2] Once they had left, he simply had to stay at school, "lonely as on any Sunday." Finally, in July 1917, when the end of term had arrived, Waugh was hit with an "insupportable blow, symptoms of mumps too manifest to be disguised." He had to spend the first two weeks of holidays in the infirmary with Roger Fulford. A nurse, Sister Babcock, attended to them, though she was "irate" about the shortening of her own vacation. Waugh's parents sent a chicken, but even this small comfort was eaten by a cat that belonged to the nurse. Waugh eventually made it home for six weeks or so with his family. He was "never bored or lonely" with them, but once his holidays were half over, the rest were spoiled by apprehension about returning to Lancing (*ALL* 113–14).

After an inauspicious start, Waugh's second term was "one of black misery." He felt "no spice of adventure in returning; merely odious familiarity." Dick Harris had gone into the army, but he had made a "final benefaction," having appointed Waugh "library underschool." The position relieved him from "all routine housefagging" and extended the "inestimable privilege" of unlimited access to the library. All other changes were for the worse. Waugh's ability put him in the Classical Lower Fifth Form, studying under a master named Howitt. Waugh found him "agreeable" (*ALL* 114), but the lessons were the same as those given to the First Form at Heath Mount (*ALL* 112). Dissatisfaction with lessons would again lead to subversiveness. In his second term Waugh also advanced in the Officers' Training Corps. Once a week he had to prepare his uniform for parade, and during exercises he had to carry a rifle, an "intolerable encumbrance." Extenuation of the war increased hardship in England, and boys had to harvest potatoes. There was even less to eat. Waiters had gone into national service, and boys had to take over, adding to the "gloom of those barbarous meals." When juniors served seniors, they were "harried and chidden;" any senior who had to serve a junior "slammed and splashed the dishes about with violent disdain." Weather also grew worse as the autumn wore on, and wind, "rain and darkness possessed the place. . . . Chilblains swelled and burst." Waugh asked his father to take him away, but Arthur "counselled endurance" (*ALL* 115).

Lonely and miserable, Waugh simultaneously felt repulsion from the place and desire to fit in somehow. When he noticed that he received more letters than most and that they were delivered with a "slight asperity," he asked his father to write less often, even though Arthur's letters were a "keen delight." Though he was afraid of standing out in any way, integrity as an individual and a Christian set Waugh apart. He "defied convention by kneeling at the *incarnatus* in the creed at Holy Communion." Waugh had been observing this practice at St. Jude's, but the boys did not kneel at Lancing. In his first term, Waugh had stayed on his feet, but during the holidays he "suffered remorse." In his second term, Waugh started kneeling, fearing the consequences, though "no one ever commented on this singularity." He thought that the boys had generally respected religion, and that they would have considered it "bad form to mock another's piety" (*ALL* 109).

Roger Fulford's memory is rather different. He recalled that when they went to bed, they kneeled down "to use the chamber pot and to address a brief word to the Almighty. Long after the pot was used, Evelyn would remain plunged in prayer by his bedside; similarly, in chapel his devotion was pronounced." His habits did not go "unnoticed," and they were "not liked." Waugh's faith probably offered even more consolation at Lancing than it had at home, as prayer gave him a chance to ask for deliverance or at least fortitude. Another cause of unpopularity seems to have been a predisposition to martyrdom he indulged then and later. He certainly had reason to indulge it at Lancing, but it was thought more proper to endure the rigors of public school with humor and stoicism. Fulford remembered that Waugh had a "strange and ungainly walk—more of a trudge than anything else. It was whispered behind his back, and . . . to his face, that he was a martyr to trench-feet." He was often the object of "spluttering, tittering and staring," but he "showed neither by the flicker of an eyelid nor by a brave smile that he noticed or minded."[3] Almost certainly he did notice, conscious of eccentricity but wishing to appear nonchalant. He remained torn by contradictory desires, neither admiring nor wanting to be like the other boys, but still wanting "to be one of them." Waugh had "no aspirations to excel, still less to lead;" he just wanted to be himself and "yet be accepted as one of this distasteful mob" (*ALL* 109).

Conflict between individuality and conformity never left Waugh, and at Lancing and later a strong sense of self often made him an outcast. On Sunday afternoons, boys usually went for a walk, Waugh left to himself or "obliged to make a rendezvous with some equally unpopular boy in another House." Lacking friends, he spent the "best hours" of his first year in the classroom, in the chapel, and in the library (*ALL* 110–11). Despondent as he was, Waugh found some use for his trials. He enjoyed performing for a London friend, "contrasting the severe life of a boarding-school with his softness as a day-boy." Waugh was always ready to dwell on the difficulties of his life, a tendency evident in *A Little Learning* and much of his fiction. When he was at Lancing, Waugh was

2: A Less Important Place than Eton, 1917–1920

so emphatic that his complaints reached Berkhamsted School in Hertfordshire, where a friend was a classmate of Graham Greene's. Whenever Greene "wishes to portray a seedy character who nurtures a pathetic loyalty to a minor public school, he attributes this emotion to Lancing" (*ALL* 120). Waugh does not mention Claud Cockburn, a friend of Greene's at Berkhamsted, but probably Cockburn also conveyed Waugh's litany of hardship.

Waugh's public-school education was in one way worse than others', because he started at Lancing during the First World War. As he wrote later, with at least a trace of exaggeration, it had been the "most dismal period in history for an English schoolboy" (*ALL* 115). He felt that his generation had received fewer rations than their successors did in the Second World War. Even those who had been schoolboys between 1914 and 1916 had had some advantage over Waugh, who claimed that the "submarine blockade became effective" only in 1917 (*ALL* 99–100). Both older boys and younger masters left for military service, so that the "boys in authority were too young, the masters too old. Everything was of necessity a makeshift," Waugh mentioning their clothes, their food, their books, and even their teachers. Waugh and his schoolmates were "cold, shabby and hungry in the ethos, not of free Sparta, but of some beleaguered, enervated and forgotten garrison." According to Waugh, even nineteenth-century brutality showed a "rude humanity" that had been absent from Lancing. He thought public schools had flourished when they had had "men and boys of good-will, imagination and enthusiasm in a time of plenty and bright prospects." Unfortunately, most of these had been missing from Lancing during the First World War (*ALL* 116). Partly for these reasons, for those already mentioned, and for considerations of social status, Waugh reacted strongly against Lancing, regarding his time there as something of an embarrassment. Fulford affirmed that the school was solidly in the "second rank of English public schools," a reputation producing a "certain swagger" and a "certain intolerance for those who could not contribute to its forward march."[4] Waugh was reluctant to display such swagger because he considered Lancing second-rate and saw no point in competing with Eton, whose superiority seemed obvious. The headmaster of Lancing, Reverend Henry Bowlby, had been an assistant master at Eton. He was rather distant from the boys and never tried to disguise his opinion that Lancing was "a less important place than Eton" (*ALL* 99).

As he grew older, Waugh became more sensitive to social distinctions. In 1919 he still seemed willing to appreciate the school for its own sake, noting that the headmaster's sermon had been "not too bad for him." The lesson had been seeking the kingdom of God and having gifts added unto one, the verses related to the status of Lancing. Waugh found the connection relevant and interesting. By 1920 Waugh was much less patient, growing critical of Lancing's pretensions. He was bored by the new men's concert, supposed to be an "old tradition" but actually "ridiculous in so modern a school." Later that year, anticipating a cricket match against Tonbridge, he decided that the "ridiculous homage of a minor school to a better is perfectly disgusting." The Lancing boys were told to "sing lustily" in chapel in front of the Tonbridge team. Waugh judged snobbery to be "fairly healthy," but "that sort of thing is most morbid" (*DEW* 21, 56, 82). Waugh always wanted to make a good impression, but he knew even then that any hint of effort or concern could ruin the effect, making one seem inept, obvious, and contemptible. Insecure about his education in 1921, he doubted his chances of winning even a small scholarship to Worcester College, Oxford (*DEW* 145), and even after he had won a larger scholarship to Hertford College he remained reticent about his public school. In 1923 he told Fulford not to talk "so much about Lancing. If you weren't at Eton or Harrow or Winchester or Rugby no-one minds much where you were."[5] Waugh thought even Hertford inferior to Balliol and other Oxford colleges, and dissatisfaction with day school, public school, and college reflects almost automatic refusal to be happy wherever he was. In 1953 he admitted that he "shouldn't have been happy at any school."[6] In adolescence and early adulthood he felt that his education had been mediocre, though almost anyone else would have considered it outstanding. Waugh's sense of inadequacy added to resentment of his family and acute insecurity.

In the fall of 1917, in the midst of his worst term at Lancing, Waugh reacted to adversity by writing, a response he would find more and more valuable. The November 1917 issue of *Drawing and Design* published a piece entitled "In Defence of Cubism." Waugh did not keep a copy, in later years supposing that the essay had been "utterly fatuous." He had known "nothing whatever of the theory of the movement," and he had seen "very few of its products" (*ALL* 121). The article is, indeed, interesting more for contentiousness than for insight. Waugh reproves the "self-satisfied Philistine denouncing Cubism as pure affectation," asserting that the "Academicians will fall and die unlamented, and Nevinson, Picasso and all the early Cubists who . . . fought to the last against all the contempt and deliberate misunderstanding of a prejudiced

2: A Less Important Place than Eton, 1917–1920

public, will take their well-deserved places among the masters who paved the way for their coming."⁷ Satisfying as it was to be published at age fourteen, the article strengthened Waugh's sense of himself as victim of exploitation. Though he had identified his piece as an article, the periodical had considered it a letter, apparently so that the editor would not have to pay him. Waugh recognized that his motive in writing was the "wish to shock," and for the same reason he later on "pretended to be a socialist," or "advocated the restoration of the Stuarts, anarchism and the rule of a hereditary caste" (*ALL* 121–22). The same wish to shock began to influence schoolwork, and early in 1918 one master reported that Waugh had to learn to "'approve those things that are excellent', not merely those that are ultra-modern" (*ALL* 117).

In his autobiography, Waugh wrote that Barbara Jacobs had inspired "In Defence of Cubism." He remembered meeting her during Christmas holidays in 1917, but they must have met the previous summer, if she really did inspire the article, since it was published in November. Barbara was then involved with Alec, whom she married in 1919 and divorced in 1923. Evelyn was attracted to Barbara's "sense of the absurd." He noticed that she was "unconventional in eschewing hats and gloves and sunshades," often "adorning herself with crude jewellery" produced by a "bearded crank." Barbara was also a proponent of agnosticism, socialism, and feminism. Evelyn had lived in an almost Victorian world of "maiden-aunts and Anglican clergy," but Barbara represented the "new age." She was "subversive by tradition," and Waugh was "stimulated by the encounter," as Barbara became the sort of friend he had not yet met at Lancing. Together they explored London, visiting exhibitions and galleries. Inspired by what they saw, they executed their own works of cubism, on the walls of Waugh's old nursery, reducing their "figures to angles and flat planes." Waugh later considered himself carried away with Barbara's enthusiasm, having become an "aesthetic hypocrite," because the new style had really been "abhorrent" to him (*ALL* 117, 120, 121–22). Probably he exaggerated the consistency of his taste from youth to maturity, for he had not yet become contemptuous toward modern art, and as a young man he was intrigued by experiments in painting, film, poetry, and fiction. At Lancing in 1917, defense of cubism probably mattered less than connection with London and an agreeable companion. Barbara Jacobs may have contributed something to the article, but it seems nevertheless characteristic of Waugh, who expressed truculence typical of *The Cynic* the year before and infatuation with the lone artist battling the conventional, dim-witted majority, a role he often saw himself playing.

Perhaps dwelling on days spent with Barbara also reminded Waugh of her sister Luned, one of his "insignificant romantic attachments." Luned was a little younger than Waugh, and she looked up to him with "gratifying respect." At Luned's house there was a large room with an oak floor, where children played a game of "undefined rules." Players divided into two groups, and, after the lights had been extinguished, they had to crawl through the other children in order to reach the far side of the room. Evelyn and Luned would find one another and hug, not kissing but indulging in "rapturous minutes of close embrace." After the game had finished, they would "exchange glances of complicity," and one or the other usually suggested "the dark game" (*ALL* 117, 120). The Jacobs sisters helped to make London more attractive than Lancing, providing kinds of relationships Waugh was unable or unwilling to pursue at school.

In other ways Waugh was beginning to show, if not exactly the wish to shock, at least the determination to stand up for his idea of justice. In the spring of 1918 he earned respect by fighting, upset by what another boy had said about Alec. *The Loom of Youth* had been published the previous summer, and many readers had been startled by the novel's frank treatment of public-school life. Evelyn's opponent "hinted that the natural corollary to such a book was to capitulate to the enemy."[8] Alec had just been captured in the Ludendorff offensive. Evelyn was never especially well-disposed toward Alec, but he was loyal to family and sometimes impelled to defend them. A little more comfortable at Lancing after a year, probably weary of trials he had endured there, Waugh was losing his fear of being conspicuous. He was well on his way toward a quest for notoriety, characteristic of his last two years at Lancing.

While the war lasted, boys were constantly reminded of sacrifices that were being made for them, and on Sundays someone would read the names of old boys who had been killed during the week. Waugh said there were few Sundays without such a "necrology" (*ALL* 113). The armistice ended these depressing recitations, and it was "boisterously celebrated." Waugh recalled remission of all penalties, parades, cheers, bell-ringing, a service in the chapel, and a bonfire. A few boys committed some sort of transgression, but Waugh could not quite remember what it had been, supposing that they might have shoved the fire engine into the bonfire. Waugh did remember Rev. Bowlby denouncing a "dingy trick." The headmaster happened to see a boy making a

2: A Less Important Place than Eton, 1917–1920   53

face, interrupting his oration to note that "Barnes laughs. Thank you, Barnes. Now we know Barnes's ideals." As he went on to explain the more serious offense, Rev. Bowlby underlined each point by saying "But Barnes laughs." Waugh considered it an "admirable performance" (*ALL* 124). Boys were still restrained in many ways, but Waugh was beginning to see that performance imposed one kind of restraint. He became fascinated with using language to capture attention, and he began to experiment in speech and writing, seeking an advantage in relations with masters and other boys.

Partly for this reason, school was more pleasant in the year 1919. Food was more plentiful, and Waugh gave in to gluttony, the "master-passion of boyhood." He and his friends aspired to fineness of taste, resembling a "circle of maiden ladies" in their preoccupation with the "brewing of tea." More important, no one aged eighteen was going to fight anymore, and younger boys no longer needed to fill the positions of greatest authority. Waugh and company found themselves blocked in their "advance to these eminences and well content to be so." They formed an "essentially subversive stratum," calling themselves "Bolshevists," a reference to the recent Russian Revolution. Later Waugh thought they had been a "body of retarded irresponsibles" (*ALL* 125–26). Joining this unconventional group assuaged Waugh's fears about his own eccentricity, persuading him that he was like at least some other people. Senior enough to command some respect, he became active in the social life of his house. He and friends formed a strong circle that worked together to deflect threats from outside. They treated younger boys with "feudal benevolence," but they "hunted as a small pack to bring down . . . equals and immediate superiors." Waugh was just learning that aggression could make Lancing less dull. He invented demeaning nicknames, such as "Dungy" and "Buttocks." Dungy became the victim of "every ingenuity to humiliate him within the bounds of law." Buttocks boasted of his family's wealth, and Waugh, perhaps enviously, wanted to punish him. Once, in front of the whole house, Waugh and Fulford sang a song dedicated to Buttocks, honoring his "large posterior, his gluttony," and "his affectation of shaving before he need" (*ALL* 130–31). In July 1920, after a formal tea, Waugh poured leftover cream into a vase on another boy's desk, intending to "stink him out" (*DEW* 89–90). Waugh recognized later that he had had an ulterior motive for all his "nasty manoeuvres," having feared that he would fall from favor and become the "object of contempt" (*ALL* 131). There seems to have been little chance that Waugh's fears could have been realized, for Fulford remembered him as a "leader in jests and gibes against masters and boys."⁹ Waugh was seldom secure about social position, at Lancing or elsewhere. Doubts about others' loyalty probably led him to take initiatives against potential rivals. He also struck at traits he noticed in himself, obnoxiousness and gluttony for instance, ridiculing excesses as a way of asserting his own normality.

Insecurity was also evident in Waugh's attitude toward his address. At Lancing he met people wealthier than he was, as he had at Heath Mount. Claud Cockburn recalled that at age fifteen Waugh once walked across Hampstead Heath in a snowstorm in order to mail a letter. A mailbox was only "a couple of hundred yards from his home," but that was in Golders Green, and Waugh wanted his letters to have the postmark of Hampstead. Cockburn added that Golders Green was "deemed grossly, laughably inferior, as an address, to Hampstead."[10] Age fifteen would correspond with 1918 or 1919, when *A Little Learning* indicates that the postal service changed Arthur's address from Hampstead to Golders Green. The village of North End, where Waugh insisted he had grown up, lay between the two suburbs, and it became absorbed in the growth of Golders Green after a tube station had opened there in 1907. Waugh, at a "self-conscious age," was embarrassed by the "slightly comic connotation" of Golders Green (*ALL* 35). He did not explain the connotation, but Golders Green had already become known as a suburb of middle-class Jews. This association was probably distasteful to Waugh, since anti-Semitism was common in English society. In 1912 Waugh had formed the Pistol Troop specifically to defend the realm against Germans *and* Jews. Alec affirmed that Evelyn had the "curious idiosyncrasy of wanting his letters stamped London N.W.3, which was Hampstead, rather than N.W.11, which was Golders Green." Alec's memory diverged from Cockburn's in one respect. Evelyn didn't have to walk across Hampstead Heath to "give his correspondence 'class.' The N.W.3 mailbox was only a little way up the hill—a No. 4 iron shot for Arnold Palmer,"[11] or, in other words, a couple of hundred yards away. Alec and Cockburn may have remembered the same mailbox and assigned it to different postal zones. It seems strange that Evelyn would bother to walk to an N.W.3 mailbox when his father's stationery had N.W.11 clearly printed on it. Perhaps he went out of his way only for special correspondents, using blank paper and the N.W.3 postmark, or perhaps he thought old, N.W.3 stationery would look ridiculous with an N.W.11 postmark. Inexact as they are, Alec's and Cockburn's memories do at least attest to Evelyn's sensitivity about social class.

Returning to Lancing in the fall of 1919 was easier for Waugh than it had been in 1917 and 1918. He had friends among the Bolshevists, and he seems to have left Luned without regrets. On 27 September he noted that she had not written, and Waugh supposed that their "ridiculous affair" was "at an end." If Luned were to have made any overtures, Waugh thought he would have "to snub her." She was "really not worth it" (*DEW* 21). Waugh was interested in the arrival of Hugh (later Lord) Molson, who had gone to Dartmouth but transferred to Lancing after peacetime reductions in naval training. Waugh found him "flamboyant from the first," with a "superb pomposity of manner and vocabulary" (*ALL* 128). On 2 October he decided that Molson had the "true aristocrat's capacity of being perfectly at home in anyone's company" (*DEW* 23). They soon became friends. Waugh had leisure to observe Molson partly because a railroad strike had created the "pleasant sensation of being besieged," a sensation that returned during strikes in 1921 and 1926, and during war in 1939 and 1940. Waugh was usually content when resisting someone else, in 1919 feeling "remote from the outer world" in a "flint-girt fortress." The strike prevented delivery of books, and Waugh found that the "slackness" began "to pall," because they were all eager to finish school (*DEW* 21, 24). Waugh never cared for schoolwork, but he knew that he had to do some in order to fulfill his ambitions.

He was hardly wasting time, however. He was exercising his facility with language, beginning to make regular entries in his diary. Waugh's intellectual development is evident in his tackling of abstractions, that of his generation, for instance. On 10 October he noted that his father was always saying that his generation had progressed more slowly than Evelyn's had. Evelyn wondered if his fellows would manage to "produce any great men," or if they would simply "fizzle into mediocrity." Waugh thought they were "more precocious if that is at all a good sign" (*DEW* 27). Perhaps new friends, as well as his father, induced Waugh to wonder about his relation to others his age. The topic preoccupied him for the next few years, and he never lost interest in it, describing many contemporaries at length in *A Little Learning*. When he was sixteen, the destiny of his generation seemed limited to either greatness or mediocrity, and Waugh feared the latter. Ability suggested that he might become great, or at least greater than other boys. Perhaps for this reason, he began to regard his diary as a self-portrait that needed to be carefully controlled. On the same day, 10 October, he "tore out and destroyed all the first part of this diary about the holidays. There was little worth preserving and a very great deal that could not possibly be read and was really too dangerous without being funny, so all this book, now reduced to a very meagre pamphlet, must be this term. . . ." Waugh resolved to be "wiser next holidays," more careful about what he wrote down (*DEW* 26). It is not known what Waugh considered dangerous, but he seems to have destroyed personal records on at least three other occasions: in the early 1920s at Oxford; in 1929, when his first wife deserted him; and in 1954, when he suffered hallucinations. Waugh was a public figure by 1929, conscious that his life might attract attention and cautious about preserving documents he considered embarrassing or deeply revealing. Self-censorship had come well before celebrity, at age sixteen, in an extraordinary case of foresight, an extreme case of self-consciousness. The same self-consciousness would plague Waugh, but also complicate his perception, for the rest of his life.

In the fall of 1919, still in the Fifth Form, Waugh began to show interest in debating. In his diary for October he twice recorded longing to speak, but he failed to "summon up enough courage" (*DEW* 24, 30). Waugh battled not only self-consciousness, but also privileges of older boys. He considered a debate in November a "flagrant instance of how those in authority can wangle themselves to win." He likened his frustration to that felt by the "unkillable children of the very poor," certain that in their position he would be a "raving revolutionary." He understood the way that "power can crush any rising." Sensing that someone was curtailing his freedom of speech, Waugh imagined himself as a member of a lower social class, recognizing revolution as one way of redressing inequality. He also found ways to support any rising. During November he defended the motion that "reincarnation of souls is the most reasonable solution to the problem of human immortality." He didn't believe in the motion, realizing that reincarnation is unnecessary, but he was pleased that the speech seemed to have been "quite a success" (*DEW* 36–38).

Speaking in favor of eccentric motions and opposing reasonable ones soon became habits for Waugh. Still he felt hindered, since the Sixth Form dominated most debates. In November Waugh and Molson formed the Dilettanti, Molson proposing a debating society for the Fifth Form, Waugh selecting the name. Waugh and Molson chose members, who met to discuss literary, artistic, and political topics. They were not interested in learning, only in talking, and they often said the opposite of what they really thought. The Dilettanti affirmed that it is easy to defend one's own interests, but that only a "clever fellow" could "find arguments for the enemy" (*ALL* 129). A paper written in February 1921 addressed "The Twilight of Language." Waugh observed that everything had been said simply, and that one had to "find something outrageous and original to say" in order to obtain "a hearing" (*EWA* 76). He assumed the "role of iconoclast" in debate (*ALL* 129), just as he had in writing at Lancing and Heath Mount.

Waugh was not interested only in hearing his opinions applauded by his friends. He continued to seek conventional success in recognized arenas. In November 1919, just after forming the Dilettanti, Waugh was invited to speak at the school debate, honored by the very boys whose power he loathed. He busied himself preparing for the debate, neglecting the Dilettanti and realizing that he had been "brought over from the democratic party by the distinction." Despite his efforts, his motion, left unrecorded, "lost hopelessly," voted down 59 to 29 (*DEW* 37–38). Private debates were, perhaps, more rewarding, leading Waugh more fully to examine accepted ideas. In February 1920 he and Molson discussed religion. Drawing on one of his favorite words, Waugh described their talk as "ridiculous," doubting that "two boys of sixteen" could come to terms with such a subject. Still, they had an "awfully interesting discussion." Surprised to learn that he was "such an individualist," Waugh found it "extraordinary how one builds up one's convictions quite unconsciously." He concluded that the "great charm is really finding one's own opinions, not other people's" (*DEW* 55). Typically, Waugh used debate as a means of self-discovery. He continued to find his own opinions in public debate, later in February voting for the motions "Manners un-make man" and "All religion is an instance of the wishing being father to the thought." The second motion suggests that Waugh was moving past early piety, though the idea might also have been especially provocative at Lancing. The same month he "insincerely" opposed the motion that "this House approves of the education of the masses" (*DEW* 59, 61).

Waugh's skill and eccentricity attracted attention, and the Upper Sixth Form invited him to speak at their visitors' debate. Waugh saw it as a compliment, but he also saw that the invitation came from a "very exclusive if not very distinguished society" (*DEW* 60). He managed to remain active in the Dilettanti, in March feeling obliged to defend David Lloyd George, his "idol" (*DEW* 62), though he had called him a "little beast" in October (*DEW* 32). Clearly Waugh considered wit and style more important than consistency and persuasiveness, and in September 1920 he opposed the motion that "This House deplores the disrespect for age by modern youth" (*DEW* 102). Various societies resisted Waugh's arguments, but the role of iconoclast accorded well with a growing sense of his own importance and a readiness to contradict commonly held notions. This role taxed his ability to argue by presenting the most difficult problem of persuasion, enabled him to characterize the majority as mistaken and inferior in intelligence, and drew attention to himself as the advocate of a strange, sometimes perverse position. If the society voted against him, he could say that they were too stupid to appreciate his point. If they happened to agree with him, he could congratulate himself on his wit and charm.

Another arrangement at Lancing irritated Waugh in the fall of 1919. Dick Harris was replaced as house-tutor in the Headmaster's House. Waugh lived there, he and his fellow residents considering themselves the superiors of boys in other houses. Changing house-tutors was normal, since the master at Head's invariably went on to take charge of the next available house. Waugh thought that this practice constituted a disadvantage, because boys in other houses usually dealt with the "same man of known idiosyncrasy. English boys resent change and are happiest with the familiar, even when odious or ludicrous." Harris was especially popular, and boys took the change as a "personal bereavement." They disliked the replacement, E. B. Gordon, who seemed "sly," as well as "capricious and inquisitive." Gordon became known as "Pussy-foot" and "Super-spy." Boys were as "pettish as a girls' school at the loss of Dick," and Waugh "withheld confidence and affection" (*ALL* 98, 100, 126). Distaste for Gordon contributed to impatience with all masters, though Rev. Bowlby's "outstanding gift was in the choice of subordinates." Years later Waugh admitted that the boys had been "very fortunate in almost all the masters he appointed" (*ALL* 99), but he was not very appreciative in 1919, and he began to irritate teachers more and more in the next two years.

In classes Waugh was often recalcitrant or even disruptive, trying to disguise his impudence as obtuseness. At the beginning of the school year, 27 September 1919 according to the diaries, Waugh and friends were doing their best to rattle a new master, Rev. F. A. Woodard, a Lancing old boy and grandson of the school's founder. Woodard had introduced the "new pronunciation in Latin," and the boys found it an "endless source for supposed misunderstanding." They came up with some "splendid attempts such as SOOBYOONGTEEWAY for the pronunciation of subjunctive." Continuing to exasperate Woodard, the boys discovered that he

2: A Less Important Place than Eton, 1917–1920   59

had the "amiable weakness of letting one get books." They stopped bringing books to class, waiting for a "stampede" back to their houses, thereby wasting ten minutes. Soon they were "arranging it in relays" (*DEW* 20, 26). On 25 October they had a fine time with Woodard, beginning with the "usual preliminary stampede." Woodard started with church history and "rashly asked for any legend . . . connected with the Early Church." Waugh recognized a "golden opportunity," and the boys "filled paper with obscure legends," then unleashed a "storm of questions as to what constituted a legend and what was the exact line between the Early Church and stories about the Disciples and minor saints generally." The hour passed "merrily by, everyone cribbing like sin" (*DEW* 32). Perhaps the master caught on, or perhaps Waugh grew weary of confusing his classroom, for he made no further mention of tormenting Woodard.

    Waugh's campaign of disruption extended to other masters. Social class continued to be a consideration, and scientists were thought to be an "inferior race." Waugh remembered that he and his friends had had "innocent fun . . . causing explosions in the laboratories." The science masters tended to make the weights into a "fetish." Boys were not allowed to touch them, for fear of spoiling their accuracy. Instead, the boys heated the weights on Bunsen burners and then dumped them "sizzling into beakers of cold water" (*ALL* 131). A master named Treble earned Waugh's enmity in February 1920, punishing him for "impertinence" after an explosion in a "legitimate experiment." Two days later Waugh did his best to be rude, but Treble was "impervious to any insult more subtle than physical assault." In May Waugh was still engaging in "guerrilla warfare" against Treble. In June Waugh's class managed to fool a master named Puttock, whom they called "Puttass." A bee flew into the room, and the boys "jumped about and yelled for sometime" (*DEW* 60–61, 77, 81). By 1921, his last year at Lancing, Waugh was a leader, responsible for the discipline of younger boys. Age and position did not increase his sympathy for those who had invested him with authority. His house-tutor, Gordon, was replaced by a "stubborn young clergyman," Woodard, who was "always at loggerheads" with Waugh (*ALL* 126). In October 1921 Waugh referred to his history master, Lucas, as a "little ass" who spent too much time on digressions and generalizations. Waugh was "sick to death of him." Ten days later Lucas "excelled himself in slackness." His lecture on Prussia was "absolutely useless" because he didn't "know a thing about it," and Waugh felt "rather wild" (*DEW* 143–44).

By autumn 1921 Waugh was cramming for a scholarship to Oxford, and he was understandably impatient with Lucas's slackness. He felt that he would have been learning more if he had been studying classics under J. F. Roxburgh (*DEW* 143), a respected master, later the first headmaster of Stowe. This attitude reveals much about Waugh's contempt for instructors. He often saw himself as an undeserving victim of a second-rate education, proffered by second-rate masters at second-rate schools. He sometimes indicated that his education had handicapped him socially for the rest of his life. He thought he deserved the best of everything, and outwitting masters seemed to show that their betters could have made more use of his intellect. Waugh was more interested in social preeminence, then and later, than in the intellectual stimulation of a leading school, but he nevertheless emphasized the mediocrity of Lancing in order to excuse his academic record at Oxford. He did not always add that he himself had made his education less valuable than it could have been, having found it more amusing to frustrate masters than to listen to what they had to say. Waugh could almost ensure that Lancing fulfilled his assessment of its mediocrity: he did not distinguish himself at Oxford because he had not gone to a better school, but he had not gone to a better school because he had helped to make his education as pointless as possible.

Waugh also enjoyed ridiculing the Officers' Training Corps, and his reasons are easier to understand. In *A Little Learning,* he explained that his coterie concentrated their attack on the OTC, pretending to be motivated by "pacifism." Actually, the OTC was a convenient target, in that it offered "immunity . . . from severe punishment." When boys committed "crimes in uniform," the only penalty was a "defaulters' parade," usually "rendered farcical." Practically required of boys seeking advancement, the OTC was widely despised, and Waugh's misbehavior mirrored that of his contemporaries at other public schools. He remembered one especially ingenious maneuver, again revealing disappointment that he had not gone to the more famous school. At Eton a platoon "paraded in horn-rimmed spectacles and numbered off: ' . . . ten, Knave, Queen, King.'" Waugh's ruses were not as "stylish," but he and his friends "outraged local tradition." Lancing was susceptible to outrage, because the school was proud of its OTC. Minor public schools had little hope of surpassing their betters in sports or scholarship, but the Corps offered another means of competing with them. Within the OTC, "boys without other distinction could by zeal achieve positions of authority." So many people taking the

2: A Less Important Place than Eton, 1917–1920   61

Corps seriously was enough to drive Waugh into subverting it. He and his friends "despised the 'Corps-maniacs,'" claiming that those who won promotion proved the "fatuity of the institution." Waugh's platoon did find original ways to frustrate Corps-maniacs, however unworthy of Eton he might have considered them later. Once they fell into formation "each with one boot scrupulously polished and the other muddy." They marched with "ostentatious incompetence, dropping rifles, turning right instead of left," and "making the movement of forming fours odd and even numbers together." During exercises, they "either hid from action or advanced immediately at the 'enemy,'" so that they were "'killed' at the first moment of battle" (*ALL* 131–32).

Ragging the OTC may have been both enjoyable and safe, but it would be a mistake to see it as only one more example of Waugh's disenchantment with the school, its pretenses, and its reverence for authority. Some obligations imposed by the Corps disgusted Waugh, in the same way that latrines had disgusted him as a new man. Sixteen-year-olds had to go through ten days of OTC Camp at Tidworth Park, Salisbury Plain in the summer of 1920. Waugh wrote that the latrines were "horrible," and boys had to "smoke in protection against the smell." Trying to clean up was one of the "torments of the damned." Waugh shuddered as he remembered "washing up army stew in cold water kneeling in mud" (*DEW* 90). In a letter to Tom Driberg, written that summer or the next, Waugh indicated that he found "small comfort in sodomy," and that camp offered him "little that is charming."[12] Waugh tended to exaggerate difficulties, but the OTC added trials to a way of life he found trying enough without it. He resented those in authority over him, whether Corps-maniacs or army officers. The officer in charge of an examination for certificates in October 1919 was the "most blatantly risen-from-the-ranks" Waugh had ever seen, "not even a Temporary Gentleman but a Permanent Oik" (*DEW* 31). Evidently Waugh resisted directions from those he took to belong to classes lower than his own, both officers and science masters. He had lost interest in science and the army. The war was over, and there seemed to be no reason to take military rigors seriously. Little wonder that Waugh exploited the OTC for the sake of amusement, surprised to learn that Molson wanted to resign from the Corps; Waugh thought it was "far jollier to stay in and rag it" (*DEW* 105). Amusement he considered slight compensation, years later still seeming to resent the OTC's demands upon his time. He remembered one argument in favor of the OTC, that it prepared boys for "immediate commissions" in case of war. When Waugh volunteered for service, however, he was not asked if he had earned his certificate. All the schoolboy drills proved useless in the "army of 1939" (*ALL* 132–33).

Diaries starting in 1919 record Waugh's participation in athletics, also expected of boys aspiring to leadership. Waugh had little confidence in his skill, and in sports he sought anonymity or bare competence, not the notoriety he sought in debate and the OTC. In November 1919 he observed that goal was a "terrible place, much too much in the fore when their forwards are strong and no look-in when they are bad." He found running more to his taste, as fewer people depended on his performance. After one race that fall, he remarked that once one had built a "reputation of being able to do better one need not sweat," so he "took things easy" (*DEW* 34, 38). Self-conscious as ever, Waugh worried about failure and its effect on his reputation. In January 1920 he would have liked to have trained prior to a match, but he decided not to work "too palpably," in case he didn't "get a place at all" (*DEW* 54). As in debate, Waugh was careful to protect himself against failure, presenting himself as a pure amateur while "secretly eager" to earn as many honors as possible (*ALL* 133). Looking back on athletic efforts, he was pleased not to have been a "total wreck," a Lancing term for an athletic incompetent. He managed to make his house team in football, boxing, swimming, and track, but he was not skillful enough to represent the college. Waugh "never enjoyed competition" and felt "glad to escape without ignominy" (*ALL* 111). Waugh did enjoy other kinds of competition, in debate, in the classroom, and in the OTC, where his impish sense of humor could show that he wasn't taking competition seriously. He could not yet turn a track meet into the Llanabba Sports of *Decline and Fall*, and athletics left him torn between sizable ambition and moderate ability. He contented himself with scraping by, devoting most energy to more congenial, more interesting pursuits.

The fall of 1919 is also important because Waugh for the first time saw that Bolshevism might prove costly in one way or another. At the beginning of the term he narrowly missed earning library privileges. Characteristically, he interpreted this fairly trivial decision as part of a dangerous trend, noting that he seemed "to miss everything by just a hair's breadth." He had also failed to make his house team, and he imagined that after death he would "miss getting into heaven by one place" (*DEW* 21). Waugh had perhaps expected too much, thinking that he deserved honors not yet within reach, but missed opportunities seem to have opened his eyes in certain ways. In October he realized that he had gone too far in writing after receiving a letter from his father. Arthur did not like Evelyn's "'Romance' essay," finding it too "satirical" (*DEW* 33). In November Evelyn "had to scrap" a paper on "Limericks" he had wanted to read to the Dilettanti, recognizing that they lacked the "right sense of humour to enjoy it and might even think they were being ragged and resent it."[13] By December, despite having won some academic prizes, Waugh was feeling "fearfully moody and melancholy" (*DEW* 39–41), probably because he was having to restrain his anarchic (or Bolshevist) tendency just when it was emerging as a prominent part of his personality.

Conflict between self-expression and self-restraint is also evident in Waugh's ambivalence about authority, which he wanted simultaneously to flout and to exercise. Waugh became junior man on a minor council in May 1920, gaining a "very shallow sort of officialdom" but losing his friends. He felt "lonely," and the deference of younger boys gave him little consolation. He sensed that it was "ridiculous to get so depressed at gaining a position" that he "should have been more depressed to miss" (*DEW* 73). If depression was often Waugh's reaction to promotion, anger was common when he was passed over. In June, staying in the Upper Dormitory of Head's House, he called Gordon an "insufferable little bounder" for keeping him "up with the children" after his friends had been moved down. Gordon had asked Waugh to stay there, but the place was undignified, preventing Waugh from taking his proper place in "House society." Gordon had managed to wound his "pride pretty severely" (*DEW* 85), because Waugh had always assumed that he would take a proper, or leading, place in the house. Such a place would have satisfied Waugh's somewhat exalted estimation of his own ability, but failure to attain it, even through the oversight of a master, would have rendered him a nonentity, indistinct from masses of boys who never did anything of note. He saw that privilege came only with moderation and the loss of at least some camaraderie, but he tried to have it both ways and, to a surprising extent, succeeded.

Sometime in 1920 he began to perceive the need for, if he did not yet begin to pursue, a middle course between anarchy and sycophancy, independent enough to preserve integrity but not outrageous enough to shut him out from advancement. He retained a love of disruption, but he knew that he could not always indulge it if he were to fulfill ambitions. Thus joy is understandable when he and friends managed to upset convention in ways that had not occurred even to his devious mind. In February 1920 his house won the football cup, though they had not been considered contenders. Relishing the triumph of fellow amateurs, Waugh noted that the "out-Houses" were "blank with amazement." His teammates' "ecstatic joy" seemed to be "worth a life of serene happiness" (*DEW* 59). Martin Stannard characterizes his "jubilation" as an "outburst of delight at the discomfiture of the authorities,"[14] and it is indeed hard to imagine Waugh effusing over a mere athletic event. Achievement was, for Waugh, necessary and expected, but in order to be enjoyable and therefore worthwhile, it had to come in the right way: effortlessly, and in opposition to authorities' opinions.

As Waugh began to move more often outside his own house, he made friends in other parts of the school. Fulford proposed that throughout 1920 Waugh's "out-of-House friends . . . fostered in him a certain fatigue with the prejudices and loyalties inside the Heads."[15] Certainly other factors contributed to fatigue, but Waugh found among these friends freedom to indulge eccentricities he felt obliged to restrain in his own house. They included Dudley Carew, Hugh Molson, Tom Driberg, J. F. Roxburgh, and Francis Crease, who practiced illumination and calligraphy in a cottage outside the school's grounds. Carew thought that Waugh in his autobiography exaggerated the importance of Crease as a way of giving himself a connection outside of Lancing.[16] Carew may be right, because Waugh's relationship with Crease did not really last very long, though Crease did affect Waugh's development in some important ways. Waugh had shown interest in script and illumination, and Gordon introduced him to Crease in the fall of 1919. Waugh started taking lessons once a week at Crease's cottage, but he was interested in more than what he could learn about the art of a scribe. He found Crease's quiet life an agreeable alternative to the noisy crowds and intrigues of Lancing. By February 1920 he thought that the "only way to get any pleasure out of life here is to cut oneself off as much as possible from the tide of events." He had tried to jump in and "enjoy the cold water," but it had been "no good. Crease's life is about the best after all" (*DEW* 56). As Jeffrey Heath points out, the need for refuge is a recurring theme in Waugh's life and fiction, and, like the "retiring characters in his own novels, Waugh constantly sought a safe retreat where he might find protection from the idiocies around him."[17] Lancing was always very demanding for Waugh, who still had, for all his brutality, a fairly delicate sensibility. Much as he relished the privacy and tranquility of Crease's cottage, he also relished the chance to escape from the role of iconoclast he had created for himself.

Difficulties of this role are evident in "Lancing Chapel," a poem

2: A Less Important Place than Eton, 1917–1920 65

Waugh wrote in May 1920. "Lancing Chapel" satirizes the poet's world, but it also expresses hope that the poet may be redeemed from the world; in these ways "Lancing Chapel" resembles *The World to Come*. The target in "Lancing Chapel" is not the First World War, but the masters of Lancing. Waugh complains that the "coin they give us rings untrue; it swells the purse but leaves us poor." Lacking spiritual guidance, the poet asks God to remember "in thy timeless love who turned to copper thy pure gold"—negligent masters, not innocent boys. In conclusion, Waugh imagines God agreeing with him, saying that they "gave thee nothing; thou hast brought thyself. Poor servant enter in." In *A Little Learning,* Waugh considered "Lancing Chapel" a "deplorable invocation," feeling certain that there had been "no sincerity" in it. He had had "no apprehensions about the final judgement nor special resentment against the clerical masters," and his poem had reflected only a loss of "taste for everything ecclesiastical" (*ALL* 141–42).

Waugh was closer to his experience than any biographer can ever be, but these comments are hard to accept. He may not have been especially apprehensive about final judgment, but both *The World to Come* and "Lancing Chapel" end as the poet achieves communion with God, a consummation Waugh seems to have devoutly wished. He was, moreover, worried about his own immortality, even in adolescence. He may not have harbored special resentment against the clerical masters, but other evidence shows that Waugh resented, or at least ridiculed, almost every master at Lancing. Even in *A Little Learning* he seemed to resent the indifferent spiritual instruction he had received in public school. Though Waugh claimed he had lost his taste for everything ecclesiastical, he had not lost his taste for illuminated script or theological debate. Over these he exercised some control, whereas during services he was only an impotent observer. His self-appointed role as iconoclast meant that he was almost obliged to lampoon ceremonies his superiors deemed serious. Waugh may not yet have been contemptuous of formal religion, but his role dictated that he should be, and it may have led to what he represented later as a loss of sincerity. Certainly "Lancing Chapel" reflects continuing difficulty in dealing with the school and the masters.

Thus Waugh concentrated on relations with Crease early in 1920. He invited Crease to spend the Easter holidays at Underhill, and Crease became the "first adult visitor" Waugh brought to his parents' house. The occasion produced a significant revelation. According to *A Little Learning,* Arthur Waugh's "most obvious characteristic was theatricality," but Evelyn did not realize it until

Crease pointed it out. Crease commented that Arthur was "entirely charming, and acting all the time." Waugh went to his mother, who "confirmed the judgement." Evelyn's "eyes were opened," and for the first time he saw his father as Arthur had "always . . . appeared to others" (*ALL* 69). Crease's comment put even more stress on an already strained relationship. Evelyn may have imagined that Arthur's acting hid his real feelings, for Alec remembered Evelyn at a party at age sixteen. He appeared in a tailcoat handed down from Arthur to Alec, explaining that it had "come down from generation to generation of them that hate me."[18] Arthur's acting certainly did begin to annoy Evelyn. In April 1921 he heard his father give a "good lecture" that was "incorrigibly theatrical as usual." Later that month he decided that Arthur had been "ineffably silly the whole holidays" (*DEW* 123, 125). Evelyn's renewed estrangement from Arthur probably shows adjustment to Lancing in his last two years, though Arthur's influence on his son's behavior may have actually increased after the Easter holidays of 1920 and 1921. Alec argued that Evelyn was "very like his father, and his father's own emotionalism put him on his guard. He must have often thought, 'I could become like this. I mustn't let myself become like this.'"[19] Arthur's example became another kind of restraint on Evelyn, at the same time heightening his awareness of how an effective actor could elicit a desired response from an audience.

Waugh's brief intimacy with Crease was almost at an end. In May 1920 Waugh continued to work at the cottage while Crease was away. Crease had hidden a precious, antique knife for cutting quills, but Waugh found it, used it, and broke it. He wrote to explain what had happened, and on 31 May he received Crease's angry reply. Waugh had "betrayed his trust and ruined his life as a scribe," for without that knife Crease would "never be able to write again" (*ALL* 151–52). Waugh felt "very hurt that he should take that line about it" (*DEW* 80) and, more than that, "radically shocked," not by "magnification of his loss," but by Crease's suggestion that Evelyn had been presumptuous. Crease wrote again to apologize and retract his statements, but after the "incident of the broken blade," their friendship was never the same (*ALL* 152). Waugh was nevertheless willing to write a preface for Crease's *Thirty-Four Decorative Designs,* privately printed in London in 1927 (*EAR* 22–25).

The incident of the broken blade suggests a striking similarity between Waugh and Crease. Waugh recalled that several years after the incident his mother had received a "distraught letter" from Crease. On his way home from church, he had been "falsely

2: A Less Important Place than Eton, 1917–1920 67

identified as a clergyman wanted . . . on charges of unnatural vice," and the police had taken him in for questioning. Crease had a "highly nervous temper," and the interrogation was a "disaster." He claimed that he could never "go to church anywhere again." Waugh saw in this episode the "incident of the pen-knife grossly enlarged" (*ALL* 156). After he had read Crease's first letter about the broken knife, Waugh wrote in his diary that the rest of the day was "fairly all wrong." He played tennis with a "borrowed ball" that he and his partner managed to lose. Waugh anticipated a "nasty letter from home" and a "bad row" at school, all that he needed "to complete the canvas." He was placing a small wager on the Derby and with "Barnsley organizing a sweepstake," fearing the loss of all his money and his "one friend." His work was going "none too well," his "script and drawing worse." Waugh had "nothing for the Art Show," and he suspected that Mrs. Bowlby had destroyed the few things he had finished (*DEW* 80). The headmaster's wife had borrowed some of his work and probably had not destroyed any of it, though he did have trouble getting it back from her. Exaggeration and, more often, imagination of misfortune point to Waugh's kinship with Crease, their tendency to represent minor setbacks as irrevocable reverses. In 1920 Waugh may not have been conscious that they shared this characteristic, but it nevertheless helped to draw them together. It also intensified Waugh's feeling of having lost both a friend and a refuge from Lancing.

Waugh was once again dependent on whatever support he could draw from Lancing itself, J. F. Roxburgh offering some. Waugh remembered going to church and seeing Crease in his "cape and soft cravat," seeming "diminished." Waugh realized that Crease and Roxburgh were "opposites," and he "transferred . . . allegiance to the more forceful and flamboyant person" (*ALL* 162). Crease asked for precise, graceful script, but Roxburgh asked for precise, assertive speech and graceful conduct. Arthur Waugh had already tried to show Evelyn the value of these things, but Roxburgh impressed the boy in a way his father never had. Waugh went to Roxburgh for Latin and French, "always in awe of him," seldom daring to test this master as he tested others. Once Waugh did try to "score off J. F." Roxburgh had given a lecture on Praed, but through Arthur's readings, Evelyn had already learned about the poet. In his next essay, Waugh quoted Praed several times, drawing on poems not mentioned in class. Roxburgh dismissed the essay as a "*mere orgy of dittography*" (*ALL* 160–62). Waugh admired the apparent self-assurance of such devastating comments, and they became characteristic of his response to anything innovative. Under Roxburgh's influence, Waugh developed tremendous respect for wit, style, and grace, and that respect never left him. Fulford remembered once having had Roxburgh to tea, a success in spite of the tea. He and Waugh were disappointed, because Roxburgh never said anything about the strange taste. Waugh told Fulford that Roxburgh had been "considerate," not wanting the boys to think that he found the tea objectionable in any way. Pleasure in niceties of language was also evident when another master reported that a boy "was pleased to belch rudely in my face." Waugh was "delighted by the well-chosen 'pleased' and 'rudely', and the words echoed round our circle to the end of our time."[20] Waugh was starting to see that words can be manipulated to represent actions, often with humorous effects. He was also beginning to recognize that speech and behavior can send exquisitely appropriate or embarrassingly inappropriate messages to one's company, depending on one's competence. Roxburgh's apparent mastery of both language and conduct made him worthy of emulation, since equally unimpeachable manners would, Waugh hoped, free him from concern about his own social standing.

Roxburgh attracted Waugh for other reasons and probably influenced him in other ways. Roxburgh was a dandy, exuding "panache of the kind to which adolescents are specially susceptible." He was "consciously pre-eminent" in the school, everything about him "calculated to impress," and boys tried hard to imitate his enunciation and witticisms. By then conscious of his father's acting, Waugh may have been more receptive to Roxburgh's. He seemed always "jaunty and fresh as a leading actor on the boards, in the limelight, demanding complete attention" (*ALL* 157–59). Conforming in some ways to stereotype, Roxburgh was also homosexual. His interest in Waugh was only "professional," as Roxburgh perceived "potentialities worth cultivating" and helped to build the boy's self-esteem. Roxburgh seems not to have sought "physical release" for his "passions," but his attachment to "individual boys" may have eroded some of Waugh's resistance to such relationships (*ALL* 160–61). Certainly Waugh showed more interest in homosexuality in his last two years at Lancing, though he remained "pure" until his second or third term at Oxford. In June 1920 he wrote a poem, "*Ars Amoris* for ———," describing love between two other boys. Waugh ironically termed it "platonic," as "pure as a Gibbs' House Grove," one of Lancing's latrines. The parody is gentle, perhaps because Waugh wanted it to be read by the older boy. He thought it was not bad, considering that he had composed it in "twenty minutes at the fag end of the day" (*DEW* 81).[21] Waugh was still criticizing others, but he was combining observation with humor instead of staying serious, as he had in "Lancing Chapel." Perhaps making fun of others' emotions helped him to suppress his own, as he continued to keep his distance from other boys.

Roxburgh seemed to be an agnostic, and, though "reticent about his skepticism," the boys thought that he "doubted the existence of the entire supernatural order." He occasionally raised a question in the debating society, asking about life after death, for instance, topics that the boys were old enough to contemplate, though Roxburgh "never suggested an answer." After the boys had sung "God Moves in a Mysterious Way" in chapel, Roxburgh led an "examination of the mixture of metaphors in that hymn" (*ALL* 157, 159). Roxburgh's appeals to the power of reason and the integrity of language intrigued Waugh, and reason and language began to supplant religion in his system of values. He recognized that Roxburgh's "religious position alone set him apart from the spirit of the school" (*ALL* 158), and perhaps Waugh saw imitation of the master as a way to affirm independence and ability. Having developed more confidence in himself, Waugh became less dependent on Christianity as an external source of direction, though he seems to have replaced it with another external source, Roxburgh. Within a year Waugh would declare himself an atheist. His spirituality remained, leading to reception into the Roman Catholic Church in 1930. Waugh thought that Roxburgh probably looked on conversion as the "betrayal of all he had tried to inculcate" (*ALL* 162), but as a Roman Catholic Waugh felt that he had been betrayed as well. He resented the nudge toward agnosticism Roxburgh had given him, resentment only occasionally revealed in an otherwise equitable portrait of Roxburgh in the autobiography. In 1965, in one of his last reviews, Waugh praised a biography by Noel Annan, *Roxburgh of Stowe,* referring to his former master as an "admirable man" (*EAR* 638).

Waugh's friendships with Roxburgh and Crease indicate how far he had come in his first three years at Lancing and how far he had still to go in his remaining two. He had moved past early, largely self-imposed isolation, risking exposure of his personality and hoping others would find something worthy of appreciation. At the same time, Waugh had focused attention on much older men, outcasts in their own ways. Neither Roxburgh nor Crease showed much more than interest in the boy's education, while Waugh was probably seeking a more personal, more profound relationship. He had some friends his own age in the Bolshevists, but none he remembered as distinctly as his "Two Mentors." Waugh's choice of terms suggests that, at that age, he preferred learning to teaching. He was beginning to assert himself in the classroom, in the OTC, in debate, and in writing, but he was still in a state of dependence, looking for models rather than striking out on his own. In Roxburgh and Crease he found two versions of what he might become, and he considered each one carefully before deciding that his own path had to be independent, not imitative. In the next two years, Waugh would become more and more independent, partly because of disappointment in Roxburgh and Crease. Even as he recognized the limitations of others, Waugh emulated whatever he found useful or admirable. Roxburgh and Crease were leading him past dependence on religion and his father. They were also fostering, if not creating, respect for certain attainments, Crease showing Waugh the dedication and self-sufficiency of the artist, Roxburgh the power of language and performance. Art, language, and performance would become more and more important to Waugh, enabling him to live as he pleased, even at Lancing. Using language in art eventually supported Waugh and his family, but initially, and more fundamentally, it offered opportunities to stigmatize sources of displeasure and to explore choices confronting him. Language also became part of performance, part of Waugh's role. The role helped him to overcome fears that his sincere self might be rejected, and it prevented others from getting too close. Performance came to serve Waugh as another form of self-protection in that it masked emotions, but it also allowed him to entertain friends, to intimidate rivals, and to court trouble he had carefully avoided as a new man.

3
Limited Bolshevist, 1920–1921 and After

In August 1920, before returning to Lancing, Waugh found time to write two pieces that have survived. One is, like many early works, a parody, of Walter Savage Landor's epigram "On His Seventy-fifth Birthday." Landor had written

> I strove with none, for none was worth my strife,
>   Nature I loved, and next to Nature, Art;
> I warmed both hands before the fire of life.
>   It sinks, and I am ready to depart.

Waugh's version is dedicated to a "decadent modernist":

> I strove with none, lest he should strive too well;
> Nature I feared, but safely toyed with art;
> I warmed both feet before the fires of Hell,
> They rise a little; comfort bids depart.
>
> *(DEW 95)*

Despite the pretense of dedication, Waugh was dealing with his own concerns. He "strove with none," lest others prove better advocates, athletes, or scholars. It is not clear why Waugh would have feared nature, except perhaps as a source of sexuality, or as an eventual cause of death. He admitted having "safely toyed with art," probably remembering time spent with Crease. Not yet having declared himself an atheist, Waugh thought he had confronted the "fires of Hell." Sensing danger, Waugh found it best to "depart"; presumably he meant to abandon whatever wickedness he had indulged during the vacation. Such self-consciousness consistently limited Waugh's natural bolshevism, making it hard for him to enjoy anything without fearing the consequences. In the next two years, he struggled to balance bolshevism against responsibilities to himself, his school, and his parents.

The other piece from August 1920 is a valentine addressed to

Horatio Bottomley, the editor of *John Bull,* a patriotic magazine. Waugh alluded to *Hamlet,* playing upon Bottomley's first name, reminding him that there are more things in heaven and earth than he dreamed of, and suggesting that Bottomley didn't believe in heaven. He added that love is not the least of these things, as "someone" had said, though "not in John Bull" (*EWA* 57). Whatever doubts he may have had about his own character, Waugh seems firmly Christian here, referring to heaven and First Corinthians in order to expose the limitations of Bottomley's patriotism. Christianity transcended jingoism, but Bottomley was himself a kind of bolshevist, and for many years Waugh found it difficult to reconcile spirituality with aggressiveness he disliked in others but recognized in himself.

Elevated to the Sixth Form in September 1920, Waugh felt "happier" than he had ever been at school, in a "greatly raised social position" (*DEW* 102). He expressed exuberance and secured his position by criticizing others. Perhaps he associated Bottomley's patriotism with the Corps-maniacs of the OTC; in October 1920 he wrote an essay on "Maps," claiming that in its "lust for maps . . . the full subtlety of the bellicose mind is revealed." Far from explaining anything, maps serve only to simplify and distort: "nineteenth century pseudo-Gothic and early Saxon churches" are "degraded to the same 'conventional sign,'" foolish equations representing the "ideals for which soldiers . . . will keep awake in military school." Waugh managed to insult the OTC even in assignments, incidentally sneering at Lancing's architecture in the reference to nineteenth-century pseudo-Gothic. As in his valentine, Waugh treated ironically what some of his contemporaries were taking seriously. He did the same in "Convention," an essay written a week before "Maps." Waugh argued that convention is only "self-protection of the mediocrities." He advised "cleverer people to respect the shams they can so easily despise. Mr. Bernard Shaw acts as a cad in offending those earnest middle classes who have paid eight and sixpence for their seats." Clearly Waugh fancied himself as one of the cleverer people, but in this case intelligence led to tolerance, not ridicule, as in the other two pieces. He went on to say that the "fundamental cynicism of life is clothed by the mediocrities; if anyone can see its true nakedness, the least they can do is courteously to look away" (*EWA* 58–59). Waugh's meaning is not quite clear, probably because he did not bother to articulate it in an assigned essay. He had argued ingeniously in favor of convention, perhaps preparing himself for transition into a senior

3: Limited Bolshevist, 1920–1921 and After

boy, perhaps realizing that he could no longer flout seniority if he were to enjoy its advantages.

In the fall of 1920 Waugh also started his first novel. He abandoned it at the beginning of 1921, but the surviving fragment contains an interesting dedication:

> To myself,
> Evelyn Arthur St. John Waugh
> to whose sympathy and app-
> reciation alone it owes its being. . . .

The "Dedicatory letter" conceived of critics as adversaries, imagining that his family's literary interests would be raised against him.

> 'Another of these precocious Waughs,' they will say, 'one more nursery novel.' So be it. There is always a certain romance, to the author at least, about a first novel which no reviewer can quite shatter. Good luck! You still have high hopes and big ambitions and have not yet been crushed in the mill of professionalism. (*EWA* 60–61)

In later years Waugh realized that his family's interests had been an advantage rather than a handicap, but a lingering sense of having been born at a disadvantage led him, at age seventeen, to see even Alec's novel as a hindrance to his career.

The story concerns a schoolboy named Peter, his hatred of the OTC, his impatience with the school's improvisation during the war, his boredom with an aging history master, and his relationship with his brother Ralf, a soldier five years older than Peter. Waugh was obviously drawing quite closely on his experience, as he would do in many later novels. Robert Murray Davis notes that Waugh made two important changes as he transformed life into fiction: he moves the "family home from Hampstead to 'the Hall' at Bulfrey Combe, a small rural village, and he makes Peter and Ralf three years older than the Waugh brothers," maintaining five years' difference in age. Anticipating my view, Davis suggests that some "Waugh critics would no doubt attribute the last two modifications of fact to Evelyn's desire to present his alter ego as more mature and more highly placed socially." Instead, Davis finds the fragment "far less self-aggrandizing than exploratory," noting that Waugh contrasts Bulfrey Combe and Bulfrey, a growing industrial town, in order to present the village as a refuge threatened by changes stemming from the war.[1] Need for refuge and threats to rural England recur in Waugh's fiction; he had felt the same need as a child, when he had seen the beginning of urban sprawl in Hampstead.

Aristocratic heroes, including Basil Seal, Tony Last, William Boot, and Guy Crouchback, also recur in his work, as Waugh often imagined himself in more privileged positions, attributing his experience to upper-class characters. Those characters usually seek refuge in country estates, and early in life Waugh seems to have put together the need for refuge, the danger to the countryside, and the aristocratic hero. The association emerges, however incompletely, for the first time in this fragment. Contrast between Bulfrey Combe and Bulfrey may have enabled Waugh to comment on a social trend, but choosing Bulfrey Combe over Hampstead also allowed him imaginatively to raise his social status, a concern for some time before 1920 and for many years thereafter.

Changing the ages of the brothers was, Davis remarks,

> based more on social history than on personal aggrandizement. In March 1918, Evelyn was fourteen and a half; Peter is seventeen and a half for two reasons: first, to allow Waugh to place him at Selchurch [the name of the school] in the summer term of 1914, so that he can contrast the opulence, ease, and intellectual distinction of that period with the privation, academic slackness, and war mania of 1918; second, so that Peter is faced with the immediate prospect of leaving school for the battlefront, and he knows and resents the fact that the Officer Training Corps . . . has not prepared him to function in that world.[2]

Sound reasons for changing biographical facts, though it seems unlikely that Waugh would have aged his hero in order to present a more mature self. He seldom dealt with any hero older than himself, focusing instead on his past and his younger self, as he does, for the most part, in the fragment. Ralf's age seems to have mattered only in that he is five years older than Peter, just as Alec was five years older than Evelyn. Waugh preserved other biographical details, transferring to Peter his own resentment of the OTC and, perhaps, his own distaste for the war mania of people like Horatio Bottomley. Spring 1918 was, moreover, the time of Alec's capture by the Germans, and something similar might have happened to Ralf if Evelyn had continued writing. Contrast between the war and the summer of 1914 became conventional in European literature, and it is also operating in the fragment. Peter's age suggests that Waugh may have imagined more than contrast. Peter would have turned eighteen in September 1918, weeks before the end of the war. Peter never reached the front lines, and there is no evidence that Waugh intended him to, but Waugh certainly had created an opportunity to be exploited. Peter realizes that "next year, if the war was still on, as it showed every sign of being,

3: Limited Bolshevist, 1920–1921 and After   75

would see him fighting. It brought everything terribly near." Peter has learned "much of what it was like over there from his brother," feeling "sure that he would not be able to stand it" (*EWA* 63), but Waugh's dates and ages suggest that Peter might have proved himself through the ordeal of battle. Perhaps Waugh envisioned a reunion between Peter and the captured Ralf.

The fragment also mentions Moira, Ralf's girlfriend. Waugh seems to have drawn this character after Barbara Jacobs, though Moira is younger than Barbara, the same age as Peter. Perhaps Waugh was also thinking of Barbara's sister, Luned. Peter leaves school to see Moira and Ralf at Bulfrey Combe, inverting Alec and Barbara's visit to Lancing in October 1919. Peter seems to admire the couple, who are free to move outside the dullness of school, but, as Davis observes, Peter has also "begun to judge Ralf's witty utterances as calculated for effect." Peter's ambivalence about Ralf undoubtedly reflects Evelyn's ambivalence about Alec, and the fragment suggests that Peter's ambivalence might have developed into an urge to compete with his older brother. Davis sees that the "fragment ends before Peter can assert himself as rival in war, love (note the effect of making Peter and Moira contemporaries), or words."[3] Waugh may have stopped writing for any number of reasons, and Davis is willing to propose a few. The fragment enabled Waugh to

> objectify in the war his fears of the adult world, his resentment of the system that was preparing him for it so badly, and his early, grudging respect and resentment of the older brother who seemed to be winning the prizes—manhood, marriage, literary success—to which Evelyn aspired by means that he could not yet clearly imagine. Perhaps this is the real reason that the novel was never completed.

Perhaps, but Waugh had been imagining manhood and marriage, if not literary success, ever since he had learned to write. Why would he suddenly stop at age seventeen? Davis goes on to suggest that, "having outlined his social themes but finding himself unwilling to face even an imaginative rivalry with Alec, [Evelyn] welcomed the return to schoolboy status."[4] No doubt he did, leaving the hard work of writing fiction, but again Evelyn had been facing actual rivalry with Alec ever since birth. Why would he refuse to represent in fiction a relationship so familiar to him? Perhaps Evelyn wished to avoid embarrassing Alec, but that hypothesis fails to explain the many cutting remarks Evelyn made about his brother.

Failure of imagination and nerve probably contributed to abandonment of the novel, but lack of curiosity may have been an even more basic reason to give up. Waugh had already written one short story about brothers, "Fidon's Confetion," and he would write one more, "Winner Takes All," in the 1930s, but few of his other works devote any attention to the relationship. The war trilogy is an exception, but Waugh uses three brothers instead of two, suggesting comparisons between himself and Guy Crouchback while discouraging connections between Alec and Gervase or Ivo. It is surprising that Waugh made so little use of brothers in his fiction, since he made so much of other relationships, with Oxford friends, his first wife, his father, and so on. He tried to make something of the relationship in 1920, intending to write a study of "a man of two minds by his brother," Alec evidently inspiring the man of two minds. The divided self continued to interest Evelyn throughout his career, but the divided self that really intrigued him was his own, not Alec's. Evelyn admired Alec to a certain extent and was loyal to him, but he had never really liked him. Perhaps ambivalence led Evelyn to try to articulate the complexity of his feelings in a novel. Evelyn's best fiction depends on a more complicated ambivalence, involving strong but delusive attraction to some person or ideal. He soon discovered that he wasn't interested enough in his brother to write a full-length novel about him. He wasn't interested enough in Lancing to write a novel about it, either, and the project ended, a few weeks and several pages after it had begun. Alec and Lancing were interesting in themselves, but Evelyn never loved them in the way that he loved other things. When love turned to disappointment, he wrote at his best, compelled to articulate what was wrong with something so apparently beautiful, and what had been wrong with himself when he had fallen under its spell.

Sensitivity about Alec's military service may also have made Evelyn eager to help break the miners' strike in April 1921. He sensed that "war fever" had broken out again, as it had in August 1914. Waugh was "anxious to get some work, but the only people . . . being called up" were "over eighteen." To his "disgust," his parents refused to let him join. Too young for the First World War, Waugh found inability to serve in 1921 "exasperating," as England was apparently headed for "civil war," with him left out of it. The situation wasn't quite as serious as he thought, but he never doubted his value to his country and his social class. As in debate, he did not admit definite values unless they served his own ends, remarking that the dispute had "ceased to be a matter of right or wrong and is merely war." If Waugh had been a miner, he would

3: Limited Bolshevist, 1920–1921 and After 77

have been "only too anxious to strike;" since he was not, he tried "to break them" (*DEW* 124). Opportunity to fight was more important than the reason for fighting, one's choice dictated by class, not by reason or emotion.

Waugh continued to write in early 1921, after he had abandoned his novel. Sometime in February he wrote a poem, "The Philosopher," celebrating a hero whose greatness makes him unintelligible to other men. The philosopher's character and intellect attract enmity, and in this way he becomes the prototype for most of Waugh's other heroes, from Paul Pennyfeather to Guy Crouchback. Waugh dwells on the philosopher's loneliness in the opening lines:

> Among the mean adventuring of men,
> Godlike he walked and like a man he died;
> He passed the taunting mediocrities
> Smiling, supreme & unaccompanied.

The philosopher overcomes loneliness in death, finding in "the Darkness . . . Great kindred spirits long misunderstood." Together, "through undivided days," they discuss "all their ills and find the talking good." The philosopher is still not satisfied;

> So far was he above the frenzied stress
> Of all the little men that hated him,
> That he could love them for their littleness.

Waugh saw himself in the philosopher, sensing his own greatness, bored by "mean adventuring" and "frenzied stress" at Lancing. He never approached love for others' "littleness," endowing an autobiographical hero with virtues greater than his own. Waugh often did the same thing in mature fiction, emphasizing heroes' innocence in order to rouse readers' sympathy. "The Philosopher" is also interesting for its promise of immortality, its faith in a better world. The poem's Latin epigram asserts that the "living power of the soul will prevail and will proceed far beyond the flaming walls of the universe" (*EWA* 72–73). Waugh was once again attributing alienation to his own superiority, seeking consolation in the prospect of deliverance not only from Lancing, but from life itself. "The Philosopher" is an early expression of "The Death Wish," explored forty years later in the last volume of the war trilogy.

Another piece from early 1921 was written for a class. In it, Waugh's narrator is listening to a painter named Lurnstein. Waugh's preoccupation with Jews is evident: the narrator notes that Lurnstein is "Jewish, of course, but with a distinguished air that made one overlook his stumpy hands and other signs of ill-breeding." Instead of just condescending to Jews, Waugh shows some sympathy for his character. Lurnstein is an artist, one of the few vocations that Waugh could respect at that stage of life. Also an outcast, Lurnstein prefigures "aesthetic buggers" in Waugh's novels, Ambrose Silk, another Jew, in *Put Out More Flags* (1942), and Anthony Blanche in *Brideshead Revisited*. Lurnstein has tried to break from his ethnic background, Waugh appreciating Jews' suspension between upbringing and new social circles, where they were often unwelcome. Lurnstein's break has been "spoilt" by a woman (*EWA* 79), and he is the first hero in Waugh's fiction to blame failure on a female character. Waugh was still almost entirely innocent of sexual experience, but he tried to explain his extreme alienation, often by creating alienated heroes. One obvious explanation was the faithlessness of women's love, discovered in this story and used consistently in the major fiction from *Decline and Fall* on.

Another product of February 1921 was Lancing's Prize Poem. Boys were told to choose an episode in Malory's *Morte D'Arthur* and recast it in Spenserean stanzas. In *A Little Learning* Waugh noted that he had avoided a "story of heroism or romance," preferring the "nostalgic disillusioned musing of Sir Bedivere after the death of Arthur" (*ALL* 137). The autobiography is based on Waugh's diary, where he had planned to make Bedivere the narrator. Actually, the poem describes the "Return of Launcelot after the Siege of Joyous Gard," based on Malory's book 21, chapters eight, nine, and ten, and told by Sir Bors, in the Holy Land many years later. Launcelot is, like the philosopher, a hero treated contemptuously by inferiors. He says he has been "great, and not unknown to fame," but now he rides "alone, weary and wet," and "slaves and peasants spit upon [his] name." The distressing spectacle is the consequence of a fallen kingdom, Bors remarking that

> Arthur is dead, and Guinever his Queen
> Gawain for hate, Tristram for love lie slain. . . .
>
> (*EWA* 88, 92)

Bors's nostalgic, disillusioned musing appealed to Waugh's sense of the past as both irrecoverable and superior to the present. Few schoolboys could have been inspired by such a melancholy passage, and Waugh's choice probably helped him to win the competition.

3: Limited Bolshevist, 1920–1921 and After   79

As he became senior, Waugh seems to have become more concerned about appearance. In early 1921 he joined the Shakespeare Society, noting with typical self-consciousness that "only two other commoners" were there (*DEW* 110). More conspicuous in school society and eager for leadership in his house, Waugh exerted himself even in athletics. In February he had decided, as usual, "not to sweat in the House Trials," but suddenly he "determined to get a place" and finished "about fifteenth." He was "disconsolate" because he had "wanted to do well." Fearing that he had shown his "exhaustion," Waugh wrote that he hated himself and had "lost confidence" in his "personality and guts." Refusing to "plead bad training," he called himself a "contemptible, clever, little coward" and, "worst of all," he knew it. Waugh was once again overreacting, exaggerating incompetence, as Fulford made clear. The race had been the "House Trial for the Five Mile and it was regarded as something of a triumph to finish." Having watched while "well wrapped up," Fulford and companions had been "amazed by Evelyn's spirit as he jumped into one of those filthy dykes, and he was loudly cheered. His independence and courage were the secret of his standing in the Head's" (*DEW* 112–13 and note). Waugh had added to his stature, but from his point of view, failure was unforgivable, especially since effort had gone into it. Feelings of inadequacy grew worse in March 1921 during semifinals of the 100-yard dash. Waugh thought that everything conspired against him, and he came in "last—bloody bad." He did better a few days later, taking third in the 220, but another boy complained that Waugh had run across him. Waugh was starting to believe in "some malignant fate" that made him foul (*DEW* 118, 121). He was again interpreting mild adversity as vast conspiracy, though athletics had never been his forte. Failure to master the playing field aggravated his insecurity and led him largely to abandon sport after he had left Lancing.

Failure in another endeavor compounded Waugh's depression. Competition for the House Shield took place in March 1921. The shield was awarded to the house making the smartest appearance in an OTC parade. There seemed to be little chance that Head's would win, given their record of sloppiness and indifference. Waugh was wondering if that needed to be changed, starting to see that "one must limit one's Bolshevism. It is no use leading a *Loom of Youth* existence, ragging everything. One's attentions must be confined to certain deserving cases such as the Corps." His judgment seemed confirmed two days later when he received a demerit during physical training. He concluded that "Limited Bolshevism" had to be their "motto." The next day, 10 March, more radical limitations seemed necessary, at least to Waugh. Woodard addressed the house, talking about the OTC and telling the boys that he would do "all in his power to stop any Bolshevist being made a House-captain." Waugh was "worried." Woodard had given him the "worst possible reason for being good," but he did want to be a house-captain. He knew that his father craved the honor, but Waugh also wanted "other distinctions like editor of the magazine and president of the literary society for which one has to be one." He pondered the problem that evening but came to "no decision." Woodard had made him "ashamed to stop" (*DEW* 115–16). Waugh was finally caught between the demands of authorities and those of his conscience, and he tried to satisfy both. He felt some obligation to family, sensing his place in a tradition described in *A Little Learning*. Perhaps he thought that by pleasing his father he could improve their relations, but his own goals were probably more important to him.

Waugh and friends discussed Woodard's threat, and though one group was in favor of "increased disorder" (*ALL* 133), someone, probably Waugh, said that it would be "witty" if Head's House won the "ridiculous shield." Several boys wanted to try, hoping to "rag the 'jerry-run'" (*DEW* 116). Winners celebrated by carrying the shield around the school, but Waugh thought that Head's could "ignore it and take no part in its transference." Waugh later regarded this plan as a "face-saving manoeuvre" to satisfy his ambitions, but other boys in Head's House also had ambitions, and they had found a compromise between stylish disenchantment and conventional obligation. In an "unprecedented performance," Waugh's circle called a meeting of the house, explained their plan, and took a vote, unanimously in favor (*ALL* 134). The house had a week to get ready, polishing buckles and cleaning rifles while Waugh fretted over his dilemma.

Insecure as always, he imagined that circumstances had been conspiring against him. At the beginning of the term, he had been "popular with almost everyone." He had been "mildly ragging the Corps" when he had been "driven into an organized rebellion against the Gods," or house-captains and prefects. Waugh didn't see how he could get out of it, feeling "pledged to the House" and his friends. He longed for something to happen, even if he had to "break an arm or get ill." He was "absolutely in a net" and "bitterly unhappy," and he "seriously began considering running away." Waugh tended to see predicaments in the most melodramatic way, and he tended to blame others for his own faults, as he did then. He

3: Limited Bolshevist, 1920–1921 and After 81

did reproach himself for alienating his friend John Longe, having watched him "gradually being broken by the God system." Waugh blamed the "extreme Bolshevism" into which he was "being driven" (*DEW* 118–19). He remained acutely observant. During the week of preparation, a master asked Waugh and Fulford about their plans for the parade, addressing them as "gentlemen." Fulford recalled that such remarks were "never wasted on Evelyn." At Lancing the boys were "always 'you men' and never addressed in the more courteous form;" Waugh thought the term indicated anxiety about the boys' intentions.[5] He remembered that the "authorities were uneasy" about his house's "ostentatious activities." They knew about the meeting, but they did not know what the boys had said. The authorities also knew that the changes had come from the meeting, not from Woodard's speech (*ALL* 134).

The parade was on 18 March, and Waugh's house took the lead after two events. For the third, the "worst section was picked," Head's suspecting a "premeditated device of the authorities" (*ALL* 134). Head's finished third. According to Fulford, the section commander had not accepted the "new doctrine," adhering to the "outmoded slovenliness,"[6] though one wonders if the boy was avenging an injury inflicted by Waugh. Defeat was deeply discouraging; Waugh noted simply that the Gods had won (*DEW* 119), but once again Fulford reacted differently. He thought the episode deserved "emphasis" as an example of Waugh's authority: "Virtually the entire House followed his leadership," and only a "man of character" could have persuaded the boys to act like soldiers.[7]

Waugh's leadership was forceful, but his purpose undermined the discipline and respect the authorities were trying to maintain. Two weeks later Woodard summoned Waugh to an interview, recorded in the diary. Woodard said that they needed to appoint another house-captain, and that Waugh was the "obvious person," with "immense influence in the House." Waugh had to "accept the attitude of a Head's House official," or his "people" would be asked to take him away. Woodard knew that Waugh didn't believe in much of what he said and wrote, and he wondered what Waugh really thought. Under some pressure, Waugh got "going on the God tradition," the "war gap," and his generation, Woodard seeming "very reasonable." Waugh said that he was "prepared, and already determined, to lead a steadier life," and that he would work "to see rules kept." He refused to drop any of his friends, and he wouldn't "put on the airs of a brat" or "play cricket." Woodard took it "like a lamb," and they "parted on the best of terms." Waugh had nearly gone too far, but he and his supposed antagonist had resolved the problem more amicably than he had thought possible. He accepted the house-captaincy and later enjoyed "watching Bevan waiting about before undressing expecting to be summoned. Poor fellow, he would love all the petty pomp of it!" Waugh had fulfilled his ambition while maintaining independence, and he was "in a way pleased." He feared that his next term might be "even less enjoyable," but he found it "gratifying" that he had "won through" in his own way. The authorities had made the "first advances," and Waugh had not worked for it, as other boys had (*DEW* 122). Momentarily satisfied, Waugh soon found his position "really impossible," considering the house-captaincy a "bribe" to make him "sober" (*DEW* 126). Constantly suspicious, he resisted any kind of cooperation, worrying that he had somehow betrayed his convictions by rising to the pinnacle of Lancing society.

Waugh examined his conflict in "The House: An Anti-climax," written for a class. The master thought Waugh should try something more serious, but to Waugh the story was very serious indeed. It concerns rivalry between two boys, Ross and Stewart: one wants the house to concentrate on the OTC, but the other chooses the five-mile run. They quarrel and the house loses both events, finishing third in parade for the Corps' shield. In the end, Ross and Stewart become reconciled to each other and to the rest of the house. The story clearly derives from disappointments Waugh had just experienced, and the two characters resemble the author more than any other boy at Lancing. "The House: An Anti-climax" is Waugh's first attempt to do something characteristic of his mature fiction, articulating different sides of his personality in the conflict between characters. Ross and Stewart both want to succeed, but in different ways, and refusal to cooperate consigns them to mediocrity. Waugh obviously saw himself in the same position, ambitious but proud and independent, needing somehow to reconcile bolshevism and his wish to excel.

A play called *Conversion* is a more complex expression of this dilemma. Started soon after his decision to accept the house-captaincy, *Conversion* was performed for Head's House and then for the entire school in June 1921. It consists of "three burlesques." Act I depicts "School, as maiden aunts think it is," a parody of his own aunts' inability to imagine a school where boys are neither pure nor amenable to the salutary influence of aunts. Act II concerns "School, as modern authors say it is," a parody of Alec's *Loom,* where intensity about football devolves into absurdity. Act III portrays "School, as we all know it is," where boredom is universal, prompting boys to torment the authorities. Waugh's hero

3: Limited Bolshevist, 1920–1921 and After 83

Townsend is, as Dudley Carew says, a "rebel fighting against the sound and platitudinous arguments of the Head of his House on the question of discipline and loyalty to institutions."[8] Clearly representing Waugh himself, Townsend rejects these arguments but capitulates to the power of his prefect. He converts to orthodoxy, his surrender symbolizing the "tragedy of Youth."

The play is interesting for a number of reasons. The first two acts ridicule misapprehensions of two generations Waugh considered distinct from his own. The oldest generation of maiden aunts obviously had no idea what was going on, but neither did Alec's generation, close to Evelyn's in age but old enough to have served in the war. It was up to Evelyn, spokesman for the youngest generation, to present the truth about school in 1921, freeing the audience from the misconceptions of his predecessors. The play also distorts Waugh's dilemma in certain ways. Townsend lacks the ambition that led Waugh to restrain himself, and the prefect is more ruthless than Woodard in threatening retribution. Waugh refrained from direct insult by making the voice of authority a prefect rather than a master. The same alteration of experience, exaggerating both the hero's innocence and the wickedness he confronts, became characteristic of Waugh's mature fiction. Presenting his experience to the public often kept him from admitting that he had provoked his opponents.

Evelyn wrote "Ode on the Intimations of Immaturity," another parody, for Alec's birthday in July 1921. After invoking the Muse, Evelyn resorted to commonplace with curious illustrations.

> Youth hot upon his flaming quest
> At length sinks sobbing into age,
> And Gordon—brave Byronic soul—
> Grows to a shrewd, sardonic sage.
>
> Let others, less profound than he,
> Indulge in vain, athletic fads
> Screening their minds paucacity [*sic*]
> In square legs, popping crease and pads,
>
> Let others dote on averages
> And yearn for centuries or ducks,
> The Sage, composed and cynical,
> Observes that all things are in flux.

Gordon is an allusion to George Gordon, Lord Byron, the shrewd, sardonic sage of the Romantic period. Waugh's title invokes another, less sardonic sage, William Wordsworth and his *Ode on the Intimations of Immortality,* later cited in the preface to an edition of Waugh's travel writing, *When the Going was Good* (1946). Gordon is also the name of Alec's protagonist in *The Loom of Youth,* Evelyn questioning the quality of Alec's fiction, suggesting that there had been little difference between author and character. Similar comparisons irritated Evelyn after he had published novels of his own. Evelyn seems to be comparing Alec with the sage Gordon grew into, commending his brother's loss of interest in cricket. That makes it hard to see how the poem intimates immaturity, suggesting that the sage continues to be Gordon, or Evelyn himself, while Alec is one of the others, "less profound than he," indulging in vain, athletic fads. Alec played cricket for many years after 1921.

The rest of the poem is also ambiguous.

> Shall he be ticketed and laid
> Deep in the dust of God's great shelf?
> No, let the angels say of him
> 'Poor chap, he grew into himself'.

Alec is not to be pawned, not to die young like a true Romantic, sentenced instead to life and having to come to terms with himself.

> So let the rhythm of the words
> Bring more familiar attitudes;
> Let him find hope for human kind
> In pantheistic platitudes.

Perhaps the most puzzling phrase in the poem is "more familiar attitudes," apparently Evelyn's judgment on Alec's writing and *The Loom* in particular, four years after publication. Alec's attitudes are so familiar that they are trite, tending toward the pantheistic platitudes of Wordsworth, unworthy of Evelyn's consideration. Evelyn seems to reject pantheism as an alternative to Christianity, Alec never having shown his brother's interest in formal religion.

The "Envoi" tells the Muse to

> Let Bergson prate of memory,
> Potential relativity
> Whatever that may be
> Alec's twenty-three.

(*DEW* 129–30)

Not quite time to sink "sobbing into age," though Byron was dead at thirty-six. Evelyn dismisses memory and potential relativity, perhaps impatient with philosophy, perhaps suggesting that it would not interest Alec. Much that Evelyn wrote about Alec is ambiguous, and the ode is no exception. Evelyn did not respect his brother's intellect, but he seems to have respected his feelings, realizing that Alec and others might read the poem, as they eventually did. He confined himself to a few provocations couched in generalities, beginning and ending with the mere fact of Alec's age. Perhaps he wanted to fool Alec, who might have mistaken veiled insult for praise, the ode only an elaborate joke. Disdain is evident, but Evelyn was either too polite or too sly to make it obvious, and he was too busy to revise the draft.

In *Conversion,* irreverence in chapel leads to the hero's difficulties. Waugh had lost his piety, on 13 June 1921 claiming that in the last few weeks he had "ceased to be a Christian (sensation off!)." He knew that for at least two terms he had been an "atheist in all except the courage to admit it." There was little anguish in this confession, only characteristic insistence on the distinction between faith and skepticism. Waugh thought it was "only a phase," worried only about alienating Longe (*DEW* 127). He said much later that he "suffered no sense of loss" as he rejected the religion that had been so important to him. He was concerned with "propriety": as he and Tom Driberg prepared the sanctuary for a service, Waugh announced his "discovery that there was no God." Driberg observed that Waugh had "no business . . . handling the altar cloth" (*ALL* 143–44). Driberg's memory of this exchange was slightly different, suggesting that loss of faith had not been as simple as Waugh had indicated. When Driberg was "fussing about the proper hang of the linen cloth," Waugh "merely said: 'Nonsense! If it's good enough for me it's good enough for God.' This may be mildly blasphemous: it is not a proclamation of atheism."[9] Waugh had proclaimed atheism in his diary, but two weeks later he entered a prayer, as if still dependent on the idea of a supreme being and the prospect of immortality. He hoped that his soul would be taken, along with his "body and brain." Waugh suggested that body and soul might be allowed to weaken together, death involving the "utter extinction" of his existence (*DEW* 129). Thoughts of death and "pagan gloom" are common in the diary for this period (*ALL* 143), but they reflect only the doubts of an agnostic, not the denial of an atheist. In July, pondering an old problem, Waugh realized that "Omnipotence is absurd. One cannot have it without omniscience and that limits it." If "one knows what is going to happen, one can't do anything at all except the things you know. Knowledge controls action and limits possibility." Nevertheless, he was willing to admit that "if one is going to allow an omnipotent being one must allow him to be illogical" (*DEW* 131).

Later in life, Waugh tended to blame his doubts on others instead of seeing them as natural steps in his intellectual development. Skepticism had been common among boys at Lancing; Waugh estimated that at least half the boys in his form had been "avowed agnostics or atheists." If boys had not been especially pious, masters had not especially encouraged piety, and Waugh thought that tolerance and indifference had led to his loss of faith. Despite the school's Anglican origin, masters had offered boys "no antidote" for doubts, and Waugh had never been advised to read a book of "Christian philosophy." Instead, boys had been told to think for themselves, and their thoughts had "in most cases turned into negations." After the incident with Driberg in the chapel, Waugh went to see the chaplain. He was "genially assured that it was quite in order for an atheist to act as sacristan" (*ALL* 142–44). After he had become a Roman Catholic, Waugh regretted his phase of agnosticism, and he found it hard to forgive the carelessness of spiritual guides at Lancing. Reflecting on relations with Crease, Waugh suggested that his life might have been different if he had come into contact with a "real, disciplined, religious contemplative" (*ALL* 155). His life might have been different, but it is hard to imagine Waugh, at age seventeen, accepting the discipline of religion when he was resisting the discipline of education and the OTC. The spiritual void of Lancing became another obstacle he had overcome in his progress from childhood to maturity.

There were other reasons Waugh's faith was waning. He was "bored with Lancing" and bored with chapel (*ALL* 141). Probably he was distancing himself from the school's ideals and the earnestness of younger boys. By the fall of 1921, Waugh was intent on getting away from Lancing by winning a scholarship to Oxford. He was studying hard, though again he followed his own course rather than that outlined by the authorities. He was "rather wayward in reading" and, "instead of pursuing the topics normally set in the examination," found himself "interested in inessentials" (*ALL* 137). One morning in October he "cut chapel." He saw it as a "serious breach of trust and all that," but he wanted to make it a "habit on Sunday mornings." He was trying to "combine rest and work," leaving "God and honour in abeyance for a time" (*DEW* 142). Waugh was not willing to deny God's existence, but youth, ambition, and cynicism were leading him away from Christianity. He

3: Limited Bolshevist, 1920–1921 and After   87

still felt important, even immortal, but leaving Lancing early and going to Oxford as a scholar seemed more stylish and assertive than kneeling at the *incarnatus* in the creed. Waugh had not yet found ways to accommodate Christian humility and joy in his aggressive and morose personality, and he found agnosticism more suited to his temperament.

Waugh's sense of importance apart from Christianity emerged in other ways in 1921. He already thought of himself as a competent critic, and in January he tried to improve Carew's fiction, offering what seemed to Carew, many years later, "remarkable criticism for a boy of 17," both "balanced and self-confident."[10] The letter included a drawing of a man's head and shoulders entitled, or perhaps signed, "RALPH." Waugh told Carew to keep it and "reproduce it in a collotype facsimile in the biography," noting that it would "add value at Christie's" (*LEW* 2). There is something whimsical about imagining one's biography at seventeen, but, as with much of Waugh's humor, there is something serious about it as well. He knew that his life was going to be interesting enough to attract biographers, and his confidence came out in the diary, not always in jokes for Carew. In August 1921 he wrote that Shaw was "really supreme in his own way. (Trite remark. Will future editor kindly omit from published version. E. A. W.)" (*DEW* 134). Self-conscious criticism, often parodic by 1921, is evident even earlier. In June 1920 Waugh used his experience as an artist to perceive that

> We are all painting or drawing our lives. Some draw with pencil, weakly and timidly, continually breaking the point and taking up another, continually trying to rub things out and always leaving an ugly smear. Some use ink and draw firmly and irrevocably with strong, broad lines. Their work is often ugly, often grotesque, but always purposeful and deliberate. Some use colour, rich and lurid, laid on in full, glowing brushfuls, with big sweeps of the wrist. Some draw a straggling haphazard design, the motive being eternally confused with unnecessary and meaningless parts. The threads pass out of the picture and are lost. The whole is an intricate incoherent maze. But some, and these are the elect, draw their design clearly and fully. No part is unnecessary. Each twist and curl of the fanciful foliage adds to and carries on the original motive. Each part works into the whole and there is no climax or end to it. (*DEW* 83)

Waugh aspired to join the elect, already beginning to see his life as a work of art, important and interesting because it was self-consciously designed.

Carew provided an insight into the origins of Waugh's self-consciousness and sense of importance. In May 1921 someone remarked that "Evelyn would be the Max Beerbohm of his age." Memories differed on the identity of the speakers, but Carew's diary indicated that Arthur Waugh disagreed, saying "No, Evelyn. You'll be greater. You're a creator."[11] Comparisons between artists and members of Waugh's family came naturally, and it was also natural to quibble about the validity of the comparisons. Evelyn had many differences with his father, but the old man, whatever his faults, did manage to instill in his son the sense of being both important and open to scrutiny. As Waugh's life unfolded, that sense proved to be both an inspiration and a burden.

The burden became oppressive in the summer of 1921, when Waugh had lost faith but had retained a sense of responsibility to accomplish something. Carew remembered that in June Waugh felt "depressed," because the people he liked never liked him. Waugh also considered it "rotten when you think you've got a touch of genius and you don't know how things are going to turn out."[12] That month Waugh's touch of genius and depression inspired a poem, untitled but addressed to his friends Longe and G. V. Hale. Self-conscious as always, Waugh imagined that he might become vulnerable to delusion.

> I suppose that when I leave
> I shall think as others do,
> Storing in my memory
> Things refreshing and untrue.
> I shall think that I have known
> Comfort in the flint and stone
> In the light the evening shews
> When I leave, I suppose.
> Light on china, white and blue,
> Memories of study teas
> I shall think that I loved these
> Just as all the others do.
> Fellowship, I shall believe
> Cheered my way when I was young;
> I shall hunger for old friends,
> I suppose when I leave.
> Yet I know that just you two
> Mattered out of all I knew—
> But I may lose the thought of you
> Just as all the others do.
>
> (*DEW* 127–28)

3: Limited Bolshevist, 1920–1921 and After 89

The poem expresses sentiment that Waugh usually tried to hide behind a facade of hardness and cynicism. It exudes a highly developed sense of individuality, so that he became wary of behaving just as all the others do. Above all, the poem expresses Waugh's misery and loneliness throughout his time at Lancing. He had not been happy during his schooldays, and he wanted to resist the temptation to imbue them with imaginary pleasures. He was always prone to embellish the past, a tendency he recognized early in life. Instead of being pleased with his progress, he anticipated departure from school, pathetically appealing to Longe and Hale, who had never really returned Waugh's friendship, not to his satisfaction. The conclusion is nevertheless ambivalent and reserved, aware of his weakness and conscious that the emotions of the moment may prove less important than they seem.

By July Waugh was thinking "a lot about suicide," deciding that he would end it all if he were "without parents." As long as they were alive, he owed them a "certain obligation." Depressed as he was, Waugh preserved his taste for the dramatic, one night sitting up until 1:00 A.M., "composing last letters." He wrote to Carew, interested in the form of his life presented to others. Waugh was afraid that his biography would be "rather short," but he suggested that Carew print the suicide note "in full to swell it." He could specify "no really definite cause" for killing himself, supposing that it was "really fear of failure." Waugh knew that he had something inside of him, but he was "desperately afraid" that it might "never come to anything. Suicide is cowardice really." He was sure that if he had genius, it would survive; "if not it isn't worth living anyway" (*DEW* 131). Waugh never doubted that he was somehow special, but pressure to prove it sometimes made suicide seem like a more attractive option. He felt the pressure keenly, but his vagueness about other motives suggests a failure to recognize his lifelong predisposition to martyrdom. Life was difficult for Waugh, and he often tried to attract sympathy for his endurance of life's tribulations. When he was seventeen, suicide seemed like one way of attracting sympathy, but he resisted its allures then and later, finding other ways to invite people to feel sorry for him.

Waugh also wrote to Longe, acknowledging that agnosticism was creating a breach but still reluctant to deny God's existence. He promised to mention Longe to God, adding that Longe's "sort of God" would know all about him already, while Waugh's sort wouldn't care. Immersed in problems, Waugh was still able to criticize himself, finding suicide notes to be the product of a "morbid taste" (*DEW* 131). The sense that he was becoming too morbid helped Waugh to refrain from suicide, though honors he received at the end of the term probably also encouraged him to go on. In July 1921 he became editor of the school magazine and president of the debating society, but he was not satisfied with even these marks of esteem. He heard that Woodard had been "very much opposed" to Waugh's editing the magazine, and it had been given to him "after it had been offered to all the conventionalists." Waugh was "piqued," and "only filial piety" compelled him to take it. He was still sensitive about his reputation and wanted to justify authorities' opinions of him. Presidency of the debating society did not please him, because Molson in his "customary parliamentary way offered to pack the house" and have Waugh elected. Waugh "could not sanction it" but said he "would be pleased if he succeeded." Later Waugh had second thoughts, feeling "ashamed of the intrigue," but Molson said it was too late to change the plan (*DEW* 132). Waugh wanted to excel, but he didn't want to seem ambitious. Success itself was not enough to satisfy his demanding standards; it had to be achieved without apparent effort and with the approbation of all involved.

Characteristically, Waugh interpreted these mixed blessings not as rewards for respect he had earned, but as evidence of frustration and failure. He felt that everything had come to him "shop-soiled and second-hand." There were only two people he loved more than himself, but both Longe and Hale had given Waugh a "third-rate friendship with many inadequacies and misunderstandings." Waugh thought he had been a "failure as a House-captain from all points of view." He had not managed to become "sound and able," but neither had he "kept gloriously" on his own path. He also reproved himself for having led an "unhealthy life," feeling "ashamed" of the "petty and silly and spiteful things" he had done. Waugh preferred the previous term, when he had been "dissatisfied enough and Bolshevik" but "dramatic," having produced a "perfect pattern." He had "ruled the House" and had run it into "indiscipline," but he had stopped "when it had gone too far; it ended in a dramatic capitulation by the authorities." That summer Waugh thought he had been "ineffectual and silly—liked, but not respected." He considered it "so much wasted time" (*DEW* 132–33). Waugh's disgust indicates the main source of his frustration with Lancing. The power of the masters detracted from his independence and his ability to create a perfect pattern. He felt confined, deterred from expressing and defining himself. He had little choice but to bide his time, doing his best to escape Lancing and to gain freedom the school withheld. In July Waugh anticipated the discipline and self-denial he would have to adopt in the fall in order to gain independence, imagining that everything would be "pretty different" in September. He planned to settle himself "into the rut for the time," promising to "work like blazes and get a scholarship and run a nice orderly debating society and a nice magazine which the clerical old boys will like." The prospect seemed as "damnable as hell has ever been" (*DEW* 133). Waugh had fulfilled every ambition at Lancing except, he thought, that of being true to himself. Failure in this respect made seniority, privileges, and honors worthless. Unhappiness with an enviable record indicates how impossibly high his standards were and why, in later years, he refused to tolerate even slight deviations from excellence.

Despite his agnosticism, Waugh was still interested in religion and churches. In August 1921, with Oxford in mind, he and Molson spent two weeks reading at Birchington. One Sunday they went to Canterbury. Waugh "liked the town but was disappointed by the cathedral." In his opinion, the "episcopal authority left much to be desired." When they tried to get in, they were told to wait for the end of the service. They came back half an hour later, finding the cathedral "shut because the service was over." The following Sunday they went to a "delightful" service at St. Nicholas. When they had visited the old church, they had seen a "funny little room out of one of the cottages with a notice up," inviting visitors to an evening service. Molson "immediately decided" that they should attend. The service started with an "execrable hymn," Waugh never having "heard such singing anywhere and so loud." He thought that "their God had endued them with a most phenomenal capacity of self-unconsciousness." As someone uttered an incoherent prayer in a working-class accent, Molson was "prostrate with laughter;" Waugh, "by repeating the diplomatic situation of 1789, managed to keep fairly quiet." The minister and another man were the "most intellectual there," though they seemed "incapable of consequent thought." Waugh realized that it was "obviously very unusual for them to have a visitor" (*DEW* 135–36).

Impatient as he was with their singing, prayer, and discussion, Waugh was more tolerant than he had been at the "horrible low" church in Brighton in 1915. As with Longe, he recognized that different people have different ideas of God, and he seems almost to have envied the congregation's self-unconsciousness. He felt sympathy when he saw that it was unusual for them to have a visitor. Uncomfortable with the working class, Waugh lacked the true aristocrat's capacity of being perfectly at home in anyone's company, keeping quiet while Molson laughed and enjoyed himself.

Suspended between two social classes, Waugh distilled the evening into a richly comic scene, not rejecting another way of life, but showing how each side's assumptions prevented communication with the other. The scene anticipates many in the travel books and novels, where idioms of native language and whims of officials confuse the protagonists, as they had confused Waugh at Canterbury.

Once they had finished reading, Molson wanted to spend one night "whoring." Waugh expressed "disapproval," but Molson was "immovable." The next morning Molson "wondered if it was worth while," prompting Waugh to speculate about a "telepathic wave" emanating from the minister praying for them. That day Waugh "wrestled with him in spirit and at last he decided it wasn't worth it." They went to dinner and *The Beggar's Opera* instead, Waugh thinking it "more profitable than an attack of syphilis." Molson "didn't really regret it" (*DEW* 136–38). Fear of syphilis seems like rationalization of Waugh's anxiety to avoid intimacy. A casual, heterosexual encounter could hardly have threatened his future, and it couldn't have hurt his standing at school. He implies opposition to whoring on moral grounds, but morality excused reluctance to try something that might have exposed incompetence. Waugh seems to have been relieved when Molson changed his mind, probably because he would have been dragged along, as he had been dragged to the funny little room.

In October Waugh thought he had adjusted to his new role. He was "conscious of behaving like a cad," and he tried to seem as "strict and dignified" as he could, given his relatively short stature. Waugh was also "extremely full of the official spirit" (*DEW* 141). Such spirit did not last long, as Waugh continued to resist seriousness and convention, diverging from the regimen he had planned for himself. The debating society devoted half its time to foppish questions, opening with Irish home rule but moving on to the motion that "The canons of good taste rather than the laws of morality are outraged by murder." The third debate proposed that "The day of institutional religion is over," and Waugh spoke in opposition. The last that term entertained the motion that "This House deplores the invention of the cinema," and Waugh once again opposed.[13] The society may have been orderly, but only through ruthlessness, as Waugh closed it to the Fifth Form. He had argued for including the Fifth Form when he himself had been a Fifth Former,[14] but he had become a Sixth Former, interested less in fairness than in imposing his personality on the proceedings. The magazine under Waugh was neither nice nor designed to please

3: Limited Bolshevist, 1920–1921 and After 93

clerical old boys. His editorial in November, "The Community Spirit," made a "direct assault upon the school's principles of comradeship."[15] His editorial in December, "The Youngest Generation," again insisted on the war's division of England into three distinct generations, imparting especial importance to Waugh's, the youngest.

Other writings also expressed impatience with convention. He had an idea for a project called "'Reconsiderations: an Oxford book of Wild Oats', consisting of essays disparaging established reputations. Dr Johnson no conversationalist, etc." He had expected scholarship to dull his brain, but it did not seem to be doing so (*DEW* 142). Waugh's interest in Oxford and scholarship stemmed from boredom with Lancing, which became stronger after promotion had separated him from the Bolshevists. Waugh was "free of the whole place" and "exempt from almost all rules," but he had "no relish for such things." Instead he showed his usual enthusiasm for organizing unorthodox groups, forming a "'Corpse Club' of those who were weary of life." Members wore black ties and wrote on "mourning note-paper." Waugh held the "chief office as 'Undertaker'" (*ALL* 137–38). Masters' opinions of Waugh in his last term are not a matter of public record, but they cannot have been very pleased by the strange and discontented example set by one of the school's leaders. Whether or not he felt compromised by his position, Waugh was still keeping his own way, finding other means of disconcerting the masters once they had cut him off from Bolshevism.

Waugh's distaste for Lancing is obvious in the diary he kept during the fall of 1921. In October he found the prospect of another term "very repugnant," since he was "really hating this term" (*DEW* 141). Sensitive about reputation and wary of anarchic tendencies, Waugh began to fear the consequences if he were to have to endure the strictness of Lancing any longer. He was becoming "susceptible to the prettiness of some fifteen-year-olds" (*ALL* 135), and by the end of October he had become "open to fall in love with someone." He thought he would have to be careful if he wanted to leave with "credit and self-respect" (*DEW* 144). Longing for intimacy is understandable, given Waugh's loneliness at Lancing. By November he was "depressed as usual," finding life "dull and unpleasant," noting that he and Longe had been "gradually breaking apart this term." Waugh was looking for an ideal relationship, not merely a sexual one, deciding that "one of the chief things that has gone out of life is friendship." Lancing seemed to be lacking in "real friends," though there were "several lusts" (Diary HRHRC).

Lack of an ideal relationship may have roused his sexuality, but he "never fell victim to the grand passions which inflamed and tortured" most of the boys, Waugh preferring to act as "astringent confidante." Sexuality became a kind of weakness, a threat to his standing. Reluctant in any case to show tenderness or caring, Waugh conformed to "public opinion," dismissing sex as "filth" (*ALL* 135).

In spite of his restraint, Waugh's sexuality aroused suspicion. He wondered how the rumor of immorality would affect his reputation, as he began to use sexuality to define himself, if only through fantasy. On 11 November 1921 he arranged an "amusing incident" when the headmaster asked to speak to him privately. Longe wondered what had happened, and Waugh said that he had been "sacked for immorality." The rumor spread, and Waugh was "repeatedly accosted with people saying, 'My dear fellow, bad luck! Who was the other man?'" Waugh claimed that he didn't "care a lot," seeing the incident as "really rather witty," since he led a "life as pure as any Christian in the place, always excepting conversation of course" (Diary HRHRC). Aside from anticipating the homosexuality Waugh would try within a year, the episode shows his lifelong tendency to cast himself as a victim. The same fascination with misapprehensions and undeserved reproaches lies behind much of his fiction, creating most of the problems for his heroes. Waugh was also cutting himself off from the other boys and imagining his eventual departure.

He contemplated departure a week later, when he was again suspected of misbehavior. His only close friend was an unidentified prefect in another house, and during the summer they had started "going out after lights-out . . . and walking down to the sea." The walks were "entirely innocent," Waugh and his friend trying "simply to get clear of the school for an hour or two." Reports of this practice reached Arthur Waugh in a "roundabout way," apparently during November, and they "provoked a rhetorical reprimand." Arthur wrote a long letter, referring vaguely to a "rotten and contemptible game," recalling that Alec had told him about the same sort of thing at Sherborne. Evelyn thought his father was "making a great ado about nothing," not understanding Arthur's fear that his younger son should be expelled for homosexuality just as his older son had been. The reason for Alec's expulsion had been kept from Evelyn, and only *The Early Years of Alec Waugh,* published in 1962, made it plain to him (*ALL* 136). In 1921 Evelyn thought his father suspected that he had been "caught in a brothel" and that he was being "blackmailed into finding an honorable excuse for

3: Limited Bolshevist, 1920–1921 and After 95

leaving." Waugh almost wished he had been compromised, since it would "at least ensure [his] release" (Diary HRHRC). Much as he wanted to leave Lancing, Waugh refrained from any discreditable sexual affair, largely because he was so ambitious, though his father's strange warnings and his own critical habits contributed to restraint. As he told Molson in December, he had "never had any keennesses . . . because they can never talk intelligently" (*DEW* 153). Among brighter companions at Oxford, freed from Lancing's restrictions, Waugh finally let himself go, becoming involved in at least two homosexual relationships and forsaking the solitude he had seldom broken at Lancing.

Waugh found it "very cheering" when his father agreed that he could leave Lancing after the fall term, though it meant "working like hell for a scholarship." Waugh felt that he would be "deliriously happy" if he won one and "abysmally depressed" if he failed, though he knew it was not a "wholly logical view to take." Waugh also noted that life was "tolerable" only because of Oxford (*DEW* 142), expressing an attitude evident throughout his life. Waugh felt dissatisfaction with anything he had to endure for long, whether it was Oxford, the aristocracy, the military, or even the Roman Catholic Church. He compensated by imagining the superiority of some other place—when he was at Lancing, he wanted to be at Oxford; when he was at Oxford, he wanted to study art in Paris. Usually impatient with the immediate environment, Waugh hoped for more amusing company and more interesting surroundings somewhere else. This attitude helps to explain not only his frequent, almost incessant traveling, but also the profound gloom he experienced near the end of his life, after he had realized that death alone held anything new for him. The attitude was already in place in early manhood.

Examinations to determine recipients of scholarships were to be held in early December 1921, and as they drew near, Waugh doubted his chances. In late November he was "confused and confounded," sensing not only "ignorance" but also "incompetence at essay-writing." A few days later he said he would not be surprised if he failed, "continuously appalled" at how little he knew. On 5 December he was traveling to Oxford, fearing that it would turn out to be a "city of lost causes." He felt "fairly hopeless of success" (*DEW* 147–48, 150). Waugh was demeaning his ability, being too hard on himself, for he did well, following advice to concentrate on "very few questions and disregard those that would expose ignorance" (*ALL* 139). He won the £100 scholarship to Hertford College, and he was naturally "not a little cheered," enjoying a "very jolly day" (*DEW* 153). Waugh was finally "free to leave; to do so, moreover, amid congratulations." The most gratifying acknowledgment came from Roxburgh, who wrote that if he used what the gods had given him, he would do as much as anyone to shape the course of his generation (*ALL* 139, 161). Waugh saved the letter for the rest of his life, pleased that a respected master should recognize ability he sensed in himself. An insecure boy, conscientious about responsibility to his parents and himself, had earned a scholarship to Oxford against all expectations and had affirmed his status as hero at a school he despised. He had left Lancing behind, along with five years of misery, boredom, and restraints on his personality.

Throughout his career in fiction, Waugh made occasional use of public-school experience, drawing on years at Lancing and work as a master in the mid 1920s. He seems to have sympathized with characters obliged to take jobs in public schools, as he had been, and as Paul Pennyfeather is in *Decline and Fall*. Half the boys in Paul's class claim to be Tangent, the other half say it's a silly name, and Paul can quiet them only by assigning an "essay on 'Self-Indulgence,'" promising a "prize of half a crown for the longest essay, irrespective of any possible merit."[16] Schoolboy ruses afflict Waugh's other masters. In *Scott-King's Modern Europe* (1947), one boy, "more ingenious than the rest," tries to get Scott-King talking about anything other than the assigned work, reporting that another master "says it's a pure waste of our time learning classics."[17] Scott-King avoids the trap, but in *Officers and Gentlemen* (1955) Mr. Crouchback answers all the boys' questions about his forebear, the Blessed Gervase, enabling them to sit back "contentedly. Old Crouchers was off. No more Livy."[18] These scenes may derive from tricks Waugh had played as a student or had fallen for as a master, but other passages seem more strongly to echo experiences at Lancing. In *Decline and Fall* he observes that anyone "who has been to an English public school will always feel comparatively at home in prison" (*DF* 254). In *Men at Arms* (1952) Guy Crouchback encounters at Kut-al-Imara House a "dining-room, soon to become familiar in every horrid aspect," with "dishes of margarine, sliced bread, huge bluish potatoes and a kind of drab galantine which Guy seemed to remember, but without relish, from his school-days during the first World War."[19]

Aside from occasional references, Waugh did not often use his Lancing years in fiction. Only two fragments deal directly with experience at public school, the one written in 1920 and another written in 1945. After his discharge from the army in September

1945, Waugh read his Lancing diaries with "unmixed shame." By early October he had started a "novel of school life in 1919—as untopical a theme as could be found" (*DEW* 636). The novel was never finished, but Waugh did make a fair start. His agents titled the fragment "Charles Ryder's Schooldays" and published it in 1982, in a volume including several other short works by Waugh. The book's appearance coincided with the showing of *Brideshead Revisited* on television. Waugh had probably intended to follow Charles from the fall of 1919 through his move to Oxford in 1922. Waugh never completed this plan, but the fifty pages he did finish indicate that he was relying on experience as heavily as he had in *Brideshead*. The fragment begins in September 1919, when regular entries started to appear in Waugh's diaries. Obviously Waugh had his diaries in mind when writing. Charles's school is called Spierpoint, a thinly disguised version of Lancing, set on the shore where the "estuary was just traceable, a lighter streak across the grey lowland, before it merged into the calm and invisible sea."[20] Spierpoint is also, like Lancing, a "product of the Oxford Movement, founded with definite religious aims; in eighty years it had grown more and more to resemble the older Public Schools, but there was still a strong ecclesiastical flavour in the place" (*CRS* 274).

Ecclesiastical flavor helps to explain the hero's matriculation at Spierpoint, just as it helped to explain the author's matriculation at Lancing. The narrative conveys both Charles's alienation from Spierpoint and, through the passive voice, Waugh's own resentment of his father's choice. He explains that the "school had been chosen for Charles because, at the age of eleven, he had had a 'religious phase'." Charles goes to Spierpoint even though the "'phase' had passed and lingered now only in Charles's love of Gothic architecture and breviaries" (*CRS* 274–75). Waugh's religious phase had also begun at about age eleven, but it had lasted for some years, until he was at least fifteen, long after he had been sent to Lancing. There he enjoyed chapel and little else. In this representation of himself, and in most others, Waugh exaggerated his vulnerability to whims like those of his father. Arthur Waugh's choice had not been quite as inappropriate as Evelyn made Spierpoint seem in "Charles Ryder's Schooldays," but distaste for Lancing and a tendency to emphasize difficulties led him to distort experience and to exaggerate his father's capriciousness. The same type of distortion is evident in Charles's relationship with his mother. She is dead in "Charles Ryder's Schooldays," in keeping with *Brideshead,* which recalls her death during the First World

War. Catherine Waugh actually lived until 1954, but the hero's mother is not important in *Brideshead* or any of the late fiction. Waugh simultaneously cuts short any consideration of this relationship and generates sympathy for his hero, having Charles remember receiving news of his mother's death in 1917. Waugh did not greatly alter experience in "Charles Ryder's Schooldays" and certain other autobiographical works, such as *Brideshead* and the war trilogy. When he did, he almost invariably altered it in the same way, making circumstances harder on his hero than they had been on himself.

Davis suggests that Waugh may have been intending to use the mother's death to explain "Charles' rejection of Spierpoint values, his outward callousness, and his inward refusal—unlike the youthful Waugh—to analyze himself or others."[21] No one knows what Waugh was planning, but this suggestion seems implausible, since Charles's mother has been dead for two years when the story begins. Waugh seems to have been simply glossing a detail from *Brideshead.* In "Charles Ryder's Schooldays," he otherwise explains Charles's alienation in ways that reflect Waugh's experience more directly than the death of Charles's mother. Charles keeps a diary, recording his feelings about the "*trivial round of House politics.*" Frank Bates, the fictional equivalent of Dick Harris, has been replaced as house-tutor by Graves, the equivalent of Gordon, and Charles maintains that they "*ought to have the best of Heads [sic] instead of which they try out ticks like Graves on us before giving them a house.*" Graves plays "*hell with the house,*" making Apthorpe a house-captain and giving O'Malley an official position. Waugh rehabilitated Apthorpe a few years later in *Men at Arms,* when a character of the same name is again promoted to captain without deserving it. Charles "*never expected to get on,*" but he thinks that he should have been ahead of O'Malley, who seems to have been derived from the unfortunate Dungy. Charles's "*only consolation*" is "*seeing the woe on Wheatley's fat face*" (*CRS* 245), like Waugh noticing Bevan's disappointment after he had failed to become a house-captain in 1921.

Charles's resentment is so obvious that Graves feels obliged to explain his decisions, having noticed that Charles feels a "little illused this term." Graves realizes that everyone in Charles's year is in "rather a difficult position. Normally there would have been seven or eight people leaving at the end of last term but with the war coming to an end they are staying on an extra year, trying for University scholarships and so on." There has been no "general move," and there has been "only one vacancy at the top." Graves suspects that Charles thinks he "ought to have had it." Charles denies the allegation, though he has already criticized O'Malley's promotion in his diary. Graves goes on to another consideration. He says that Charles has "plenty of personality. O'Malley isn't at all sure of himself. He might easily develop into rather a second-rater. You're in no danger of that" (*CRS* 256).

Charles's ability and the master's recognition of it clearly derive from the ability Waugh felt he had shown at Lancing. Even ability becomes a handicap in the fragment, blocking Charles from advancement and relegating him to the same subversive role that Waugh had filled at Lancing. Charles vents frustration in the same way Waugh had, by ragging superiors. The first night O'Malley is in charge of the dormitory, Charles and friends cause a disturbance by taking too long over their prayers. They insist that O'Malley honor the custom of saying good night, so that he interrupts one boy still pretending to pray. The next night they insist that they've said their prayers before O'Malley asks them to, earning a beating from a master despite being within their "*rights*" (*CRS* 290). They also embarrass O'Malley by refusing crumpets left over from a formal tea. O'Malley has to offer them to everyone according to seniority until they are finally eaten by the most junior, most inconsiderable boys. Graves sees that "all you little beasts in the Upper Dormitory have been giving him hell" (*CRS* 287), but the manuscript ends soon after this remark, and there is no resolution of the conflict between Ryder and O'Malley. Probably Waugh meant to educate Charles as he had in *Brideshead Revisited,* showing him the mistake of trying to rag everything, undercutting obsession with himself, and making him more considerate through exposure to human deficiencies, perhaps through the demise of O'Malley. Waugh was certainly not using Charles to obscure his own abrasiveness at Lancing.

Waugh's abrasiveness is also evident in Charles's relations with masters. Charles or one of his friends admits that ragging a master the previous term had left him "quite exhausted" (*CRS* 251), and Charles, like Waugh, advocates absurdities to disconcert those in authority. He tells Graves that the "invention of movable type was a disaster" because it "destroyed calligraphy." Graves says that Charles is a "prig" (*CRS* 257). Graves is, as Davis observes, one in a "series of models for young Ryder," among them the "masculine and intellectual" A. A. Carmichael, based on J. F. Roxburgh and "contrasted with the almost maternal" Frank Bates. Graves appears between these two extremes and "attempts to draw Ryder out of his contemptuous rejection of human responses."[22] Graves is related to other masters in the fragment, but he is also related to Gordon, a master in Waugh's past. Waugh had been cruel to Gordon, having withheld confidence and affection after he had replaced Dick Harris, having called him Pussy-foot and Super-spy, but Gordon had never responded in kind. He had introduced Waugh to Francis Crease, one of the few friends Waugh valued at Lancing. In "Charles Ryder's Schooldays" Graves introduces Charles not to a scribe, but to a printing press, as Gordon himself had done for Waugh. The printing press in the story allowed Waugh to concentrate on Charles and Graves, instead of Charles's relations with some other character. Charles affects indifference, but he is fascinated by the printing of attractive books. Another boy suggests that they may have "misjudged Graves" (*CRS* 258), noting that "when he wants to be decent, he *is* decent" (*CRS* 259), and though Charles demurs, the fragment is obviously preparing for recognition of Graves's qualities. The source of the story indicates that Waugh was recognizing Gordon's qualities twenty-five years too late, portraying his character in "Charles Ryder's Schooldays" more fairly than he had in his diaries.

Charles's interest in calligraphy is also Waugh's, and their talent is about the same. Waugh said that he lacked the discipline needed to be a good painter or calligrapher, and Charles realizes that his work is going "too fast—a monk would take a week over a single letter" (*CRS* 277). Reference to the superior discipline of a monk is intentional, for Waugh exploits the irony of his own past agnosticism. Charles inscribes a "secular, indeed slightly anticlerical, lyric" (*CRS* 275), Ralph Hodgson's "The Bells of Heaven," without realizing that the poem is "not perfectly suited to the compressed thirteenth-century script in which he had written it" (*CRS* 276). The mature Waugh considered the thirteenth century a time of superior craftsmanship and Catholic unanimity before the Reformation. An anticlerical lyric in thirteenth-century script would be an artistic failure, the sentiment inappropriate for the method of representation. Charles's inscription turns out to be "absolutely beastly" (*CRS* 278). Waugh's understanding of historical coincidence between form and sense may have been reductive, but it did give him one way to explain his failure as a graphic artist.

The most important similarity between Waugh and Charles becomes apparent when a boy named Curtis-Dunne confronts Charles in the library. Unhappy with limited library privileges, Curtis-Dunne wants to extend them, and he asks Charles to sign the proposal. Charles hesitates because the "suggestion outraged Spierpoint taste in all particulars." The

3: Limited Bolshevist, 1920–1921 and After 101

intrigues, blandishments and self-advertisements . . . employed by the ambitious . . . were always elaborately disguised. Self-effacement and depreciation were the rule. To put oneself explicitly forward for preferment was literally not done. Moreover, the lead came from a boy who was not only in another house and immeasurably Charles's inferior, but also a notorious eccentric. A term back Charles would have rejected the proposal with horror, but . . . he was aware of a new voice in his inner counsels, a detached, critical Hyde who intruded his presence more and more often on the conventional, intolerant, subhuman, wholly respectable Dr. Jekyll; a voice . . . from a more civilized age, as from the chimney corner in mid-Victorian times there used to break sometimes the sardonic laughter of grandmama, relic of Regency, a clear, outrageous, entirely self-assured disturber among the high and muddled thoughts of her whiskered descendants. (*CRS* 281–82)

Charles signs, recognizing a rebellious tendency like the one Waugh developed in the school year of 1919–20. One cannot be sure, but it seems safe to say that in the rest of the novel Waugh wanted to explore the conflict between expression of self and obedience to authority. Probably the conflict would have resolved itself in some sort of compromise, as it had in *Conversion* and in Waugh's own case at Lancing.

Waugh never finished the book, for any of several possible reasons. Davis suggests that the "complexity of character, especially in the conception and treatment of Charles, created what proved to be insuperable problems," such as incongruity between Charles's early coldness and later nostalgia.[23] Charles is nostalgic in *Brideshead Revisited,* not "Charles Ryder's Schooldays," however, nostalgic about Oxford, not Spierpoint. It seems unlikely that Waugh would have found it too difficult to portray a character with different attitudes in different stages of life, especially since changes in Charles's attitudes mirror those in Waugh's own. Davis also suggests that Waugh could "not bring himself to deal directly with the causes of his own coldness and misanthropy."[24] Those causes are open to speculation, but "Charles Ryder's Schooldays" certainly points to some—poor choice of school, sense of having been passed over, and temptation to rebel.

A more practical reason to abandon the story may have been its ambition. The fragment covers only five days of entries in Charles's diary, and Waugh probably realized that he could not continue to cover Charles's schooldays in such detail if he wanted the story to extend to December 1921, when he had left Lancing. To do so, he would have had to turn the novel into something on the scale of the war trilogy, and Waugh was not interested in such an extensive project at the time or in writing so much about Lancing. He usually managed to revise work until he found it acceptable, seldom abandoning anything outright. Presumably he lost interest in any fictional representation of his experience at Lancing. His agnosticism there and Charles's agnosticism in *Brideshead* meant that Waugh could not explore his hero's or his own relationship with God in "Charles Ryder's Schooldays." He claimed to be more interested in that relationship after *Brideshead,* and he was probably dissatisfied with having to make only ironic comments about past skepticism. Lancing had never generated the ambivalence Waugh felt for other things in his life, natural but delusive attractions lying behind his most complicated fiction. He had never really liked Lancing, and he obviously had no interest in writing about nonexistent attraction or understandable revulsion. Unfinished as it is, "Charles Ryder's Schooldays" is definitely uninspired, full of schoolboy slang and public-school jargon, and hard to follow without the aid of Waugh's Lancing diaries. The old conflict between independence and obedience still intrigued him, but it was not enough, by itself, to sustain him through a story of public-school life. He could deal with the same conflict in stories more immediately relevant to his adult life, stories involving the military and the Church.

Waugh's only full treatment of experience at Lancing appears in his autobiography, his last major work. To write it, he had to review early diaries, which he found to be "painful reading. Most adolescent diaries are naive, trite and pretentious," and Waugh's was "lamentably so." The "shame of re-reading" came from "deeper sources," however, as the diaries indicated that Waugh had been "conceited, heartless and cautiously malevolent." He hoped that he had been "dissembling a more generous nature," that he had "absurdly thought cynicism and malice the marks of maturity." Waugh prayed that it might have been so. Still, he found "damning evidence . . . of consistent caddishness." He felt "no identity with the boy who wrote it" (*ALL* 127). Time and achievement had completely allayed the ambition, frustration, and resentment that had consumed Waugh at Lancing. Embarrassment in rediscovering his adolescent self may have made him more indulgent toward his old school. He "revisited Lancing after an interval of forty years and wandered about with a few tremors of nostalgia." He noticed several changes, rock gardens having "horribly appeared," the chapel "spotted with a miscellany of pictures." The boys no longer wore black coats, and Waugh even saw one small boy running on the school grounds. Changes did not provoke his usual lament about the decline of Western civilization, Waugh perhaps conceding that more freedom in his own day might have made Lancing more pleasant. He was willing to admit the possibility of improvement, noting the "startling change . . . in the environs. Little red houses were everywhere, some of them on the school property." The "austere isolation deliberately sought by the founder" had been "entirely lost," and Waugh thought the change was for the better (*ALL* 104–5). He praised Lancing Chapel, claiming that he knew "no more spectacular post-Reformation ecclesiastical building in the kingdom" (*ALL* 98). Finally able to see some good in the place, Waugh reached his most balanced, most complex perspective of Lancing, which had at last stimulated enough interest to appear in a publication.

Waugh never wrote the second and third volumes of his autobiography, but in fiction he had already used parts of his life that they would have covered. In this sense, *A Little Learning* begins to look like an act of completion, the pacification of Waugh's lifelong impulse to analyze himself. He returned to youth, the only part of his life that had not inspired publishable fiction, almost as if he were searching for the origins of his peculiar personality. If he was, he would have found not only consistent caddishness, but also imaginative habits that would characterize the rest of his life and most of his fiction, developed long before he wrote *Decline and Fall*. As a child, Waugh had sensed that he had something to say, expressing himself in various ways and preserving his scribblings for a lifetime, so that we can see continuity between juvenilia and more mature, more subtly critical work. Awareness of intelligence had made him, at an early age, extremely critical of his work and conduct. Critical reflex is evident in his novels and private appraisals of acquaintances' behavior. From the beginning he had seen himself as a victim of discrimination, and in later years he often transferred his predicaments to fiction, where autobiographical heroes usually suffer more than Waugh had in life. Disadvantages he perceived in birth and education had made him very sensitive to distinctions between social classes, a preoccupation in his fiction and in his life. In youth as in age, Waugh usually remained convinced of his righteousness and innocence even when he had provoked retribution that he took as a sign of others' unfairness.

Waugh the *provocateur* found representation in Basil Seal, an exceptional hero in his fiction, never a victim, appearing in three different works. The last is a long short story, *Basil Seal Rides Again,* published in 1963, a year before the autobiography and two years after *Unconditional Surrender,* the last major novel. The novel is notable for, among other things, Madame Kanyi's interpretation of the Second World War, so stirring to Guy Crouchback, so crucial to Waugh's understanding of himself. According to her, there had been a "will to war, a death wish, everywhere" in 1939, when danger had "justified privilege."[25] Danger had always justified privilege for Waugh; in other words, difficulties had made him a martyr and a hero. He had consistently operated on this assumption—as a child, at Lancing and elsewhere—and this passage is one of the few indications that he understood his tendency to derive individual worth from the amount of hardship endured. Guy asks for divine mercy because he has looked to the war for redemption, and perhaps Waugh thought only his attitude toward war had been mistaken, failing to see the other ways he had equated hardship with worth.

It is more likely that Waugh noticed the connection between Madame Kanyi's comments and his entire life. After *Unconditional Surrender*, in the five years left to him, Waugh never attempted to write another novel typical of his fiction from *Decline and Fall* through the war trilogy, another novel involving an innocent hero in the midst of corruption. Waugh had complained about the difficulty of writing before *Unconditional Surrender*, but he complained even more afterward, and it seems reasonable to attribute declining productivity to abandonment of his usual plot and representation of himself. He turned to Basil Seal, the devilish side of himself he had explored in only two novels, and to his "still unravished boyhood" (*LEW* 432), finding it "quite impossible to identify . . . with the lonely schoolboy of this chill time" (*ALL* 109). Composition of *Unconditional Surrender* had been enlightening for Waugh, enabling him to appreciate how often he had obscured guilt by emphasizing hardship, impelling him to try other ways of representing himself. He often felt that life at Hampstead and Lancing had been a waste of time, but it had helped to form an imagination that sustained a lifetime of writing, exhausted only at the very end.

4
Et in Arcadia Ego, 1922–1924

On 21 June 1930, capitalizing on the success of *Vile Bodies,* the *Daily Mail* published an article by Evelyn Waugh entitled "Was Oxford Worth While?" After dismissing any "monetary returns" from a university degree, Waugh decided that Oxford *was* worthwhile, primarily because it kept undergraduates from getting jobs before they were emotionally prepared to do so. Oxford gave them a chance to "grow up gradually." Undergraduates could "learn to get drunk or not to get drunk;" they could "edit their own papers and air their opinions;" they could "learn how to give parties;" and they could "find out, before they are too busy, what really amuses and excites them." When they were finished, the graduates could go to the "dreary and futile jobs that wait for most of them, with a great deal more chance of keeping their sense of humour and self-respect."[1] After he had left Oxford in 1924, Waugh had been obliged to try a series of dreary and futile jobs, until he gained some popularity as a novelist with *Decline and Fall* in 1928. Clearly he never lost his sense of humor, and generally he maintained self-respect. Doubtless Oxford was valuable to him for these reasons, but it was even more valuable to him because experience there impelled him to grow up, however gradually. At Oxford Waugh developed his aesthetic sense, observing architecture, drawing for friends, arguing about the virtues of this or that artist, and writing fiction for student publications, such as the *Isis,* the *Cherwell,* and the *Broom.* Powers of argument and a taste for the absurd showed when Waugh spoke at the Oxford Union, a grander form of the Lancing College Debating Society. These activities amused and excited Waugh, unlike the interests of his father and brother. Oxford allowed Waugh to live as he pleased, almost independent of family, the way most young men like it.

Waugh found independence intoxicating, and he did not always react responsibly. He indulged in alcohol and sex, neglected his studies, and spent far more than his scholarship and allowance could cover. Indulgences, paradoxically, were what made Oxford worthwhile, in that Waugh grew up by recognizing their incapacity to provide him with a satisfying, meaningful life. Waugh perceived the shallowness of his life while still at Oxford, and he renounced most habits acquired there well before or shortly after coming down. He never lost his taste for alcohol. He did, however, fall in love twice and then recognize the shortcomings of the loved ones and the inadequacy of homosexuality. He discovered that he was no scholar and, having accepted it, turned instead to art, though he drew more than he wrote. In his second year he realized that he was spending too much, began to live more modestly, supplemented his income with literary and artistic work, and settled his debts with his father. The years after Oxford were full of drinking, orgiastic parties, and new debts; Waugh was too young and too rebellious to settle down completely. Already at Oxford, however, well before conversion to Roman Catholicism, there were signs of dissatisfaction with the hedonist's life, signs of readiness to seek fulfillment elsewhere, even if that search required discipline. Oxford was important to Waugh because it taught him to look beyond whatever was superficially pleasant, beyond carefree existence, to investigate kinds of experience that might provide more permanent value. Oxford itself was permanently valuable in a way that was hard for Waugh to articulate. He went back after he had left, though he knew that revelry interfered with his progress, and for years he ruthlessly blamed others for having spoiled his happiness at Oxford. The problem of Oxford's insidious attraction occupied Waugh for the rest of his life, and in fiction he expressed his ambivalence toward the university more profoundly than he could for the *Daily Mail*.

In 1921 Waugh wanted to go to Oxford primarily to escape from Lancing, but the university attracted him in other ways as well. He appreciated its architecture; as early as September 1920 he recorded a visit to Oxford and exclaimed that he had "never seen anything so beautiful." Waugh knew that he would be following family tradition by going to Oxford, and the exploits of predecessors were impressed upon him. He saw the platform where his father had recited the Newdigate Prize Poem and the gate of Trinity College, which his great-uncle had climbed at 2:00 in the morning. Evelyn was in duty almost bound to go to Oxford, especially since Alec had never made it, but he welcomed the challenge. He also visited the Oxford Union, where he hoped to speak (*DEW* 100–01). Perhaps even then Waugh recognized that his family had taken different paths at the university, any one of which he could pursue

4: *Et in Arcadia Ego*, 1922–1924

as his own. He was only half-inclined to follow his father's example of literary effort, and he began to see Oxford as an opportunity for self-expression greater than any at Lancing or in what was by then Golders Green. Alan Pryce-Jones suggested that Waugh valued Oxford because it "removed him for good from Golders Green—not the Golders Green of reality but the bourgeois citadel of legend."[2] Michael Davie agreed, noting that Oxford created "contempt for the bourgeois, literary Hampstead world to which his father and brother were proud to belong." Davie added an important qualification. Waugh's contempt for his father's life developed only after he had gone up to Oxford at the beginning of 1922. After 1923 Alec found Evelyn "increasingly aggressive and cantankerous."[3] Diaries and letters do not indicate that Waugh saw Oxford as an escape from Golders Green, and it does not seem logical that he would have done so. Since age thirteen he had spent most of his time at Lancing, and impatience with school as he passed his eighteenth birthday was clearly the most important reason to seek a new life at Oxford. Still, once he had been to Oxford, he found his father's milieu unattractive by contrast. In a letter probably dating from May 1922, Waugh wrote that after Oxford, London and the suburbs seemed "indescribably dreary" (*LEW* 9). Oxford was the first place he had really liked since he had wandered through his aunts' house as a child.

Oxford was agreeable because Waugh could exercise liberties he had never dared to try at Lancing or Golders Green. From the beginning Waugh associated the university with freedom and license. When he went with Molson to take scholarship examinations in December 1921, Waugh described the week in Oxford as one of the happiest he had ever known (*DEW* 151). Forty years later, he recalled in his autobiography that they had stayed at a hotel, the first time he had done so on his own (*ALL* 138). He had a vague notion of entering New College, where his father had been, but Hertford was also giving examinations for scholarships. Waugh noticed that scholarships at Hertford were worth more than those at New College, and he listed Hertford as his first choice. He was awarded the £100 scholarship, "to the surprise of all able to judge" (FS HRHRC). His choice sounds like pure financial consideration, but again he may have been intent on distinguishing his experience at Oxford from his father's. Back at Lancing, Rev. Bowlby announced Waugh's scholarship and described Hertford as a "very rising college" (*ALL* 164). Waugh's father found Bowlby's phrase funny, both awkward and patronizing. Bowlby's condescension and Arthur's amusement probably irritated Evelyn. He was pleased with his scholarship, but others' reactions made him sensitive about the reputation of his college.

Once Waugh had gone up in January 1922, alcohol became his favorite indulgence. He had probably had a few cups of punch at Lancing, but he never became interested in alcohol until he went to Oxford, where he got drunk for the first time (*ALL* 166). In February he drank most of a bottle of wine, along with some port and cider, and later tried to recite poetry in the quad. He started to advise Tom Driberg "most seriously . . . to take to drink." Waugh extolled the "aesthetic pleasure of being drunk" and claimed that if it were done in the right way, one could "avoid being ill next day." That lesson was the "greatest thing Oxford has to teach" (*LEW* 7, 10). However he might rationalize it as aesthetic pleasure, drunkenness was for Waugh above all a form of rebellion, against Lancing and Golders Green. As he wrote later, there had been in the 1920s a "real danger of Prohibition in England." He remembered an "element of a Resistance Group about the drunkards of the period." Drinking offered Waugh membership in a certain group, badly needed in his new situation. He soon joined the "drinking set," partaking in the "convivial swilling of beer and wine" (*ALL* 191). Drinking was also a form of rebellion against the university itself. One way to undercut education is to identify the university's greatest lesson as the avoidance of a hangover; another is to inhibit study by making noise at night on the grounds. Drinking destroyed whatever inhibitions Waugh retained, and other undergraduates soon became accustomed to his clamor. Cyril Connolly once found him "making an abominable row outside the gate of Balliol College" and asked why he was so consistently loud. Waugh said that poverty impelled him to be,[4] alluding to other undergraduates' wealth and to frustration at the limits of his background.

Another way to undercut education is to avoid doing any work, and Waugh found it hard to study in such an open, agreeable place. In May 1922, after his first term, Waugh told Driberg that he had enjoyed it "immeasurably," largely because he had done "no work" and did "not propose to do any next term." Instead, he tried to learn a "little during the vac." By the middle of his second term, facing preliminary examinations, Waugh had to start studying, and it did not agree with him at all (*LEW* 9–10). In his autobiography Waugh wrote that he had regarded his scholarship as a "reward for work done, not as the earnest of work to come." He also blamed lack of industry on the atmosphere of the university. He had been typical of other undergraduates in his "indifference to work." Half

4: *Et in Arcadia Ego*, 1922–1924

of them had been sent to Oxford "simply as a place to grow up in." They had pursued various interests, some involved in sports, some in "acting and speech-making," some in "pure pleasure." Waugh had known everything about his friends' "political and religious opinions, their love affairs, finances, homes, families, their tastes in food and clothes and drink," but he "would have thought it indelicate to inquire what school they were reading." It is hard to believe that one's field of study had been the only subject considered off-limits. Perhaps Waugh and friends had not discussed theirs because they had honored the "prevalent illusion that a man of parts could idle for eight terms and at the end sit up with black coffee and master the required subjects in a few weeks" (*ALL* 171–73). Waugh had probably been more serious about studies than he later claimed, at least in his first few terms. He had worked hard for a good scholarship and kept it for eight terms, but scholastic success had soon paled beside other possibilities presented by the university.

Waugh's studies suffered in two other respects. First, he and his tutor immediately disliked each other, which detracted from his interest in learning and led them to discontinue their meetings. Second, Waugh was bored by lectures and set books. He had "faint interest in History as it was taught," since the "curriculum seemed to have been designed to show that the British parliamentary system at the turn of the century was the consummation of human wisdom and that the affairs of other countries were significant so far as they showed an approach to this ideal." Students had to choose a special subject for further study, and Waugh described his choice as "unconsidered." When his tutor asked which subject he wished to pursue, Waugh, probably because he hadn't bothered to acquaint himself with the options, could remember only one subject, representative government. The "peculiarities of the various democratic constitutions of the world" failed to interest him; in fact, nothing could have been "drearier" (*ALL* 172). Waugh said that he would have been interested in the cities of the Italian Renaissance, but he had no acquaintance with them in 1922, and one wonders if he was imposing later taste on an earlier time. He had already been bored by constitutional history at Lancing, but he may have chosen representative government in order to get by with minimal work. Attribution of failure to a hasty choice, which probably could have been changed anyway, seems like simplification and whitewashing.

Waugh's tutor was C. R. M. F. Cruttwell, a surname familiar to readers of the early novels. Waugh described him at length in *A*

Little Learning, explaining that Cruttwell's "appearance was not prepossessing. He was tall, almost loutish, with the face of a petulant baby. He smoked a pipe which was usually attached to his blubber-lips by a thread of slime." During their meetings, Waugh would be "distracted" by this thread, so that he was often "inattentive" to Cruttwell's words. After forty years Waugh was still blaming Cruttwell's appearance for his own inability to concentrate on scholarship. His description is not entirely hostile, as Waugh also tried to delve into Cruttwell's nature. He seemed to be a "wreck of the war in which he had served gallantly," behaving "as though he had never cleaned himself of the muck of the trenches. His conspectus of history was narrowed to the few miles of the Low Countries where he had fought, and the ultimate, unattainable frontier towards which he had gazed through his periscope over the barbed wire." Cruttwell was "obsessed by the Rhine," and Waugh's confession that he was "ignorant of its course" caused the "first, sharp difference" between them (*ALL* 173-74). Waugh's shortcomings in other areas also caused problems. In his first term Waugh noted that his tutor had said "Damn you you're a scholar. If you can't show industry I at least have some right to expect intelligence!" Waugh had just translated *Eramus* as Erasmus, and it had been "too much for his scholarly manners" (*LEW* 6). Cruttwell had been largely, if not solely, responsible for awarding Waugh's scholarship, and he became frustrated when he realized that he had wasted it on an indifferent and ill-prepared student.

If the incidents reflect Waugh's inadequacy as a student, they also reflect Cruttwell's inadequacy as a teacher. In *A Little Learning,* Waugh remembered Cruttwell's "frustrated pugnacity," his "violent rages," his "frenzies of exasperation." Cruttwell was a "misogynist," and he "refused to have women at his lectures. . . . If one slipped in, he drove her out, crimson faced, by his obscenities." Waugh may have exaggerated Cruttwell's belligerence, always aroused by the "antipathy" between them (*ALL* 174-75), something Alec described as "dislike . . . mutual, instinctive and irrational as love."[5] Still, Cruttwell tried "to show kindness" in Waugh's third term, telling him that being "conspicuously drunk" was not the "best way of ingratiating [himself] with the college." Waugh became "fatuously haughty" and later thought that their "mutual dislike" had then become "incurable." Though he tried to read with Cruttwell for final examinations, Cruttwell soon refused to see him, and he was left "without tutoring of any kind" (*ALL* 175). Alec pointed to the bias behind his brother's characterization of Cruttwell, describing it as an "attack" that inspired letters from

4: *Et in Arcadia Ego*, 1922–1924

those who had had "different experiences of the Dean." Alec also noted that Cruttwell must have had "considerable merits" in order to have climbed as high as he did.[6]

Evelyn refused to recognize any merits, resenting Cruttwell's treatment of him and trying repeatedly to embarrass his tutor. These attempts, some remembered by Waugh, some by contemporaries, contributed to Cruttwell's loathing of his scholar. Waugh wrote that Terence Greenidge "first imaginatively imputed to Cruttwell sexual connection with dogs" (*ALL* 177), a connection Christopher Hollis derived from a lecture. Cruttwell had made an "incidental observation" that "a dog cannot have rights."[7] The statement developed into a running joke when Greenidge bought a stuffed dog in a junk shop and, with Waugh, placed it in the quad as an "allurement" for Cruttwell. They also used "rather often to bark under Cruttwell's windows at night" (*ALL* 177). Hollis recalled that Waugh had "invented a ridiculous rhyme":

> Cruttwell dog, Cruttwell dog, where have you been?
> I've been to Hertford to lie with the Dean.
> Cruttwell dog, Cruttwell dog, what did you there?
> I bit off his penis and pubic hair.

Waugh would "shout this across Hertford Quad."[8] Claud Cockburn remembered another version of the joke, suggesting another reason Cruttwell irritated Waugh. One morning he and Waugh were sitting in Waugh's rooms,

> looking at the rain, drinking whiskey against the enervating climate of Oxford, and listening to the intrusive sounds of patter and thump from the rooms above. The rooms, Evelyn explained, were those of his enemy, the dean of the college, whom Evelyn, as a blow in the feud, accused of having sexual relations with his dog. "Now he's raping the poor brute. And at this hour in the morning."

Cockburn thought the noise might have come from a "faulty vacuum cleaner," but Evelyn had "no doubt" about the source, expressing pity for "that unhappy dog."[9] The dog story seems to have been in part revenge for having been disturbed by Cruttwell's noise. The fantasy of bestiality also reflects Waugh's uneasiness about sexuality at Oxford. Attracted to other men and wondering if he were normal, Waugh accused others of perversions greater than any he feared in himself.

Waugh did not limit persecution of Cruttwell to a series of sexual jokes. In *Isis,* ordinarily the heartiest of the student magazines,

Waugh congratulated "the Dean of Hertford on his recent bowling successes. The following headline has been suggested to us: 'Crutters collects Considerable Kudos in County Cricket. *Macte virtute esto,* "Googly Dean."'" He also insulted Cruttwell in "*Isis* Idol," a column celebrating the accomplishments of undergraduates. Waugh impudently dealt with a don, deciding that Cruttwell's intellect was at its best "with a dose of pungent hops in him," finding that the dean "doggedly changes his ground in defence of superstition and prejudice."[10] By the end of Waugh's education, there was no longer any point in trying to be polite. After Waugh's final examinations, Cruttwell and another tutor gave a dinner party for those in the history school. Waugh arrived "tipsy and further alienated their sympathies by attempting . . . to sing a Negro spiritual." Cruttwell still tried to be decent, even when writing the letter that withdrew Waugh's scholarship because his performance on examinations translated into a third-class B.A. Cruttwell could not say that Waugh's third did him "anything but discredit: especially as it was not even a good one; and it is always at least foolish to allow oneself to be given an inappropriate intellectual label." He hoped that Waugh would soon "settle in some sphere" where he would give his intellect a "better chance than in the History School" (*ALL* 208). Like Roxburgh, Cruttwell knew that Waugh was bright, but he was disappointed and puzzled by his inability to arouse any sense of responsibility or curiosity.

Somewhat surprisingly, Waugh continued to take pleasure in Cruttwell's discomfort long after he had left Oxford. Alec reported that Evelyn had been "jubilant" when, in Abyssinia in 1935, he had received word that Cruttwell had been defeated in the election for the Oxford University seat in Parliament.[11] Cruttwell had run as a Conservative and had lost, even though the seat had been thought to be safe (*ALL* 175). That year Waugh had contributed to Cecil Hunt's *Author-Biography,* claiming that his favorite book had not been published and that it might be "years before it was completed." The book was to be a "memorial biography" of Cruttwell, a "labour of love to one whom, under God," Waugh owed "everything."[12] Waugh was being sarcastic, alluding to Cruttwell's death, but he was also serious, having by then converted to Roman Catholicism and having recognized that Cruttwell's discouragement of his academic career had helped move him toward writing. Waugh was hardly grateful, continuing to obsess himself with Cruttwell's idiosyncrasies. Hollis recalled that Waugh once had to "fill in a form, for some work of reference, of books which he had composed. Evelyn amused himself by entering *The Mind and Face of Cruttwell, Cruttwell from Within* and similar absurdities."[13] Waugh didn't need to invent books to embarrass Cruttwell, since actual writings did the same. "Mr. Loveday's Little Outing," a short story that lent its name to the collection published in 1936, was, according to Alec,

> originally entitled 'Mr Cruttwell's Little Outing'. Evelyn was anxious that Chapman & Hall should write to the Dean, saying that they were proposing to use this title for a collection of short stories. The Mr Cruttwell in the story was a homicidal lunatic; if the Dean of Hertford thought he would be mistaken for this character, they were prepared to alter the title. But the letter was never written. It was felt that the joke had gone far enough, and by then the victim had suffered an adequate humiliation.[14]

The story appeared twice with Cruttwell's name in the title, in *Nash's Pall Mall Magazine* and *Harper's Bazaar*.[15]

Waugh found other ways of using Cruttwell in fiction. His name appears in each of Waugh's first five novels, given to characters such as Toby Cruttwell, the jewel thief in *Decline and Fall,* and Mr. Cruttwell, the bonesetter in *A Handful of Dust.* Cruttwell did not take his "valedictory bow" until publication of "An Englishman's Home" in October 1938, appearing as a "dishonest treasurer for the Wolf Cubs of Much Malcock."[16] John Jolliffe pointed out that it was 1942 before Waugh published a novel, *Put Out More Flags,* "without dragging in the name of a man whose form of immortality is perhaps not much to be envied."[17] Cruttwell's death in an insane asylum in 1941 seems to have been the only reason Waugh stopped using his name, though it is possible that Waugh felt some remorse. Waugh lost interest only at that point, after almost twenty years of abusing Cruttwell, showing how durable his bitterness could be.

Waugh did not confine attacks on Cruttwell to fiction. He also went out of his way to insult the dean in *Labels: A Mediterranean Journal,* a travel book published in 1930. Waugh decided that his guide in Pompeii looked like Mussolini, inferred that the "lower orders often grow to resemble the public figures of their generation," and noted that a don at his college looked "exactly like a prominent murderer."[18] Waugh refrained from using Cruttwell's name, but the original title of "Mr. Loveday's Little Outing" leaves little doubt as to whom he was referring. Cruttwell seems to have preoccupied Waugh, who found that the cathedral at Malaga reminded him of the chapel at Hertford, "evoking long suppressed memories . . . of all those gentle and wise men who directed [his] youth with who can tell what insight and sympathy." Waugh associated the chapel with a "venerable figure," his history tutor, "ill at ease in his starched white surplice, biting his nails, and brooding . . . on all the good he intended for each one of us" (*L* 191–92). Waugh is clearly ironic when he contrasts the dean's supposed concerns and unattractive appearance and stresses too strongly his faith in the man's virtue. Cruttwell represented authority and discipline Waugh had loathed at Oxford, and he blamed Cruttwell for incompetent tutelage and loss of his scholarship. By the time he wrote *Labels,* Waugh was enjoying some success as a writer, using almost every publication to embarrass the man who had dismissed him from Oxford.

Given Waugh's refusal to study and his conversion to Roman Catholicism in 1930, his relentless assault on an evidently insecure man might seem to be rather cruel. In one way the attack was little more than amusement for Waugh, who enjoyed making people uncomfortable, especially if he disliked them. Waugh's campaign against Cruttwell was more than a joke, however, even at Oxford. According to Hollis, Waugh had once said that "Cruttwell is rather better than most of the Dons. But one must have someone to persecute."[19] Finding someone to persecute is reminiscent of Waugh harassing masters and boys at Heath Mount and Lancing. Persecution enabled Waugh not only to undermine others' pretensions, but also to become the center of a subversive group, which at Oxford included Greenidge and Harold Acton. Subversiveness was enjoyable in itself, but it also ensured acceptance by some and contention with others, both essential to Waugh in order to avoid boredom. Waugh's love of a fight does not explain continuation of his campaign after he had left Oxford. Alec remembered that Evelyn had come down from Oxford to live with his parents, "his fortunes at their lowest." He had been

> knocking on innumerable doors. At one point he had been interviewed by the headmaster of an excellent preparatory school. He had liked the headmaster; the headmaster had said 'You seem to be exactly the man I'm looking for.' Evelyn had returned home jubilant. 'Mr Toad on top,' he told his mother. But the headmaster knew Cruttwell and that was that.[20]

Lady Burghclere also interviewed Cruttwell when Waugh wanted to marry her daughter, Evelyn Gardner. Waugh naturally began to blame Cruttwell for interfering with his marriage and his search for agreeable work. Cruttwell had no reason to be anything but

4: *Et in Arcadia Ego,* 1922–1924

honest with anyone who asked, but Waugh hated Cruttwell for what he had said, and he spent years exacting one form of revenge or another.

Waugh was unlucky in having Cruttwell as his tutor. He didn't "want an academic career,"[21] but a milder man might have directed Waugh's intellect in some way both interesting and rewarding, instead of driving him away from studies. Admittedly, it is difficult to see how such a tutor could have prevailed upon the freedom Waugh was apparently determined to enjoy at Oxford. Cruttwell's successor, T. S. R. Boase, "preserved the politeness" that Waugh had "supposed was universal," but he "did not learn very much from him" (*ALL* 175). By then he wasn't interested in studying, and he used Cruttwell's temper and appearance as excuses not to do so. Later he represented himself as the innocent when he had in fact wasted his time carousing, indicating that he had been "unfortunate" because the Hertford dons "did not captivate the imagination" when compared with J. F. Roxburgh (*ALL* 173). The statement may have stemmed from failing memory, or it may have been deliberate distortion. In 1922 Waugh had been telling Driberg that Roxburgh's brain seemed "inconsiderable when one is daily taught by dons of real education," having reached the "conclusion that J. F. is thoroughly second-rate" (*LEW* 9–10). Waugh may have been trying to appear worldly wise in front of the Lancing crowd, but it seems that interest in education, if not dedication to it, persisted during his first two terms at Oxford. In his third term, starting in September 1922, Waugh began to realize how liberating Oxford could be. The few restraints the university imposed, such as reporting to a tutor, incited further excesses in someone so naturally disruptive. The system worked for most, but Waugh refused any restraint at Oxford, resisting Cruttwell's attempts to constrain exuberance and resenting them for years.

Waugh also lost interest in studies because he became quite closely attached to several other undergraduates; he found himself in love with two of them.[22] Friendships developed gradually: Waugh remembered living "unobtrusively" during his first term, in a "subdued fashion" during his first two terms (*ALL* 165–66). No diary exists for the period, making it difficult to follow Waugh from term to term. The autobiography indicates that Waugh's first two terms were quite ordinary. He dined in the college and did "all that freshmen traditionally did," buying a "cigarette box carved with the college arms and the popular printed panorama of the *Towers and Spires of Oxford;* learning to smoke a pipe; . . . walking and bicycling about the surrounding villages; making an unremarkable maiden speech at the Union; doing enough work to satisfy the examiners in History Previous." Still there seemed to be a "quintessential Oxford" that he "knew and loved from afar and intended to find" (*ALL* 166–67). Waugh was somewhat disappointed in Hertford, which had "no scholar of importance among the dons; among the undergraduates, no member of the Bullingdon, no President of the Union or of the O.U.D.S.; no Blue; the boat never came near the head of the river." In the "generally recognised order of precedence among the colleges," Hertford was "halfway up, on a par with Oriel and Exeter." Among his contemporaries, Waugh could identify an ambassador, a bishop, a Dominion Chief Justice, a film actor, a queen's counsel, and a "popular composer." He did "not know of any other notables" (*ALL* 164).

Letters also express Waugh's dissatisfaction with the company he had kept so far. Early in 1922 he was "very shy and a little lonely still," wishing he could find some "congenial friends." A little later, alluding to an ambition, he wrote that he was "not yet the centre of any group but on the fringes of many." As late as 31 May 1922, beginning his second term, he was still happy to lead a "solitary and quiet life" with enough friends to keep him from being lonely and not enough to bother him (*LEW* 4, 6, 11). Waugh went up to Oxford in the Lent term beginning in January, whereas most wait until the Michaelmas term in September. Almost no one there was his age, the same position he had been in when he had started at Lancing. He had planned to study art in Paris for at least a few months, but his father, in his mid fifties and anxious about money, decided to send him up immediately. Arthur himself had gone up in a by-term, and years later Evelyn still wondered about his father's decision. It seemed "curious" that Arthur saw the "disadvantages of his own experience" and still set Evelyn on "precisely the same road." Evelyn was "eager enough to go," and his father was "showing his habitual impatience to get a task finished." Arthur was also "growing weary of the routine at Chapman and Hall's and looked forward to retirement." When Evelyn finished his education, Arthur thought he would be "so much the nearer to leisure or to less exacting work." Evelyn may have resented his father's decision more than he admitted, since he never studied in Paris and later considered it his "life-long impediment" that he had never gained "some command" of French (*ALL* 163). Initial loneliness at the university may have been another source of resentment.

Still, Waugh represented himself as happy in his letters, perhaps only to impress friends still at Lancing. One written sometime in

4: *Et in Arcadia Ego*, 1922–1924

1922 describes life at Oxford as "very beautiful," "almost perfect" except for the "menace of Schools," or examinations, at the end of the term (*LEW* 10). In another, perhaps dating from May 1922, Waugh characterizes himself as "too happy," deciding that "life is good and Oxford is all that one dreams" (*LEW* 8). Temporarily relieved of the pressure to prove himself, Waugh became indifferent and serene. He invited Carew to come up for an examination and "have a bust" (*LEW* 4), later advising him to "take things as they come. That is the lesson of Oxford. Nothing matters at Oxford."[23] Sent to the university as a "lone explorer" and insecure anyway, Waugh at first depended on friendships formed at Lancing, writing often to Carew and Driberg. Interest in those friends soon waned, and, recognizing that he had "little choice but to rove," Waugh began to make new friends, many of them from nearby Balliol College. Toward the end of his second term, Waugh estimated in his autobiography, he began to show "indiscriminate *bonhomie*" (*ALL* 163, 171), and his circle of friends expanded rapidly. That term Waugh had changed his way of life and had started to study, not wanting to lose his scholarship by failing History Previous.[24] Once he had passed the examination, Waugh apparently felt entitled to a reward. Hollis remembered that shortly thereafter Waugh "first blossomed forth as a public figure in undergraduate life," in the "Michaelmas term of 1922,"[25] Waugh's third term.

One of his new friends was Terence Greenidge, another Hertford man. In Waugh's second year, he and Greenidge were the "nucleus" of the "Hertford underworld." This group collected in Waugh's rooms, "drank large quantities of beer and made a good deal of noise" (*ALL* 178–79). More important for Waugh, Greenidge introduced him to the Hypocrites' Club. Clubs were popular, since undergraduates could not enter Oxford pubs. The Hypocrites' name came from their motto, meaning "water is best," though most of them drank beer.[26] Waugh explained that the "original members were heavy-drinking, rather sombre Rugbeians and Wykehamists with vaguely artistic and literary interests." When he joined, however, the club was undergoing "invasion and occupation by a group of wanton Etonians who brought it to speedy dissolution." The Hypocrites became "notorious not only for drunkenness but for flamboyance of dress and manner which was in some cases patently homosexual" (*ALL* 179–80). Driberg added that the Hypocrites had been known for "lively and drunken revels ('orgies', were they?), mainly homosexual in character." He had been dancing with someone named John, "while Evelyn and another man rolled on a sofa with (as one of them said later) their 'tongues licking each other's tonsils.'"[27] The Hypocrites became for Waugh the "stamping-ground" of half his Oxford life and the "source of friendships still warm" (*ALL* 181). Membership in the club coincided with the beginning of Waugh's homosexual phase, though it is unclear when he joined. He seems to have joined at the beginning of his third term in September 1922, or, at the earliest, at the end of his second term in June or July.

It is difficult to come to terms with Waugh's homosexual phase, something he obviously regretted in later years. He destroyed the diary he had kept at Oxford, apparently because he had recorded at least some of his homosexual experiences, and he did not mention his own homosexuality in his autobiography. At Lancing Waugh had grown weary of pretending to be strong and solitary, and at Oxford, momentarily dazzled by the brilliance of other undergraduates, he relaxed the standards he used to define and defend himself, opening up for the first time, risking romantic involvement with another person. In the almost exclusively male world of Oxford in the 1920s, it was natural that his love focused on other men. Waugh's homosexuality was never definite or exclusive: just as agnosticism did not rule out an occasional prayer, homosexuality did not prevent him from admiring women. At Oxford and for some time after, he felt attracted to good-looking, intelligent people regardless of their sex. Relationships with such people at Oxford helped to determine Waugh's later views of the university, its value, and its danger.

Waugh was candid with friends about his homosexual phase, writing Nancy Mitford in 1954 to say that he had gone to Oxford and had visited his "first homosexual love, Richard Pares, a don at All Souls" (*LEW* 435). Born in 1902, Pares went up as a Balliol scholar, finished with two first-class degrees, married Janet Lindsay in 1937, and became Professor of History at the University of Edinburgh in 1945. If Pares is any indication, Waugh's early circle at Oxford had been more interested in scholarship than he admitted in his autobiography. In his diary for 25 December 1924, Waugh noted that Christmas always made him "feel a little sad," partly because his "few romances" had "always culminated in Christmas week—Luned, Richard, Alastair" (*DEW* 194).[28] "Richard" is Richard Pares, indicating that Waugh's first homosexual affair lasted less than a year, having begun sometime after he had gone up in January, the climax having been reached in December 1922. Though unusually ready to accept undergraduates on their own terms in his first year, Waugh nevertheless proved too demanding

4: *Et in Arcadia Ego,* 1922–1924 119

for Pares. He had been entrusted with Waugh's "full devotion," but Pares did not like to drink, and for that reason they "drifted apart" (*ALL* 191). It is not clear if "full devotion" means only emotional commitment, or if Waugh is coining a euphemism for sex. Harold Acton thought it unlikely that Pares and Waugh had ever had sex, and Martin Stannard, generally ready to minimize Waugh's homosexuality, describes their relationship as "idyllically platonic."[29] The question of sexual activity is in many ways the least interesting aspect of the relationship, focusing on physical instead of emotional and intellectual needs. Waugh preferred drinking to Pares, not because he was an alcoholic, but because drinking could involve a lot of company and a lot of noise. Quiet intimacy was one thing, but Waugh preferred unrestrained camaraderie, something he had not enjoyed at Lancing or Hampstead, and something Pares could not provide either.

Homosexuality was in this sense a reaction to the emotionally straitened years of Waugh's adolescence. He felt deprived of affection at home, where his father demanded attention from his mother and clearly favored his brother, though Alec also experimented with homosexuality. "Prancing," in the language of the day, subverted the modest, respectable upbringing that exasperated Evelyn. He had not been happy at Lancing either, and loneliness made him especially vulnerable to other men's charms. Homosexuality, like drinking, was a means of gaining acceptance within a certain group at Oxford. It was then a "male community," and "girls were very rarely to be seen in the men's colleges." Most undergraduates were "well content . . . to indulge in light flirtations during the vacation and deep friendships during the term." Waugh reported that "fewer than ten per cent" of his contemporaries had had "'girl friends'. Some had made a single, pleasureless adventure with a prostitute abroad. Few had any serious interest in women" (*ALL* 168–69). Hollis confirmed that "males had for the most part no great wish for feminine company and did not admit them into their societies."[30] Anthony Powell added that the authorities had discouraged heterosexual relationships, most necessarily outside the university, but had been "indifferent to homosexuality." Powell had received a warning after he had been seen talking to a waitress in the street one evening. Peter Quennell admitted that he had "spent a night in term-time with a woman." Even though it had been "some distance from Oxford," Quennell was "rusticated (sent down for a term), and in consequence never returned to Balliol or bothered to take his degree."[31] Given little chance to worry about women, Oxford men concentrated on alignments within the university. They divided into three groups fairly equal in size, "hearties," intellectuals, and aesthetes. Waugh was not much of an athlete, and his first friends in the university seem to have been intellectuals. Waugh found them dull, and after two terms he moved on to the aesthetes, who used homosexuality to shock everyone else.

Waugh wanted to be part of a group, but he also wanted intimacy. Alastair Graham was Pares's "successor as the friend of [Waugh's] heart." He was in one way more attractive to Waugh, for Graham had "no repugnance to the bottle," and they "drank deep together" (*ALL* 192). Waugh seems to have been more sexually active with Graham than he had been with Pares, and their intimacy lasted until Graham suddenly left England for Africa in September 1924.

Harold Acton was in many ways the leader of the aesthetes. A wealthy Etonian and flamboyant homosexual, Acton had lived in Chicago and Florence and had already published some poetry. Waugh was a "little dazzled by [Acton's] manifest superiorities of experience" (*ALL* 198), embarrassed by his own relatively modest background. Waugh fell under Acton's influence soon after Acton had come up in the Michaelmas term of 1922, making Acton the subject of another "*Isis* Idol," emulating Acton in some ways but never becoming quite so outrageous. Though not as self-assured as his new friend, Waugh nevertheless admired Acton's independence, his determination "to stir us up," his "scorn for the bogus." Acton "loved to shock and then to conciliate with exaggerated politeness. He was himself shocked and censorious at any breach of his elaborate and idiosyncratic code of propriety" (*ALL* 196–97), and Acton's example encouraged Waugh to behave in the same way. Graham also led Waugh to adopt the aesthetes' point of view, appealing to Waugh's "natural frivolity, dilettantism and dissipation," exposing "worldly ambition" as "vulgar and futile" (*ALL* 193). Aesthetes had a wide range of cultural interests, but none fell within courses of study outlined by dons. Aestheticism was thus a way of distinguishing oneself from conventional scholars, rejecting studies as insufficiently interesting, and trying "to create a new ambience in which art and literature could flourish without social constraints."[32]

They paid as little attention to parents as they did to dons. Acton had started a "vogue for Victoriana," derived, Waugh thought, in part from the "wish to scandalize parents who had themselves thrown out the wax-flowers and woolwork screens," which the aesthetes "ardently collected" (*EAR* 597). Aesthetes didn't care about money either, an attitude that distinguished Waugh from his father. Waugh's scholarship meant that he was "earning nearly a third of the normal expenses of an undergraduate," but he "regarded this sum as the reward for a brief period of intense effort at school," not as a way to reduce his father's expenses. Evelyn considered himself "entitled to some self-indulgence," though he realized later that he had been "exorbitant in this claim." With "some exaggeration," Arthur saw himself as "toiling" so that Evelyn "might enjoy luxuries which he denied himself." Evelyn thought Arthur would have "submitted happily enough" if father and son had shared the same interests, if Evelyn had been "playing Hamlet in the O.U.D.S. or touring the countryside in a cricket team." He had been a "pure waster," however, and later he could not say that Arthur's "resentment" had been "unjustified" (FS HRHRC).

Playing Hamlet or cricket was impossible for an aesthete, and Waugh was soon spending more than his scholarship, allowance, and other income could cover, buying clothes, books, and wine, living like the irresponsible aristocrat he always wanted to be. When Claud Cockburn started complaining about his finances, Waugh lectured him on "improvidence." Cockburn had made the "mistake of not buying enough, on account, from tailors, wine merchants, booksellers, and others." Waugh supposed that when bills had come in, Cockburn had "panicked, sought to economize, stopped buying." Waugh's debts were even larger, but he "kept the creditors quiet in the traditional Oxonian manner of the day by simply ordering more and more goods."[33] Arthur Waugh resented his son's extravagance, since he was paying and "money is the root of almost all family differences" (FS HRHRC). Relations between Arthur and Evelyn, never easy, became almost openly hostile, as Evelyn began to see his father's financial worries as philistine and bourgeois, antithetical to aestheticism. By 1925, after he had injured himself during a drunken visit to Oxford, Waugh was "far from gracious" to his parents, though he had to spend three days on a couch in his father's "frightful house" (Diary HRHRC). Joining the aesthetes at Oxford gave Waugh the chance to declare intellectual, if not economic independence, inviting him into another sort of contest, opposing the money-grubbing middle class.

Arthur was not the only opponent. By this time Alec also belonged to the middle-class literary establishment, and, as Evelyn said, he "*makes money* out of writing." Cockburn explained that that was a "serious charge," implying

> vile philistinism, betrayal of all artistic principle. Evelyn, who had feelings of warm affection for his brother, regarded him in this respect the way a delicately nurtured girl might have regarded an older sister

who made good money as a whore. One still was as fond of her as ever. Probably she had done the best she could. But the least she could do was to use the money for the benefit of worthier, finer members of the family.

Cockburn thought that some of Waugh's critics were "inadequately aware of how potent, how absolute that way of thinking was when he was nineteen or twenty and at Oxford." Making the most of his disregard for money, Evelyn decided that Alec should loan Cockburn whatever he needed to pay his debts. The Cockburns and Waughs were related, but they were not especially close, and Alec refused, pleading poverty. Evelyn thought Alec needed a "lesson in gentlemanly comportment," he and some friends going to London and "mocking Alec." They

> spied on Alec and dogged him. Sometimes they would be lying in wait just as Alec and some young woman got out of their taxi. They would then rush forward shouting, "Boo to Alec the bald-headed lecher!" Once, . . . they hid just outside the windows of the apartment, waited until the girl was reclining on a couch while Alec lowered the lights, and then burst in with their offensive slogan.

Evelyn observed that "Alec's women" were "apt to be rendered frigid by anything unconventional."[34]

Alec remembered that Evelyn had once "missed his last train to Oxford" and, "needing a roof above his head," had started searching the building for Alec's apartment, "shouting into each bedroom as he passed, 'Is the baldheaded lecher sleeping here?'" The management had asked Alec to "seek another home." Alec did not remember the request for a loan, the "campaign of minor persecution," or the "invasion of young Oxonians" interrupting a "discreet essay at gallantry." Cockburn's cable in reply reached *The Atlantic* in time for printing, insisting that "THOUGH GOOD COUSIN ALEC'S OTHER POWERS HAPPILY UNIMPAIRED HIS MEMORY FLAGS STOP HE HAS MISDATED ENTIRE EPISODE WHEREOF MY ACCOUNT ENTIRELY FACTUAL."[35] It is not possible to tell whose memory was more accurate, or if Evelyn had given Cockburn an exaggerated account of exploits in London. At least Cockburn and Alec agreed that when he had been at Oxford, Evelyn had been unusually aggressive toward his brother. Cockburn believed that aggression had stemmed from Evelyn's contempt for Alec's indifference to art, contempt that had been encouraged by other aesthetes. Remarks about Alec's lechery are also interesting, again reflecting Evelyn's tendency at Oxford to defend his own sexuality by stigmatizing another's as unnatural or excessive.

4: *Et in Arcadia Ego*, 1922–1924

Alec also came in for abuse because, like his father, he enjoyed cricket. In September 1923 Evelyn published "The National Game" in *Cherwell*, recounting a match from the long vacation. There had been some confusion about the site, and Evelyn detailed his boredom: he had worn himself out, he had seen "nothing and no one of any interest;" he had "suffered acute pain" in his big toe; he had walked "several miles;" he had drunk "several pints of indifferently good beer;" he had "spent nearly two pounds;" he might have "spent that sum in dining very well and going to a theatre;" he might have "made that sum by spending the morning, pleasantly, in writing or drawing." Alec nevertheless "maintained that it had been a great day. Village cricket, he said, was always like that" (*EWA* 151). Besides dwelling on his discomfort in a way characteristic of all his writing, Evelyn pointed to the huge difference between his and his brother's sensibilities, evident in one's aversion to sport and the other's enthusiasm for it. At Lancing Waugh had been occasionally interested in sports, but once he went up to Oxford he avoided them, again under the influence of the aesthetes. Aesthetes were in one way the rivals of the intellectuals, but they were even more seriously the rivals of the "hearties," athletes ill at ease with the aesthetes' theories and affectations. Sometimes rivalry broke into mild violence, the athletes dumping Harold Acton in one of the fountains, and Waugh again found himself in the midst of contention, opposing not just the bourgeois mind prevailing outside Oxford, but also the insufficiently radical students within the university itself.

Waugh did not stop at antagonizing athletes. He delighted in ridiculing almost any other undergraduate, protecting himself from criticism and using his sense of humor as a social advantage. Anthony Powell remembered that Waugh, when drunk, had been

> making a great deal of noise one day lunching at an undergraduate club. The rather pompous president (or secretary) came over and said: 'Unless you are quieter, I am afraid you will have to leave—people can't hear themselves speak.' Waugh rose, not without difficulty, staggered across the room to where a member of the club was sitting alone at a table. He put his hand on this mild-looking man's shoulder and asked beseechingly: 'You *can* hear yourself talking to yourself, can't you?'[36]

Christopher Hollis remembered Philbrick,

> who had confessed, or was alleged to have confessed, that at school he had derived pleasure from the beating of smaller boys. Evelyn had

got hold of this story and very mischievously spread all round the University the tale that Philbrick was an unbridled sadist. It happened shortly afterwards that at a film shown at one of the Oxford cinemas about African life there was a shot of some poor African being flogged. When this was shown on the screen there were cries from every quarter of the cinema of 'Philbrick, Philbrick'. The episode must have caused him very considerable embarrassment.

This joke, and probably others, went too far. When Hollis was elected president of the Union, he gave a party in Balliol. Waugh was there, and the next day Hollis found a "large parti-coloured South Sea Island walking-stick which it was Evelyn's habit to carry around with him." Hollis went to Hertford to give it back, Waugh telling him that "Philbrick and Basil Murray had waylaid him . . . and beaten him up. 'We did not attack you in Chris's room,' they said, 'because it would have been embarrassing for him, but we have had as much of you as we can stand and now, by God, you're going to get it.'" Waugh got revenge in *Decline and Fall,* using Philbrick's name for the enigmatic butler who tells fantastic stories about his past. Prendergast, the name of the novel's doubting clergyman, also comes from Oxford, where, according to Hollis, it belonged to a "wholly virtuous and inoffensive aesthete who had never . . . done any harm to Evelyn except once, it seems, make some remark to Peter Quennell about the undesirable bohemian company which he entertained when he found Evelyn in Quennell's room."[37] Basil Murray is supposed to have been one of the models for Basil Seal.

Obnoxious as he was to other undergraduates, Waugh more often offended authorities. He belonged to the White Rose, an "occasional dining-club devoted to the Stuart cause." The club had been banned since 1745, when two members had been "reputedly hanged on Magdalen bridge." Waugh and friends "commemorated their anniversary, the Restoration," and the "birthday of the Bavarian pretender," sending "loyal greetings." Their gatherings were "regularly raided by the proctors" (*ALL* 183). Waugh frequented the New Reform Club, supported largely by David Lloyd George, in an attempt to encourage Liberal politics among undergraduates. Two politicians showed up to see the club for themselves, probably because they, or Lloyd George, had heard some strange reports. Having drunk "at least a bottle" of champagne, Waugh responded to the inquiry. Though "ill-wishers" had portrayed the club as a "meeting-place of homosexuals," Waugh insisted that almost every man in the room had a "complete orgasm" every time he passed a woman in the street. Cockburn remembered that the "former Cabinet minister took offense because he supposed this was some oblique, satirical joke at Lloyd George's own sex life. The nonconformist leader was shocked for more obvious reasons, and both walked out of the club, no doubt to report adversely on its tone."[38] Another defensive sexual joke, another unnecessary conflict.

Waugh's favorite club was the Hypocrites, and membership led to more difficulty with authority. The club's reputation meant that it was condemned by the colleges' deans, especially "Sligger" Urquhart of Balliol, who "rightly regarded it as a rival attraction to, and source of corruption of, his own sober salon" (*ALL* 180). The sober salon may have opened the breach between Urquhart and Waugh, as Hollis remembered that Urquhart had "asked Evelyn to lunch in the days of his companionship with Richard Pares and offered him barley water to drink—an error not easily to be forgiven."[39] Pares soon joined Urquhart's circle of sober intellectuals, cutting himself off from Waugh and giving him another reason to dislike Urquhart. Waugh recognized Urquhart's opposition to the Hypocrites, and he began to abuse the dean in the same way he was abusing Cruttwell. Urquhart's sexuality was fair game, though Waugh's accusations were more bitter than absurd. He "alleged that Sligger lusted after Pares himself."[40] Peter Quennell remembered Urquhart's "deep affection for clever, attractive youths" but believed that he remained a "natural innocent." Waugh was an "especially vociferous critic." Whenever he went to Balliol at night, the "walls would echo to his chantings. '*The Dean of Balliol sleeps with men!*'"[41] Perhaps Waugh had reason for resentment; perhaps his account of the break-up with Pares, attributed to Pares's distaste for alcohol, obscured Waugh's jealousy and homosexuality. The account in the autobiography seems more likely to be true, simplified perhaps, but neither as heated nor as hysterical as Waugh's outbursts at the time. Then and later, he was likely to attribute failure in love to interference from a third party, not to any fault in himself. Waugh also blamed Cyril Connolly, another undergraduate, for the break-up with Pares, claiming that he had been "cuckolded by Connolly."[42] Waugh seldom preferred dull accuracy when he could invent a sensational story instead, and there is little reason to believe his wild accusations, especially since he found betrayal such a compelling subject, in life as in fiction, at Oxford and afterward.

Other signs of weakness also inspired ridicule of Urquhart. Hollis recalled that Urquhart had

gone to Cambridge to deliver a lecture, but, arrived there, had been unable to deliver it because of an attack of hiccups. For some reason this intensely amused Evelyn and he caused us to parade around Balliol Quad, singing:
Gawd help Urquharts on a night like this
Oop goes the Urquhart.[43]

The shouting and insults were extreme forms of the bolshevism Waugh had tried at Lancing, no longer limited at Oxford because he was often drunk, but also because he had fulfilled his ambitions and had no reason to fear punishment.

Urquhart and others succeeded in closing the Hypocrites, apparently in the spring or summer of 1924, toward the end of Waugh's time at the university. Waugh resented this move and got even by writing a screenplay to be produced by Greenidge. *The Scarlet Woman* makes fun of Urquhart's religion, portraying him as an agent of the Pope in a "gigantic attempt at the conversion of England." The scheme falters when Urquhart's contact, the Prince of Wales, develops an interest in Beatrice de Carolle, a "cabaret-queen" played by Elsa Lanchester. Waugh himself played the Dean of Balliol, wearing a blond wig in imitation of Urquhart's hair, petting the prince whenever possible. They were filming at the end of July, about the time of Waugh's *viva voce,* but Waugh and the rest left Oxford after examinations were over. Filming continued on Hampstead Heath and in the garden at the Waughs' house, Arthur watching with interest and Alec taking a part. At the beginning of September, the film was "not finished owing to the desertion of [Viscount] Elmley," and Waugh felt "no enthusiasm to finish it" (Diary HRHRC). Waugh was depressed by his performance on examinations and his limited prospects, but undergraduates began to see the film as representative of a cause. There were no film societies at Oxford, and authorities were resisting students' requests to allow them. In October 1925 the *Cherwell* was complaining about Oxford's "conventional restraints" and hoping that Greenidge would "finish the film made in collaboration with Mr. Waugh."[44] Waugh went back to work, perhaps because the film offered another chance to embarrass authorities at Oxford, perhaps because he had little else to do. They finally finished in November, and *Isis* reviewed the film favorably on 2 December 1925.

The Scarlet Woman is obviously satirical, ridiculing machinations of the Roman Catholic Church and whims of the royal family. The film is more fundamentally personal, as Waugh hits back at the Dean of Balliol, who is given a "vacation haunt" in Golders

4: *Et in Arcadia Ego*, 1922–1924   127

Green. In a film filled with alcohol, the dean drinks lemonade. In his portrayal of the dean, Waugh exaggerates Urquhart's interest in other men. Through Urquhart, Waugh seems to have been mocking his own homosexuality and the pain that had come from it. When the prince meets the cabaret queen, Waugh turns to the camera and admits to a "far, far deeper hurt than I have ever felt before." In *The Scarlet Woman,* as in earlier and later work, Waugh splits himself between two characters, the Dean of Balliol and Lord Borrowington, a "penniless peer, master of the Prince's revels" and procurer of the cabaret queen. Again, the characters seem to have represented different aspects of Waugh himself, on one side a jilted homosexual, on the other an asexual aristocrat. Greenidge also played two roles in the film, and Lord Borrowington is a small part, perhaps insignificant. Waugh wrote the script and supervised most of the production, however. He clearly enjoyed playing Urquhart, and if he had had no interest in playing Borrowington, Waugh could have taken another part or could have found another actor. The Dean of Balliol is a much larger part, and it allowed Waugh not only to vent spleen but also to indicate the predominance of homosexuality, in his art as in his life at Oxford. The dean and the prince get their comeuppance when they are poisoned by order of the king, Waugh's comic revenge against Urquhart. Perhaps he was also trying to kill the homosexual side of his own nature.

The Scarlet Woman is the last uncomplimentary portrait of Urquhart in Waugh's writing, partly because Waugh converted to Urquhart's faith in 1930. Waugh thought that Roman Catholics had more than their share of problems in England, and he suppressed delight in embarrassing Urquhart, perhaps compensating by continuing to ridicule Cruttwell as long as the man lived. Waugh certainly had opportunities to do the same to Urquhart, who lived until 1934. He did not deal with Urquhart again until the late 1950s, when he wrote a biography of Ronald Knox, including a portrait of Sligger considerably different from that in *The Scarlet Woman.* Urquhart's religion had become grounds for commendation, for Sligger had been the "first Roman Catholic since the Reformation to be elected Fellow of an Oxford college, and he made it a point of honour to refrain from any suggestion of proselytism." Waugh did not try to exaggerate Urquhart's qualities: he had been neither a "wit; nor an Oxford 'character' of whom people treasure and embellish memorable sayings." Still, Waugh had come to appreciate virtues he had disdained at Oxford. Urquhart had drawn "people to him by his simple, unselfish affection," with "half a dozen or more in his rooms every evening talking among themselves as much as to their host." There had also been "people outside his circle who derided what they took to be its cosiness and softness."[45] No portrait of Urquhart appears in Waugh's autobiography, only three brief references, none of which could be called unfair.

Apparent objectivity or even mild praise is rare in Waugh's written treatment of dons. In writings of the late 1920s especially, he often went out of his way to accuse dons of incompetence or corruption. In his biography of D. G. Rossetti, Waugh noted that William Morris had gone up to Oxford in 1853, when the dons had been "idlier than those of to-day and more widely ignorant" but "no less tedious." Waugh also reported that until Morris died, "don" and "Oxford" had been "two of the most bitter words in a vocabulary glowing with oaths."[46] Waugh's experience certainly influenced his choice of evidence. It also seems to have influenced his behavior in one of *Labels*' comic scenes. On a cruise in the Mediterranean, Waugh met a Greek who asked "searching questions" about "aestheticism" at Oxford. The Greek had been at Christ Church, but he said with a "shade of regret that he had not found any 'aestheticism' in his day." He wondered if "aestheticism" spoiled Oxford's performance in athletics. Waugh indicated that the "evil was deeper than that," and that there was a "terrible outbreak of drug-taking at the University." The Greek asked why the dons didn't stop it, Waugh answering that dons were the "origin of the whole trouble." The Greek observed that there had been "practically no drug-taking at the House in his time" (*L* 147). The conversation may have been embellished, but the story shows Waugh's delight in slandering dons. Given his capacity for fantasy, it seems likely that he told similar stories many times. It is also interesting that Waugh implicitly defended aestheticism, blaming Oxford's problems on dons, first of all, and on drug-taking, one thing that hadn't hurt him at the university.

As self-important, authoritative figures, dons were ideal characters in Waugh's comedy, and he thoroughly enjoyed exposing their weaknesses. During the Second World War, Waugh was a guest on the Brains Trust, a popular radio show. He described a regular member of the panel, Professor C. E. M. Joad, as "goatlike, libidinous, garrulous." Waugh was "delighted to observe the derision in which he was held by all the BBC staff" (*DEW* 520). On the subject of soldiers' pay, Waugh, then on active duty, suggested that the panel should accept only one third of their usual wages, a scale proportional to that paid for other war work. The panel was "aghast

4: *Et in Arcadia Ego*, 1922–1924

but ashamed to dissent," and later they "ratted," taking their pay as usual. Waugh wanted to "give the press the full story with details," hoping to "do something to discredit Joad (which is greatly in the national interest)" (*LEW* 159). In 1951 Waugh questioned the knighthood conferred on his friend Maurice Bowra, warden of Wadham College since 1938. Waugh thought it "very odd as he has done nothing to deserve it except be head of the worst College at Oxford and publish a few books no one has ever read" (*LEW* 344). In 1953 Waugh sent the first of three letters to the *New Statesman*, disputing the claims of Hugh Trevor-Roper, then student of Christ Church, in "Sir Thomas More and the English Lay Recusants" (*LEW* 641). Trevor-Roper was beginning a long and distinguished career, appointed Regius Professor of Modern History at Oxford in 1957, created Lord Dacre in 1979. His views on church history differed from those of Waugh, who dubbed Trevor-Roper the "demon don" (*LEW* 415). Even in middle age, Waugh refused to admit that any don knew more or deserved more recognition than he did.

Waugh also made fun of dons because he carried a real grudge against them. They had made him feel guilty by expecting preparation when he had been busy drinking or clowning. They had interfered with the festive life he had led at Oxford, and he blamed them for having had to leave the university. In later years Waugh probably realized that most dons had combined ability and discipline. Waugh knew that he had comparable ability, but at Oxford he had not been able to show the same discipline. Waugh's jokes about dons' stupidity and sexuality begin to look like insecure attempts to minimize their ability and discipline as a means of emphasizing his own. Waugh could also identify particular dons responsible for some action he found repugnant, loathing Cruttwell for inadequate tutelage and Urquhart for stealing Pares. These men lingered in his imagination until he had given them some unkind artistic representation, though his resentment of and preoccupation with Cruttwell were clearly greater.

Aside from Pares, very few dons acquainted with Waugh failed to attract ridicule. One was R. M. Dawkins, a professor of modern Greek at Oxford. Waugh never studied Greek there, and he and Dawkins never met as student and tutor. Dawkins had provided an "aegis" for the Hypocrites, having served as senior member because all clubs were in theory required to have faculty supervision. Dawkins was most valuable to Waugh in the summer of 1925, when Waugh was teaching public school in Wales. Lonely, poor, and miserable, Waugh had just attempted suicide when Dawkins went home for the long vacation and seemed like a "rescuer sent to . . . the desert from that green country." Waugh was desperate for Dawkins's "openhanded hospitality and companionship," and gratitude to this "much loved, learned, fidgety, humorous bachelor" persisted for forty years, until he finally recorded it in "A Little Hope," the short manuscript intended to be the second volume of his autobiography.[47] Waugh's respect for Dawkins was the opposite of what he felt for most dons, testimony to Dawkins's congeniality and Waugh's unhappiness as a schoolmaster.

Waugh lost interest in studies, but still he needed stimulation, finding some at the Oxford Union. He made his maiden speech in his first term, opposing the motion that "This House would welcome prohibition." *Oxford Magazine* said that he had made a "good impression,"[48] but Waugh considered himself "no success as a speaker" (*ALL* 182). He seems to have been intimidated, deciding in May 1922 that he could not "go down in that House." He felt "very nervous," and *Isis* observed that "Mr Waugh appeared unaware of his audience" (*LEW* 11). He was still outrageous and occasionally ridiculous, intervening "spontaneously and ineffectually," usually in favor of some extremely conservative idea. Waugh proclaimed himself a Tory despite his ignorance of Tory policies. The Labour party had attracted "many of the best brains," including Richard Pares. Waugh remembered telling a "middle-brow socialist" that he would find the "competition too hot and that he had better make his appearance as a Conservative." Waugh followed the same course, joining Conservatives at the Oxford Carlton Club. The club was "social rather than political and more than party loyalty was required for membership," as the Carlton tried to achieve in "miniature the atmosphere of a London club." Conservative politics offered Waugh social advantages he was reluctant to turn down. He belonged to both the Liberal New Reform and the Conservative Carlton Clubs, as well as the Chatham, a "small, ostensibly *elite* Tory discussion club without premises" (*ALL* 182–83). Waugh enjoyed meeting sons from rich and powerful families, who were, presumably, less common in more liberal settings. He enjoyed access to the Carlton Club, and he had found a way to distance himself from Richard Pares.

Waugh was also politically conservative later in life, and regardless of the opportunities his views may have offered him, he seems to have embraced conservatism mainly to make a spectacle of himself. At Oxford in the 1920s, "extreme Tories were very much in the minority, and were branded 'Die-Hards'." By Waugh's "third term he was describing himself as a Die-Hard; by his fourth he was uttering what *Cherwell* . . . called some of the most outrageous reactionary sentiments the Union had ever heard."[49] He changed positions on one issue: in November 1922 he defended the motion that "the Introduction of Prohibition would Benefit this Country."[50] Waugh's bluster did not impress Oxford as it had impressed Lancing, and inebriation probably detracted from some speeches. Later he noted that an "'Oxford Union manner' is reprobated in the House of Commons as frivolous," but it was "far too grave" for Waugh to maintain. He claimed to have been "too ignorant," not having heard any "political talk at home," not having read the "political papers," knowing "nothing of personalities, statistics or social questions" (*ALL* 182). It is hard to imagine Waugh contributing much to many of the debates: "Policy of the Government in the Near East," "Return to Party Government on Party Lines," "British Sovereignty in India," and so forth.[51] He nevertheless attributed failure to the limitations of his background, obscuring the extremity of positions he had advocated. He insisted on running for president of the Union in June 1923; he finished last with 25 votes while Christopher Hollis won with 309.[52] Obviously he had no chance to win. Perhaps Waugh wanted only to show his father that he had no hope of conventional success at Oxford, that his progress would have to be measured in some other way. He was still eager to perform, dictate, and contend, and he wanted others to acknowledge his effectiveness. Waugh was too insecure to succeed at the Union, but even after he had lost the presidency he remained fascinated with others' competence and control, continuing to attend almost every debate as "part of the multifarious life" he led (*ALL* 183).

Waugh compensated for inadequacy as a speaker by reporting debates for *Isis* and *Cherwell* (*ALL* 182), and he soon became one of the leading journalists at Oxford. Journalism offered another opportunity for control, since he could represent the debates in any manner he chose. More interesting than his reports are stories and verse, which began to appear early in 1922. These pieces have been dismissed as ephemeral, written only for money or amusement, but in one way or another, Waugh's writing is almost never ephemeral, consistently concerned with defining himself and his relations with others. These pieces are his first attempts to represent Oxford in fiction, and they are very ambivalent, suggesting that something might be wrong with the place. He was still connected to Lancing, writing to friends and sending literary work. Probably the first story Waugh wrote at Oxford is "Legend: A Sequel to Twelve Years On," referring perhaps to a story written at Lancing by Waugh or Carew. In an undated letter to Carew, Waugh showed how Lancing might remember his circle. Characteristically concerned with reputation, "Legend" depicts Lancing after the departure of Waugh and his friends, though most were still there. The story is nostalgic and even wistful without being sentimental, lamenting the absence of amusing boys. As usual, Waugh tended to idealize the past. In 1921 he had been eager to get away from Lancing, but once he had gone, he began to regret separation from a school he had consistently criticized. Somewhat dissatisfied with friends at Oxford, Waugh maintained contact with Carew and Driberg, perhaps hoping that their arrival would brighten his social life. Writing to Lancing also enabled Waugh to intimate the strange, wonderful things he was learning and the unfathomable gap between public school and university, his friends still subject to stupid masters. Carew asked for lectures on art and conduct, and Waugh exuded the pedantry he despised in others.

The first piece to deal directly with the university, and to express distaste for it, appeared in *Isis* in May 1922, at the beginning of Waugh's second term. "History Previous" alludes to preliminary examinations Waugh was not eager to take and consists of three verses denigrating St. Simon's *Memoirs,* J. S. Mill's *Principles of Political Economy,* and Rousseau's *Social Contract.* Bored by required reading, Waugh proclaimed that John Stuart Mill made him ill. If Waugh were "shipwrecked on some coral shore," where "print and paper" could not reach him, he would "gladly live a literary Crusoe / Devoid of books, if so devoid of Rousseau" (*EWA* 121–22). Waugh published another bit of light verse, "A University Sermon to Idealists Who Are Serious Minded and Intelligent." This piece reproves "fierce young men" who study hard, explaining that Waugh and others averse to scholarship

> do not wish, we men of dust
> To bear more burdens than we must,
> We leave the clouds for you to bear
> And earth is heavier than air.

(*EWA* 123)

Waugh found it hard to admit that others could succeed where he was failing, and he argued that the lessons he was learning were somehow more important than those set by faculty.

Waugh criticized the single-minded obliviousness of intellectuals such as "Jeremy" in "Portrait of Young Man with Career," published in *Isis* in May 1923. Jeremy is the antithesis of an aesthete, practical and graceless, so boring that "Evelyn" imagines smashing his head with a poker. Jeremy wants to meet Richard Pares because "he is a man to know," but Evelyn is reluctant to introduce them, as Jeremy usually calls acquaintances "by their Christian names." Evelyn describes Pares as an "amiable rogue" and insists that he hardly knows him, though Jeremy is always seeing them together (*EWA* 125-26). By using his own name, Waugh invited readers to see his character's opinion of Pares as his own. Five months after the culmination of their romance, Waugh publicly pointed to the distance between them, indicating that he knew Pares to be a rogue while most people did not. Such connections between reality and fiction helped to make Waugh's novels notorious in the 1930s, as readers tried to equate characters with public figures, a game still played by some critics.

The apparent resentment of Pares supports Stannard's argument that Waugh's next story, "Antony, Who Sought Things That Were Lost," expresses some of his frustration at the end of their affair. Published in the *Oxford Broom* in June 1923, the story explains that Antony "seemed always to be seeking in the future for what had gone before" (*EWA* 129). Antony's continual disappointment may reflect Waugh's forlorn attempts to recover the happiness he had known with Pares. The story is violent, like the earliest ones, but the moral is less explicit. Antony finds himself locked in a dungeon with his love, Lady Elizabeth, but she gives herself to the turnkey to secure her release. If the story does derive from Waugh's experience with Pares, it is interesting that the characters are definitely heterosexual: Waugh refused to deal with homosexual inclinations in a published story. In this attempt to depict love between a man and a woman, Waugh makes the woman betray the man, an action almost inseparable from his representation of love in the rest of his fiction. The recurrence of betrayal indicates how readily Waugh saw himself as a victim of others' infidelity, suspecting Urquhart or Connolly of seducing Pares. Antony manages to strangle Lady Elizabeth, and though Waugh probably never wanted to murder Pares, the resolution is a kind of fantastic vengeance for the pain of separation that Pares had helped to bring about. Pleasant as Oxford was, it was not perfect, and Waugh was beginning to delineate imperfection in fiction.

Waugh kept himself busy with "The Seven Deadly Sins," drawings for *Cherwell* in October and November 1923. He made his own version, and some are not surprising: "The Horrid Sacrilege of those that Ill-treat Books" and "That Dull, Old Sin Adultery." In some more suggestive choices, Waugh stigmatized "The Intolerable Wickedness of Him Who Drinks Alone," excusing his own practice of drinking with a noisy crowd. He depicted "The Wanton Way of those that corrupt the very young," feeling no inclination for that sort of deviance. Resentment of Arthur may have inspired "That Grim Act Parricide," and "The Grave Discourtesy of such a man as will beat his host's servant" may be an attempt to amuse upper-class friends. The other sin is a curiosity: "The Hideous Habit of Marrying Negroes."[53] Nothing indicates that Waugh knew anyone who had married a black person, though mixed couples caused a few sensations. On the other hand, he did sing a spiritual for Cruttwell, and he played a black clergyman in a film called *666*, shot at Oxford in 1924.[54] As with Jews in Golders Green, Waugh tended to ridicule anyone who was obviously different, but he also identified with minorities to a certain extent, sensing alienation similar to his own. "The Hideous Habit of Marrying Negroes" may have been reassuring, Waugh stressing that some heterosexuals choose unconventional lovers, somewhat like the aesthetes at Oxford. The hideous habit lingered in his mind until Sebastien Cholmondley appeared with Margot Beste-Chetwynde in *Decline and Fall*.

Waugh had also written four stories published in *Cherwell* in August and September 1923, returning to some themes he had already introduced, but also beginning to move in new directions. "Edward of Unique Achievement" is perhaps the best. Like Waugh, Edward feels "essentially different from the other young men in Old Wykehamist ties in the Carlton Club," being a "student of the cinematograph and one who, until his second failure in History previous (through his inability to draw maps) had been a senior History scholar." Waugh did not fail history previous, but he did not pass by much. To him it seemed an exercise in trivia subject to arbitrary judgment, success depending on irrelevant skills such as map-making. Edward, frustrated, kills Mr. Curtis, who seemed, "considering that he was a history tutor, a pleasant young man enough" (*EWA* 133). By this time Waugh's fantasies of revenge included not only rival undergraduates and estranged lovers, but also faculty. He had not done the work expected of a history scholar, but he was reluctant to admit slackness, accusing dons of incompetence and caprice, hating them so much that he imagined killing one. Waugh's resentment of Cruttwell seems to have inspired Edward's resentment of Curtis, but Curtis's youth and pleasant manner seem to have been derived from Boase. Already Waugh was drawing on attributes of different people to create fictional characters, avoiding simple portraiture and confusing the simple-minded in their search for models. He was also embellishing the depravity of people he didn't like. By mistake the dons charge Lord Poxe with murder because Edward has been careful to provide himself with the alibi of speaking at the Union. Thus Waugh imagined not only the crime but also getting away with it. The warden punishes Poxe with only a small fine, becoming servile before the young lord's name and family. Waugh envied others' advantages, but he makes the dons worse than sycophants. They are also conspirators, fining Poxe to cover up murder and sexual relations between Curtis and the warden's wife. Waugh revelled in fantasies of dons' corruption, and distaste for dons never left him.

The second story, also from August 1923, is slight and apparently incomplete, entitled "Fragments: They Dine with the Past." The narrator is enthralled to hear that Imogen is in London, wondering if she is with "*him*" and hinting at another betrayal. Somewhat more interesting are two stories from September, "Conspiracy to Murder" and "Unacademic Exercise: A Nature Story." The first concerns Guy Legge, who goes mad after convincing himself that his strange neighbor plans to murder him. The story is Waugh's first study of madness, a recurring interest in his novels. Guy's madness suggests that there is something inherently unsettling about Oxford, an idea Waugh raises again in "Unacademic Exercise." Some undergraduates perform a ceremony intended to turn one of them into a werewolf. They apparently succeed, and the subject of the experiment emits a cry that threatens the witnesses with the loss of their sanity. The story ends abruptly, and Waugh explains in a note that the rest had been "omitted owing to blind stupidity of editor and printer" (*EWA* 148). Besides reviving childhood interest in magic, the story alludes to a kind of forbidden knowledge, available at Oxford but specifically unacademic and dangerous to those who seek it. Insanity may be one consequence of this knowledge; suicide may be another. In "Edward of Unique Achievement," Waugh claimed that most "undergraduates would kill themselves sooner or later if they stayed up long enough, very few would kill anyone else" (*EWA* 133). Waugh had already flirted with suicide at Lancing, and two years later he thought Oxford threatened his stability. Much as he resisted it in youth, discipline was essential to Waugh's survival, his control of doubts and fears. He was too independent to accept direction from dons or set books, but he was only beginning to find discipline in writing and drawing. Later he would see Roman Catholicism as another kind of acceptable discipline.

Waugh's actions and other writings also show ambivalence about the university. Even in 1922 he recognized the validity of Carew's decision not to go to Oxford. In some ways Waugh envied Carew, feeling trapped as a student for three years while Carew would be "carving a position in literary society." Carew would be "worldly wise," while Waugh would be only an "ingenuous B.A. . . . blinking at life through the smoked glasses of scholarship." Carew might even be "married with an enormous family" by the time Waugh was "trotting down to schools in a white bow tie." Waugh noted that Carew wouldn't "lose everything by missing Oxford."[55] By 1923 Waugh was wondering if he would do better to join Carew, realizing that he could not continue the life he had led for the last few terms. He began to make changes, especially financial ones. He had not been able to live within an annual income of about £350, the "average expenditure of undergraduates" at the time (*ALL* 206), but he admitted improvidence and tried to live more modestly. Peter Quennell reported that most undergraduates spent too much money on clothes, and that Waugh in particular dressed like a "modern dandy." Waugh also decorated his rooms with expensive prints and editions of poetry. Quennell witnessed a "startling change," however. After he had "overspent his allowance," Waugh held an "uproarious private auction of all his more valuable books and pictures, and retreated to the smallest, darkest, gloomiest set of rooms" in Hertford, exchanging "earlier dandyism for a somewhat truculent bohemianism."[56]

Waugh managed to make a "modest income by contributing to the *Isis*, by designing book-wrappers for Chapman and Hall and book-plates for various acquaintances" (*ALL* 206), but not enough to pay his bills, and he left Oxford owing about £200. He wrote later that "embarrassment" would not have been the "right term" for his predicament. He did not "fret much or often about this condition," but it was an "occasional source of gloom, annoyance and frustration" (*ALL* 207). Fretting over money would not have been appropriate for an aesthete, but Waugh found it very annoying to have to concede that he could no longer maintain his carefree existence at Oxford. Still, attempts to live more prudently reflect his growing maturity and his realization that, much as he might enjoy it, Oxford was not the proper place for him. Alec thought that Evelyn had admired the

> number of brilliant and elegant young men from a larger way of life who showed him in how narrow a world he had moved at Heathmount, Lancing and at Underhill. For a year he was enchanted at moving in this brighter wider world, then he realized that he did not belong to it,

that he was only a sojourner, that if he wanted to stay in this world after he went down, he would have to win his place there.[57]

Besides dealing with debts, Waugh began to distance himself from the drunken parties of Oxford. He started going to the Ruskin School of Art (*ALL* 190), demonstrating at least some concern for his vocation. He loved the irresponsible life of the student, but by his second year he knew that he could no longer afford it, financially or morally. He had enjoyed a year of drinking, but he saw little point in another year of hangovers. Waugh was probably also troubled by homosexual relationships, and he began to look beyond Oxford to some style of life that would impose greater discipline and make better use of his talent.

Waugh's sixth term began with a request to leave the university. The Michaelmas term of 1923 was about to start when Waugh, "struck by conscience and a momentary restlessness" and knowing that he was "doing no good" at his studies, wrote to his father and asked to go to Paris and learn to paint. As at Lancing, Waugh enjoyed success in almost everything he tried at Oxford, making many friends and some enemies, but also writing and drawing for undergraduate publications. After a year and a half, Waugh was tired of this existence and anxious to try something new, much as he tired of Lancing and wanted to go to Oxford, much as he tired of everything else he immersed himself in. In 1923 Arthur Waugh insisted that Evelyn stay at Oxford and take examinations in the summer of 1924. Waugh recalled that this "reasonable verdict" gave him the feeling that he was in Oxford "under protest." He "perversely regarded it as the *laissez-passer* to a life of pure pleasure" (*ALL* 175). Once again, Waugh was having trouble accepting other points of view, particularly those of people in authority. He felt aggrieved and entitled to rewards because he had not had his own way.

Pure pleasure is apparently what Waugh pursued in the fall of 1923, trying to find in alcohol and frivolity some salve for his restless spirit. He found the experience disturbing rather than satisfying, telling Carew that he was "highly depressed." He seemed to be a "worthless [?] fellow and quite broke and rather stupid and quite incredibly depraved morally." He had also "quite lost all self Respect—at least momentarily."[58] Waugh was disappointed whenever he was unable to live up to high moral standards, and he was obviously unhappy in October 1923, a "man disillusioned with human conduct, a man without ambition, living a life apart from the world." Waugh had "consciously withdrawn from earlier University activities of a popular sort, undergraduate journalism, the Union, OUDS."[59] Waugh was unhappy partly because he had been expelled from the Hypocrites "for having smashed up a good deal of the Club's furniture with the heavy stick he always carried."[60] He may have been angry because he found it hard to resist the temptations of the Hypocrites, but being cut off from temptation added to his depression.

By early 1924 Waugh was almost desperate. His handwriting is wild and sprawling, far different from the compact style of later manuscripts. The effect was probably due to alcohol, but it is possible that mental disturbance had something to do with it. In an undated letter he wrote that his life had been "extremely precarious 'unstable equilibrium' vide lux." He was keeping his balance but feared that he might "crash [?] any moment." In another, apparently written somewhat later, he noted that he had been "living very intensely the last three weeks." For two weeks he had been "nearly insane," though he had become a "little saner." His diary had been "destroyed." He wanted "to go down for good," but he could not explain, and his parents were "obdurate" (*LEW* 12). In one of his last letters from Oxford, Waugh could not "yet explain all the things" about him: "St John has been eating wild honey in the wilderness." He did not know how things were "going to end," though they were "nearing some sort of finality." He promised to tell Carew things that would surprise him and "sell an edition of the biography if faithfully recorded."[61] Waugh seems to have been caught in a vicious circle: desire to leave encouraged licentious behavior, and depression over this behavior added to his desire to leave. It seems odd, though, that Waugh evidently wanted to escape from a life he had enjoyed. In his book on prisons as metaphors in Waugh's fiction, Jeffrey Heath argues that Waugh's

> riotous life at Oxford taught him to distrust his own unguided impulses. There, he learned that complete freedom was its own kind of imprisonment. Undoubtedly because of the anarchy he sensed not far below his own nature, Waugh frequently argued that discipline, or "imprisonment," was beneficial to the creative faculties.[62]

Heath is probably right about the way that Waugh came to understand his experience at Oxford, though Waugh was only beginning to develop that understanding in 1924. Sometime early that year he tried to curb his impulses by adopting some discipline. He spent a lot of time studying for final examinations, hoping to overcome two years of indifference in a burst of intensive effort.

4: *Et in Arcadia Ego,* 1922–1924

In fact, he "increased his debts . . . by panicking about his academic work and buying large quantities of history books on credit."[63] He wrote to Carew on a Sunday at 5:45 A.M. Waugh had been studying since 10:00 P.M., and at the "ragged end of a nights work," all his "sins" seemed to crowd upon him. He hoped it was "only the effect of Caffeine & whisky & Political Philosophy," conceding that it would have been "idle to pretend" that he was enjoying the term.[64] Waugh never enjoyed studying, and in 1924 he studied only to stay at Oxford, just as in 1921 he had studied only to get there. He hoped for a second-class performance on examinations, which would have preserved his scholarship while he finished his degree in his ninth term. Clearly he was concerned about his reputation, finally getting to work once failure was at hand, but he also seems to have retained some scholarly ambition. He discounted this motive in his autobiography, having anticipated only a "ninth term . . . of pure pleasure," and having imagined that one term's "comparative seclusion . . . would be amply compensated" (*ALL* 207). Since he was obliged to stay at Oxford, Waugh was making the best of things, and trying to avoid embarrassing himself.

Waugh's seclusion also shows alienation from a way of life he had found invigorating. Characteristically, he began to represent Oxford as a disadvantage rather than an enviable opportunity. In *Isis* in February 1924, Waugh asserted that undergraduates had "just no chance of . . . being able to earn a living, or at least a living decent enough to allow any sort of excitement or depravity." They were all confronted with "bills, over-fastidious tastes, and a completely hopeless future." What could they do "but long for a war or revolution?" (*EAR* 21). Concern about money is unusual in Waugh's writing at Oxford, probably a sign that his time there was drawing to a close, probably also a sign that he sensed the futility of studying for a second-class degree. Even as he longed for war or revolution, he also longed for society and alcohol, and probably he broke out of seclusion to enjoy them. He was still very young even in his third year at Oxford, not yet twenty-one years of age, not yet ready to settle down to a life of order and sobriety. Even in his fifties, Waugh liked to break up quiet, productive stays in the country by going to London, seeing his friends, and drinking a great deal.

Waugh took written examinations in late June, feeling "uneasily aware . . . that the questions had been rather inconvenient." He rewarded himself for work he had done, attending a large party in Balliol College, being "lowered on a rope by Patrick Balfour at 1

A.M.," and climbing back into Hertford. His *viva voce* was not until the end of July, and the questions were "purely perfunctory" (*ALL* 208). He wired his parents to inform them of his "certain third" and set off for Ireland, accompanied by Alastair Graham.[65] There he received Cruttwell's letter revoking his scholarship, and his father decided that a third-class degree was "not worth the time and expense of going up for a further term." The memory of Arthur's own "failure in the schools tempered his reproaches," and he arranged to send Evelyn to an art school in the fall (*ALL* 208).

5
Oxford Revisited, 1924 and After

WAUGH was back in Oxford in September 1924, but he didn't enjoy it. He decided that it would be his last night there for some time. Everything seemed "inexpressibly sordid," and he hated the Hypocrites' Club for its "discomfort and . . . associations." A few weeks later he met Tom Driberg on his way to Oxford; anyone going that way had Waugh's "sympathy" (*DEW* 178–79, 182). Waugh knew that Oxford was no good for him, but his remarks are also bitter, apparently jealous of people who could go there while he could not. Waugh was living with his parents, attending Heatherley's Art School, where most of the students were "respectable girls who . . . were believed at home to be 'artistic'. The few men had ambitions of commercial draughtsmanship. No one seriously aspired to High Art" (*ALL* 210). Waugh was also bitter because of separation from Alastair Graham. Graham had converted to Roman Catholicism on 13 September 1924, and on 18 September he went to Kenya to live with his sister and her husband. Waugh was despondent, finding small comfort in vows of "poverty, chastity and obedience" (*DEW* 179). He started writing once again, working on a novel called *The Temple at Thatch*. Waugh burned the manuscript in 1925 when Harold Acton expressed distaste for it, remembering only that it had centered on an undergraduate, who "inherited a property of which nothing was left except an eighteenth-century classical folly where he set up house and . . . practised black magic" (*ALL* 223). Little to go on, but the undergraduate seems to have been a projection of Waugh's self. Waugh often imagined himself the heir to a decaying legacy, epitomized in his aunts' house at Midsomer Norton. Black magic may have aided the undergraduate in avenging himself on his enemies, and writing may have helped Waugh to assuage anger and frustration.

Waugh seems to have found more comfort in alcohol than in writing. On 12 October he was "much the worse for drink," suspecting that his cousins could not have "formed a very high opinion of [his] reformed London life." He drank for the rest of the week, though the "next week due chiefly to poverty was much more quiet" (Diary HRHRC). Waugh turned twenty-one on 28 October, but his "coming of age . . . was not celebrated" (*ALL* 209). He claimed that he "became a man and put away childish things," but he resented having been "signally neglected" by friends from Oxford. Two weeks later friends invited him to Oxford and, though hesitant, Waugh went, revisiting the Hypocrites to drink whisky and to see *The Scarlet Woman,* still incomplete (Diary HRHRC). His recollections of that night were "somewhat blurred." He had acquired a "sword from somewhere and got into Balliol somehow and was let out of a window at some time." He went back to Oxford the following weekend, finding it still blatantly homosexual. Undergraduates were wearing a "new sort of jumper with a high collar." Waugh found it "rather becoming and most convenient for lechery because it dispenses with all unromantic gadgets like studs and ties." The jumpers also hid the "boils with which most of the young men [had] encrusted their necks." Though enjoying himself, Waugh seems to have kept his distance. He "drank a good deal but went to bed eventually alone and fairly sober." Next evening one of his friends had a "male prostitute" with him, and Waugh "passed a quiet night unmolested" (*DEW* 187–88). Ambivalent as he was about Oxford, Waugh was bored at Heatherley's, getting away at every opportunity.

In early December he was back in Oxford, going to the Hypocrites, where he found an "enormous orgy in progress." He and Billy Clonmore "unearthed a strap and whipped Tony [not Powell]." Everyone was "hideously drunk except strangely enough" Waugh himself. Next day he started a "vastly expensive career of alcohol." He spent three more days in Oxford, one sober but two drunk, finally "feeling deathly ill" and returning to London "having spent two months' wages" (*DEW* 189–90). He resolved that a "gay life [was] not to be borne" and asked James Guthrie to accept him as an apprentice (Diary HRHRC). Guthrie's printing press involved too little craftsmanship and too much photographic reproduction to satisfy Waugh, but he had at least taken a step in the right direction, moving away from alcoholic oblivion, accepting discipline and seclusion to keep from wasting ability. Waugh knew that he was not being challenged at Heatherley's, and he also knew that his ability would never amount to anything unless it were challenged. For some time after Oxford, he sought challenge in various places, asking others to impose discipline on him, avoiding the self-discipline it takes to be a writer. Waugh's love of society

5: Oxford Revisited, 1924 and After 143

and leisure was great, his temptation to pursue them strong, but his sense of importance and determination not to waste talent were greater, so that he managed to impose discipline on himself for most of his life.

Waugh's resolve was shaken by the sudden reappearance of Graham on 5 January 1925. He had "contracted malaria in East Africa, run short of money and returned third class, completing the journey across Europe without eating. He was unshaven, unwashed," and "without luggage" (*ALL* 216). They had recognized that they debilitated each other, but the attraction was too strong for either to resist. Waugh was glad that Graham had returned, but he was also distressed because he had committed himself to teach in Wales in late January. Working around Waugh's stints as schoolmaster, he and Graham spent most of the next two years together. Waugh's diaries for 1925 and 1926 are largely records of where he went and what he did with Graham, punctuated by expressions of despair whenever they were separated. They drank a lot, and they visited Oxford several times. Waugh earnestly loved Graham, who seemed to appreciate him when no one else did. The strength of Waugh's feelings drew him back to Oxford and the festive life he had known there, in spite of intentions to become more responsible.

There was some strain between Waugh and Graham, but Waugh at least was willing to forgive and forget differences. The first sign of difficulty occurred in July 1924, just before Waugh's *viva voce*, when others went on a "quest," leaving Graham and Waugh "to quarrel alone." Graham's conversion in September 1924 seems to have created a breach after his return from Africa. At the end of March 1925, Waugh noted that Graham wanted him to go to an "island of monks near Ireland" (Diary HRHRC). Instead, he spent Easter holidays on Lundy Island with the Plunket Greenes, going to visit Graham at his mother's house in Barford before the end of vacation. They were together most of that summer, though on 20 September, according to Waugh, Graham and Christopher Hollis engaged in a "conversation of incredible inanity" that lasted for six hours and nearly drove Waugh "mad." Three days later, after Graham's departure, Waugh was afraid that he had been "exceedingly disagreeable all weekend" and felt "sorry for it." Again, on 8 March 1926, after Graham had been away from England for over a month, Waugh anticipated his friend's return, having "missed him more" than he had expected. In July Waugh wrote *P.R.B.*, his essay on the Pre-Raphaelite Brotherhood, and Graham printed it, incompetently. On a trip to France in August, Waugh spent little time with Graham, thinking that he had seen "too much of Alastair lately" (*DEW* 223, 248, 263). Waugh was a natural critic: he could hardly suppress tendencies to nitpick, which strained this relationship and others important in his life. Waugh still loved Graham enough to visit him in Athens over the Christmas holidays, Graham having entered the diplomatic service. Waugh was appalled to find Graham's apartment "usually full of dreadful Dago youths called by heroic names such as Miltiades and Agamemnon with blue chins and greasy clothes who sleep with the English colony for 25 drachmas a night." He returned to England, "sorry that the Athenian adventure had been such a failure" (*DEW* 275–76). The most intense phase of their relationship was clearly over at the beginning of 1927, though in 1929 Waugh cruised the Mediterranean with his first wife and again visited Graham in Athens. Graham had already gone to Waugh's aid when his wife had been in the hospital at Port Said, having lent Waugh £100 to cover expenses (*LEW* 31).

The end of Waugh and Graham's sexual relationship is difficult to date. Stannard thinks it ended when Graham went to Africa in 1924,[1] but the amount of time they spent together in 1925 and 1926 suggests that they continued sexual relations. In August 1925 Waugh was at Graham's house, where they "did much that could not have been done" if Graham's mother had been there (*DEW* 218). The affair was almost certainly over by the time Waugh went to Athens in December 1926. The end may have been caused by Waugh's impatience with Graham in August, by Graham's decision to move to Athens, by Waugh's disgust with Graham's apartment there, or by any number of other things, but it seems likely that Waugh's growing interest in women had something to do with it. As early as July 1924, while still deeply involved with Graham, Waugh had noticed a "very beautiful girl," Rachel Mayne, at Dudley Carew's twenty-first birthday party (Diary HRHRC). Carew wrote later that Waugh had been "off his balance at that time," suggesting that "Rachel set him wondering whether he ever would achieve a normal relationship with a woman."[2] In October, depressed by Graham's departure, Waugh broke from his "reclusion" when Alec took him to a "woman called Hansard" and Evelyn fell "immoderately in love." Mrs. Hansard was "all pearls and lace & ivory," and she seemed to be a "most intelligent collector." By Christmas he had met Olivia Plunket Greene, wondering if he were "falling in love with this woman." In early January 1925 he "made love to Olivia in a corner" (Diary HRHRC). He had "fallen in love with an entire family," having focused his "sentiment upon the only appropriate member, an eighteen-year-old daughter." Waugh thought he had lacked the "experience and force of purpose to

5: Oxford Revisited, 1924 and After

prosecute a real courtship," and their relationship developed into "intimate friendship," with Waugh "doting but unaspiring" on one side, Olivia "astringent" on the other (*ALL* 216). Waugh may mean that he was not yet sure of his sexuality, still attracted to Graham but wondering if their relationship could last. The women he began to notice in 1924 indicate that his homosexual tendencies were waning, that he was becoming more comfortable with heterosexuality. In January 1926, Waugh wrote in his diary, Elizabeth Ponsonby "made vigorous love" to him, and he was "sorry" that he had not accepted it (Diary HRHRC). The next year he met Evelyn Gardner and proposed marriage in December 1927. Waugh's homosexuality had been predominant at Oxford from 1922 to 1924, becoming something more like bisexuality after he left. Heterosexuality clearly began to predominate in 1926, though some sexual ambiguity persisted, probably contributing to the failure of marriage to She-Evelyn in 1929.

Waugh found homosexuality inherently wrong and at least faintly ridiculous, even at Oxford. Diaries and letters, even in his phase of agnosticism, are full of regret for being depraved or for having committed sins. His reaction to others' homosexuality was, perhaps, an even stronger deterrent. He saw how others behaved, and he tried to refrain from seeming equally offensive. In June 1924 he and Graham met the "foul Tasha Gielgud," accompanied by a "pert young woman dressed almost wholly as a man." Waugh and Graham got rid of them by "leaving the restaurant . . . and putting them to Lesbianize in a taxi." Waugh's critical reflexes meant that relationships were primarily intellectual, only rarely emotional. In November 1925 another man revealed that "throughout the giddy whirligig of his life . . . the one constant thing that had remained inviolate in spite of all else had been his love" for Waugh. All that "took some time in saying" and bored Waugh "inexpressibly." Sometimes other considerations seem to have held him back. In December 1925 Waugh was in a brothel in Paris. A boy dressed as an "Egyptian woman" began to caress Waugh and then started to kiss him. Waugh thought him "attractive but had better uses for the 300 francs which the patron . . . demanded for his enjoyment." He took a taxi back and went "to bed in chastity." He thought he did not "regret it" (Diary HRHRC).[3] Insecure, extremely self-critical, and strongly moral regardless of religious beliefs, Waugh could never accept homosexuality in the way Harold Acton or Brian Howard could. Affairs were agreeable, but he held back in each case, never feeling that they were quite right, not for him. Waugh's uneasiness with homosexuality shows, perhaps even more persuasively than the testimony of his friends Hollis and Christopher Sykes, that he was neither naturally inclined to homosexuality nor made unhappy by the need to repress it in later years.

Waugh was unhappy in the summer of 1925 and attempted suicide at the beginning of July. Near the end of an unpleasant stretch as schoolmaster, he had just received Acton's dismissal of *The Temple at Thatch*. He had hoped to go to Italy to become secretary for C. K. Scott-Moncrieff, the translator of Proust, but Alec, having raised his brother's hopes, discovered that there was no such position. Still in debt, Waugh tried to settle worldly obligations, and he "even approached kindly feeling" for his father, agreeing to "surrender [his] allowance in exchange for [his] debts" (Diary HRHRC). Waugh felt hopeless and abandoned, especially by Oxford friends. In January, Hugh Lygon and John Sutro had sent a telegram to encourage him, "On, Evelyn, on" according to *A Little Learning,* "On, Waugh, on" according to a letter written at the time (*ALL* 221; *LEW* 21). Graham had visited in February, and Acton was a frequent correspondent, but Waugh expected more attention, resenting what he took to be neglect. One night he planned to swim out to sea, writing down the "quotation from Euripides about the sea which washes away all human ills," going to the "trouble of verifying it, accents and all, from the school text." Before he had "reached the point of no return," he was stung by a jellyfish, then by another. Frustrated even in his attempt at suicide, he returned to shore, tore up his "pretentious classical tag," and "climbed the sharp hill that led to all the years ahead" (*ALL* 229–30).

Waugh's brush with death and estrangement from Oxford troubled him so much that he started to write again. In August 1925 he finished a story called "The Balance," which he had started in May. He thought it was "odd but . . . quite good" (Diary HRHRC). "The Balance" acknowledges Waugh's feel for the university's mystique. Part is a screenplay with captions, explaining that the setting is Oxford and quoting the traditional lines "KNOW YOU HER SECRET NONE CAN UTTER; HERS OF THE BOOK, THE TRIPLE CROWN?" The romantic mood dissolves in the next few frames, an "Art title showing Book and Triple Crown; also ox in ford." In the first scene Waugh hints that reputation differs from reality, presenting a "General prospect of Oxford from the train showing reservoir, gas works and part of the prison. It is raining."[4] Waugh dwells on industrialized ugliness instead of medieval architecture, and the resident he introduces is not very attractive either. Mr. Macassor is a bookseller who cajoles one customer into buying an expensive first edition supposed to have belonged to Horace Walpole. When the hero, Adam Doure, tries to sell his books, Mr. Macassor examines them "like some morbid lover fastening ghoulishly upon every imperfection." He gives Adam about half of what they are worth, and that way Mr. Macassor's "son at Magdalen is able to keep his rooms full of flowers and, during the season, to hunt two days a week" (TB 301). Waugh still resented undergraduates with more money than he had had.

Adam needs money because he is in town for his farewell party. As Adam tries to entice acquaintances to drink with him, Waugh indicates that Oxford has no basis for intellectual pretensions. First Adam visits Lord Basingstoke, who, "contrary to all expectations, is neither drinking, gaming, nor struggling with his riding boots." Instead, he is busy writing a "Collections Paper for his tutor" (TB 302). The camera cuts to the paper, Lord Basingstoke affirming that "MARSHAL LAW IS UNKNOWN IN ENGLAND" (TB 303). The paper is due the next day, and Adam is obliged to move on to Mr. Egerton-Verschoyle, who has had a luncheon party that has left him lying almost unconscious on the floor. Adam tries Mr. Furness, but his rooms are "empty and dark. Mr. Furness has been sent down" (TB 304). Desperate, Adam goes in search of Ernest Vaughan, who is "somewhat surprised," Adam never having "shown any very warm affection for him" (TB 307). Ernest is an aesthete of the kind Waugh had known at Oxford, and his rooms are "interiors of almost unsurpassed debauchery," decorated with "inscriptions and drawings, ranging from almost inspired caricature to meaningless or obscene scrawlings," all of which "attest Ernest's various stages of drunkenness" (TB 306).

Like many aesthetes, Ernest is homosexual, and he and Adam have to walk through a "cluster of men who mutter their disapproval like peasants at the passage of some black magician" (TB 307). In spite of prejudice, homosexuality is common at Oxford. Later in the story, Mrs. Hay "cannot understand why all the boys aren't in love" with Imogen Quest, though she notices that the undergraduates are not "quite the 'marrying sort' somehow" (TB 322–23). The university as it appears in "The Balance" is close to the university Waugh had known in the early 1920s, though Waugh emphasizes Oxford's least attractive features. Modern industry, stupidity, drunkenness, and homosexuality all belong to the seamier side of a university celebrated for beauty, intelligence, and tradition, as Waugh undermines popular conceptions and explains his own estrangement. Waugh's hero, Adam, also feels estranged from friends and their activities. Depressed, Adam attempts suicide, just as Waugh had done shortly before he finished the story. Like Adam, Waugh returned to the university after he had left, and though friends welcomed him back more enthusiastically than Adam's do, Waugh did find it painful when jobs and other commitments kept him from pleasures he had known. Adam's act of desperation certainly reflects Waugh's own.

Like Waugh, Adam survives his attempt, and as he walks away from Oxford, the life he has led seems more and more unreal: "All round him a macabre dance of shadows had reeled and flickered, and in and out of it Adam had picked his way, conscious only of one insistent need, percolating through to him from the world outside, of immediate escape from the scene upon which the bodiless harlequinade was played, into a third dimension beyond it" (TB 318). Adam falls asleep, waking to confront his reflection in a pool. The reflection asks about his attempted suicide, but Adam sees the act as that of another man, "as though the being who survives, . . . with very great clearness in [his] memory, was born of a dream, drank and died in a dream." Difference between one's present self and some earlier self recurs in Waugh's fiction. He felt impelled to articulate different selves, to explain earlier behavior by attributing it to the predominance of some other self. When the reflection learns that Adam has "found no secret" while asleep, it asks if the "balance of life and death" is "so easily swayed" (TB 320). Adam refers to the "balance of appetite and reason. The reason remains constant—the appetite varies." He decides that there is "no appetite for death . . . which cannot be appeased by sleep or change or the mere passing of time," an idea that Waugh doubted in later years. Adam recognizes neither "honour to be observed to friends" nor "interpenetration, so that you cannot depart without bearing away with you something that is part of another." Art is only a product of the "appetite to live—to preserve in the shapes of things the personality whose dissolution you foresee inevitably," merely part of "the balance then—and in the end circumstance decides" (TB 321).

Ideas in this story are rather bleak, but they reflect Waugh's state of mind in 1925. Oxford is a fantastic place, dreamlike when drunk, seamy when sober, and in both cases chaotic, fleeting and unendurable. Severing oneself from Oxford's friends can be traumatic, and it may even lead to suicide, but the step is necessary if one is to understand the balance between life and death, the relationship between appetite and reason. Little in life encourages one to endure in adversity, except rest, patience, and art, at best the preservation of one's personality in some form that may survive the artist's death. Waugh was still determined to make an impression on the world: he could no longer rely on others' memories, since friends seemed to have forgotten him, so he turned to art, the individual effort of creation, which also gave him a larger public. He had not yet settled on Roman Catholicism as a source of order and meaning, but he had convinced himself that life at Oxford, though pleasant, was meaningless and lacked the purpose he needed. If we can judge from "The Balance," only a few things kept Waugh going between 1925 and his conversion in 1930: circumstance, in the form of jellyfish that stung when he tried to drown himself; art, which makes order possible amid chaos; and love of others, especially Alastair Graham, Olivia Plunket Greene, and Evelyn Gardner. Waugh had survived one brush with death, and though he was not enthusiastic about the life ahead of him in 1925, he had found a few reasons to carry on. He could produce art, make order out of chaos, and project his personality, not only by drawing, but also by writing. "The Balance" is his first serious attempt to produce a work of art in fiction.

Understanding art does Adam little good in the story, for friends desert him, having decided that he is "getting rather impossible" (TB 322). Waugh was discouraged by having to teach at second-rate schools some distance from Oxford, but his friends were not as inconsiderate as Adam's. Waugh was already doing something characteristic of most later work—transforming experience to make the hero who represents himself suffer more intensely than he had. Though Oxford is awful in "The Balance," lost in meaningless revelry and populated by faithless friends, living there does confer distinct advantages. Waugh takes some trouble to describe the audience watching the film of Adam's experiences, and a voice with a *"Cambridge accent,"* coming from the *"more expensive seats,"* says, *"Expressionismus"* (TB 282). Silly as Oxford is, undergraduates there would not stand for such pretentious, continental criticism. Those who attend no university at all are even less able to understand Adam's tribulations; the audience includes Gladys and Ada, the "cook and house-parlourmaid from a small house in Earls Court" (TB 281). Gladys and Ada have preconceived notions about what they want to see, though no more preconceived than the person with the Cambridge accent. When Ada says there is *"too much talk in this picture,"* the voice with the Cambridge accent says something about *"elimination of the caption"* (TB 287). The film is unsatisfactory in other ways, and for the "fiftieth time" that evening Gladys calls it a "soft film." They would rather see "something really funny," such as Larry Semon or Buster Keaton, and it has been a "disappointing evening on the whole. Still, as Ada says, with the pictures you has to take the bad with the good" (TB 313). The critics add to Adam's isolation—they have not gone through his experience, and they do not appreciate it. Like many characters who represent Waugh's self, Adam is misunderstood, and endurance in spite of misunderstanding makes him a hero and a martyr. Oxford has been important to Adam; it has made him more inquisitive and more sensitive than others, but it has also made him incomprehensible to them. Tempted as he was to disparage Oxford, Waugh regarded it as a special experience, one that set Oxonians apart. He would come back to Oxford's special quality several times in the next forty years.

There is almost no suggestion of this quality in the next work to deal with the university. Still without prospects, Waugh started *Decline and Fall* in September 1927, two years after "The Balance." The novel is overwhelmingly hostile toward Oxford. Social life at the university is dominated by the Bollinger Club, infamous for drunken exploits such as a dinner three years before, when a "fox had been brought in in a cage and stoned to death with champagne bottles" (*DF* 1). Suspended after this achievement, the club gathers for its first meeting since, Oxford filling with

> epileptic royalty from their villas of exile; uncouth peers from crumbling country seats; smooth young men of uncertain tastes from embassies and legations; illiterate lairds from wet granite hovels in the Highlands; ambitious young barristers and Conservative candidates torn from the London season and the indelicate advances of debutantes; all that was most sonorous of name and title was there for the beano. (*DF* 1–2)

Mr. Sniggs, the junior dean, notes that they "always attack" the rooms of "unpopular undergraduates," and true to form the Bollinger

> broke up Mr. Austen's grand piano, and stamped Lord Rending's cigars into his carpet, and smashed his china, and tore up Mr. Partridge's sheets, and threw the Matisse into his water jug; Mr. Sanders had nothing to break except his windows, but they found the manuscript at which he had been working for the Newdigate Prize Poem, and had great fun with that. (*DF* 3–4)

The Bollinger Club also meets Paul Pennyfeather, bicycling "happily back from a meeting of the League of Nations Union," where

5: Oxford Revisited, 1924 and After

he has heard a "most interesting paper about plebiscites in Poland" (*DF* 5). The Bollinger proceeds to tear off his clothes, forcing Paul to run through the quadrangle *"without his trousers"* (*DF* 6).

The Bollinger Club behaves so badly and makes Oxford so awful because those in charge are either cowards or in favor of indiscipline. Most dons have deserted Scone College, leaving Sniggs and Mr. Postlethwaite, the domestic bursar, "alone of the senior members of Scone . . . at home that evening." The others seem to have realized that the "annual Bollinger dinner is a difficult time for those in authority" (*DF* 1). These two are hardly up to maintaining order, and Sniggs, in his room overlooking the quad, tells Postlethwaite that it might be better to turn out the light (*DF* 1–2). When the Bollinger catches Paul and Sniggs proposes intervention, Postlethwaite reminds his "impetuous colleague" that they have the "prestige of the senior common room to consider," that in the Bollinger's "present state they might not prove amenable to discipline," and that they must "at all costs avoid an *outrage*" (*DF* 6). Sniggs and Postlethwaite are adept at rationalizing, but they choose to do nothing partly because some "highly prized port in the senior common-room cellars . . . is only brought up when the College fines have reached £50." Sniggs anticipates the "fines there'll be after this evening," while Postlethwaite predicts at least a "week of Founder's port" (*DF* 2).

Weakness for port may be only a minor flaw, but Sniggs and Postlethwaite are truly reprehensible in their treatment of Paul. They apparently misrepresent Paul's behavior, for the master upon his return describes the "case of Pennyfeather" as "flagrantly indecent. It is *not* the conduct we expect of a scholar" (*DF* 6–7). The two witnesses do nothing to correct this misapprehension and suggest fining Paul "really heavily," but the master doubts "whether he could pay." Paul is "not well off," and the master says it would be "far better to get rid of him altogether" (*DF* 7). Paul is sent down for indecency, and though the chaplain encourages him to take to the "great world of business some of the ideals" he has learned at Scone (*DF* 8), Paul has learned only that dons are self-interested and that undergraduates are treated according to how much money they have. Paul considers the authorities insane, unable to recognize the gulf between supposed ideals and actual pettiness. Later, when the medical officer at Blackstone Gaol asks if he has ever been "detained in a mental home or similar institution," Paul answers that he has been at "Scone College, Oxford" (*DF* 220).

If Oxford is unattractive morally in *Decline and Fall,* it is insipid intellectually. Interests of students are trivial and ridiculous, as becomes apparent when Paul, teaching school in Wales, gets a letter from Arthur Potts, an acquaintance at Scone. Potts reveals that another undergraduate is planning to read a paper on "Sex Repression and Religious Experience." A "row" is expected, because someone else is "keen . . . on the mystical element," something the reader is "inclined to discount" (*DF* 55). The structure of the novel implies that Oxford never changes; its concerns remain tedious and removed from the world of affairs in which Paul has been moving. Near the end of the novel, after Paul has gone back up, he rejoins the League of Nations Union (*DF* 286), and a new acquaintance, Stubbs, says that someone presented an "interesting paper . . . about the Polish plebiscites" (*DF* 289). Social life also stays the same, and outside there is a "confused roaring and breaking of glass," as Paul observes that the "Bollinger seem to be enjoying themselves" (*DF* 289). Those who guide undergraduates remain as insensitive as ever. When Paul, having grown a mustache, explains that a cousin named Pennyfeather had been there before him, the chaplain describes this cousin as a "thoroughly degenerate type," assuring Paul that there is "no resemblance" between them (*DF* 285).

Oxford is a maddening place in *Decline and Fall:* undergraduates get drunk and riot or become incredibly earnest about dull subjects; cowardly dons indulge in greed and spread misinformation. Eccentrics are subject to persecution, but even innocents are not safe, since undergraduates are judged according to wealth and social connections. Oxford is, moreover, persistent in its folly, the same before Paul leaves and after he returns, largely because students have no sense of relative value and interest themselves in everything. Paul's experience in the outside world has given him some such sense, but he is content to resume old interests. Dons might impart the ability to discriminate between the important and the trivial, but they prefer to indulge their appetite, and their judgments are all mistaken anyway.

Waugh represents Oxford so viciously in *Decline and Fall* partly for artistic reasons. Waugh's first five novels are primarily comic, and exaggerating the silliness of undergraduates and the stupidity of dons is one way to be funny. Another reason can be ascribed to Waugh's temperament. He seldom showed much reverence for anything or anyone, especially as a young man, and he took pleasure in exposing foibles of Oxford, just as he took pleasure in exposing foibles of marriage, aristocrats, secondary education, and religion in other parts of the novel. Consideration of Oxford in

Decline and Fall also needs to take account of the novel's relation to Waugh's life in the late 1920s. Rather lonely and often miserable, he missed the friends he had enjoyed at Oxford, and he was still bitter because he could not spend more time there. Fancying that he had been, like Paul, a victim of injustice, Waugh portrays Oxford as a place where social status is more important than innocence or intelligence, where dons do not hesitate to play favorites. Waugh's representation of dons certainly derives from Cruttwell and Urquhart, but neither was as deferential to upper-class undergraduates as Sniggs, Postlethwaite, and the Master of Scone are in *Decline and Fall*. Instead of drawing directly on experience, Waugh distorts it, emphasizing dons' snobbery as an explanation of why he had not done better at Oxford, blaming them for failure to take a degree. He had done something similar in "Edward of Unique Achievement," middle-class status continuing to cause resentment and jealousy.

There is one interesting difference between *Decline and Fall* and an earlier representation of Oxford. In the novel, dons mistreat the hero, whereas in "The Balance" the hero suffers mainly from the neglect of friends. There are no dons in "The Balance," and Paul, unlike Adam Doure, has no friends at Oxford except the nonentities Stubbs and Potts. Perhaps Waugh expected less of friends by the time he wrote *Decline and Fall,* and perhaps bitterness toward dons had increased since "The Balance." Resentment seems indiscriminate in these two works, however, aimed first at one group he had known at Oxford, then at another. In fiction he blamed others, both friends and dons, for the misery of life after Oxford, accusing them, imaginatively, of mistreating and boring him. Waugh may never have believed that others caused his own decline and fall, and contentious, disrespectful behavior at the university suggests that he was often inviting retribution, looking for something to avenge later. Fiction gave him an opportunity for vengeance, first in the rather crude violence of undergraduate stories, then in the more sophisticated comedy of "The Balance" and *Decline and Fall*. Fiction also gave Waugh an opportunity to come to terms with failure by attributing it to the faults of others.

Waugh's resentment of Oxford also contributed to his characterization of Paul Pennyfeather. Paul suffers continually despite his innocence: he is sent down though he has done nothing wrong; he is disinherited by his guardian because he has failed to stay at the university; he is sent to jail for acting ignorantly on behalf of Margot Beste-Chetwynde's prostitution ring; and he is unceremoniously dropped by Margot because he can no longer satisfy her sexually. Paul's innocence contrasts sharply with the image of Waugh at Oxford, often drunk and unruly, and the contrast becomes even sharper when one considers this passage from *A Little Learning*. Hertford was "agreeably free both from the schoolboyish 'college spirit' which was the bane of many small colleges and of the hooliganism which on occasion broke out against the eccentrics in the larger. . . . No one was ever debagged or had his rooms wrecked or his oak screwed up" (*ALL* 164). Scone College is much more susceptible to such outbursts in *Decline and Fall,* one causing Paul's expulsion. Tom Driberg noted that "innocent outsiders" have wrongly regarded Waugh's description of a "bump supper and its aftermath" as "wildly exaggerated," insisting that it was, "if anything, a mild account of the night of any Bullingdon Club dinner in Christ Church."[5] Waugh never fell foul of the Bullingdon in the way Paul falls foul of the Bollinger, and Scone, the product of Waugh's imagination, is more hazardous than Hertford was in the early 1920s. In the same way, Paul, another product of Waugh's imagination, is more innocent than Waugh had been, though he suffers more than the author did. Waugh later pointed to differences between himself and Paul, admitting that he had had a "much nicer time than the hero."[6] Waugh's representation of Oxford in *Decline and Fall* obviously stems from conscious artistic decisions. He could most dramatically show the arbitrariness of dons and other authorities by making the hero innocent of all crimes, achieving mild revenge in the most effective way. It would, however, be a mistake to dismiss Paul as the naif of satirical convention. Waugh often saw himself as the innocent victim of others' corruption, and he usually represented himself that way in fiction. His heroes resemble many others in the genre of satire, but Waugh chose this representation of himself primarily for personal, not only for literary, reasons. Emphasizing his innocence and others' vices enabled Waugh to obscure unfortunate parts of his past and to excuse his alienation from such a knavish, repulsive world.

Waugh differs from Paul in one other important respect. Paul returns to Oxford to finish his degree, whereas Waugh had had neither opportunity nor desire to do so. Paul is, as Jeffrey Heath points out, returning to a "false refuge,"[7] a tactic preferred by early heroes, such as Tony Last and William Boot. Paul, who is studying theology, takes comfort in condemning heretics without recognizing that he may also be condemned, just as he is still vulnerable to violence from the Bollinger Club. More personally, Waugh's relegation of Paul to Oxford represents a positive change in his attitude toward the university, movement beyond simple criticism

5: Oxford Revisited, 1924 and After

of friends and tutors. Paul's quiet life as a scholar is very dull, but the alternative is dissolution and anarchy in the Bollinger Club, represented early in the novel by Alastair Digby-Vaine-Trumpington and later by Peter Pastmaster. Waugh had been both scholar and drunkard at Oxford, and neither way had satisfied him. More than three years after leaving, Waugh began to recognize that he and the university were incompatible. Two years earlier, in "The Balance," he had dealt with the unsettling effect of alcohol and had vented frustration against inconstant friends. By the time he wrote *Decline and Fall,* Waugh was still very bitter about his departure, exaggerating the elite's advantages and the dons' unfairness. He still saw the dangers of alcohol, but he was also ready to go further, resentment beginning to fade a bit as he sought more thorough understanding of himself.

In August 1927 Waugh had been in Oxford, finishing *Rossetti* before starting *Decline and Fall.* He had been "happier and felt better" than he had in months. He was spending most of his days in the Union Library, finding it "very quiet and nice without all those gawky young men." Waugh no longer felt much kinship with undergraduates or their interests, noting that the "central figure" seemed to be Wilfred Moon, a "scorbutic baronet" with a "smart car," surrounded by "hosts of disreputable men." Moon was "just the sort of man" Waugh had "adored" four years before; in 1927 Moon was a "bore" because Waugh wanted to work. He had also "lost the capacity for swilling down pint after pint of watery beer. How priggish that all looks" (*DEW* 287). Waugh had realized that he was better off writing than drinking in Oxford, making order out of chaos instead of letting dons do it for him or letting himself slip into the bodiless harlequinade of drunkenness. He had written some fiction at Oxford, but he had come to see that too many people expected him to play too many different roles there, distracting him from his vocation.

Oxford almost disappears in *Vile Bodies: Decline and Fall* had been enough of a statement for a few years. Oxford reappears briefly in *Black Mischief* as a silly, irrelevant place. Its most interesting figure is Basil Seal, whose "luncheon parties lasted until dusk," and whose "dinner parties dispersed in riot. Lovely young women visited him from London in high-powered cars. He went away for week-ends without leave and climbed into College over the tiles at night. He had travelled all over Europe, spoke six languages, called dons by their Christian names and discussed their books with them."[8] Already a successful novelist when *Black Mischief* was published in 1932, Waugh no longer had any interest in attributing failure to unfair treatment at Oxford. Instead, he drew on drunken exploits there to evince the irresponsibility of Basil. Much time and effort have been expended in order to identify Basil as a portrait of either Peter Rodd or Basil Murray, but the character is not only a portrait. Basil Seal is primarily an aspect of Waugh's self, a representation of experience at Oxford. Basil is obviously different from Paul Pennyfeather—confident and worldly, capable of accomplishment in spite of misbehavior. Basil embodies Waugh's anarchic self for the first time because, having attained prominence, Waugh was beginning to confront the disreputable side of his past. Waugh exaggerated Basil's irresponsibility in order to magnify his own success as a novelist, just as he exaggerated Paul's innocence in order to emphasize the corruption of antagonists. Neither character is very close to Waugh: Paul is too innocent and Basil too worldly, but they do reflect his very different artistic interests in 1928 and 1932. Paul and Basil are similar in that they are both heterosexual. Basil's interest in women is introduced immediately, whereas Paul's develops later. Waugh was not yet ready to deal with sexual ambiguity in his own past.

Whatever progress Waugh had made by 1932, he still seemed to resent Oxford, for it remains intellectually absurd in *Black Mischief.* The university fails to teach anything to Seth, one of its products, the emperor of Azania at the beginning of the novel. To Seth, Basil stands as the "personification of all that glittering, intangible Western culture to which he aspired" (*BM* 147). Seth claims to embody "the New Age" and "the Future," citing attendance at the "great tattoo of Aldershot, the Paris Exhibition, the Oxford Union," knowledge of "modern books—Shaw, Arlen, Priestley," and advocacy of "woman's suffrage, vaccination, and vivisection" (*BM* 22). Waugh is making the point that an Oxford education is funny outside the society that gives it meaning, useless to someone like Seth, an "undergraduate of no account in his College, amiably classed among Bengali babus, Siamese and grammar school scholars as one of the remote and praiseworthy people who had come a long way to the University" (*BM* 146). Even to Basil, Oxford is essentially meaningless, somewhere to spend a few years when young, a place of no particular importance. The view is in keeping with Waugh's sense, in 1932, that he had succeeded in spite of Oxford, not because of it. The view is also in keeping with the 1930 article "Was Oxford Worth While?"

Oxford recedes again in *A Handful of Dust, Scoop* (1938), and *Work Suspended,* only to reappear in *Put Out More Flags* in a brief passage that derives permanent value from the university.

5: Oxford Revisited, 1924 and After 157

Ambrose Silk, depressed by loneliness, the war, and the sterility of his art, reminisces about Oxford, remembering that he had

> ridden ridiculously and ignominiously in the Christ Church Grind, and Peter Pastmaster had gone to a *palais de danse* in Reading dressed as a woman. Alastair Digby-Vaine-Trumpington, absorbed in immature experiments into the question of how far various lewd debutantes would go with him, still had time when tippling his port at Mickleham to hear, without disapproval, Ambrose's recitals of unrequited love for a rowing blue. Nowadays Ambrose saw few of his old friends except Basil. He fancied that he had been dropped and sometimes in moments of vainglory to the right audience, represented himself as a martyr to Art; as one who made no concessions to Mammon.[9]

As in "The Balance," a character attributes present misery to the absence of friends from Oxford, playing the martyr as Waugh often did himself. In 1941, Waugh was also beginning to feel how permanently he had lost many friends from Oxford years. The passage laments something else as well. Heath sees the novel as a conflict between three aspects of Waugh's self, noting that "in the person of Ambrose Silk the uncommitted artist is bundled off into unhappy exile, and in the person of Cedric Lyne the ineffectual aesthete is liquidated. It is Basil Seal, the man of action, who now emerges triumphant." Heath adds that "behind Waugh's sardonic account of Ambrose's banishment flow powerful cross-currents of regret, and we may conclude that the exorcism of Ambrose and aestheticism from Waugh's character was no simple matter."[10] I would add that Ambrose represents not only aestheticism, but homosexuality as well. In novels Waugh often seems to have imagined himself as he might have been if he had made different choices at certain times. Paul Pennyfeather, to take one example, represents the quiet scholar Waugh might have remained. Waugh might also have developed into Ambrose Silk, if he and Alastair Graham had stayed together. Ambrose had been exorcised sometime in the mid 1920s; in 1941, the third year of the war, Waugh, happily married and an officer in the commandos, saw himself, rather hopefully, as Basil Seal, man of action. Selection of this role did not preclude regret for what he had been and for what he might have become. Knowledge that he had lost part of himself, made more poignant by awareness that he could never recover that part, is only latent in *Put Out More Flags,* but it dominates Waugh's next novel, *Brideshead Revisited.*

Brideshead's understanding of Oxford is radically different from that of *Decline and Fall*. Waugh represents Oxford as a beautiful place, paradise lost, preferable to the unfortunate present, as his narrator, Charles Ryder, suggests. Oxford is "submerged now and obliterated, irrecoverable as Lyonnesse, so quickly have the waters come flooding in." In the 1920s Oxford was

> still a city of aquatint. In her spacious and quiet streets men walked and spoke as they had done in Newman's day; her autumnal mists, her grey springtime, and the rare glory of her summer days . . . when the chestnut was in flower and the bells rang out high and clear over her gables and cupolas, exhaled the soft vapours of a thousand years of learning.

Charles senses that this "cloistral hush" gave their "laughter its resonance, and carried it still, joyously, over the intervening clamour."[11] Studious undergraduates are no longer ridiculous, and one of Charles's first friends at the university is Collins, an "embryo don, a man of solid reading and childlike humour" (*BR* 27). Robert Murray Davis notes that Collins serves as a "foil to Sebastian."[12] Biographical perspective suggests a different reading. Collins resembles Richard Pares, and, in Waugh's life, Pares had acted as foil to Alastair Graham, as in the novel Charles's friendship with Collins precedes friendship with Sebastian Flyte. Charles feels that friendship with Collins is "not all that Oxford had to offer" (*BR* 28), and events soon prove him right. Undergraduates still drink too much in *Brideshead,* as they all try to learn, "by trial and error, to carry [their] wine." This time the "not uncommon sounds of bibulous laughter and unsteady steps" start friendship instead of exile (*BR* 29). Sebastian, the son of a marquess and the "most conspicuous man of his year by reason of his beauty, which was arresting" (*BR* 28), vomits into Charles's room. Attempting to apologize, Sebastian initiates Charles into what his cousin Jasper calls the *"very worst set in the University"* (*BR* 41). Charles asserts that he happens to "*like* this bad set" and "getting drunk at luncheon" (*BR* 43). It seems as if he is being "given a brief spell" of something he has never known, a "happy childhood, and though its toys were silk shirts and liqueurs and cigars and its naughtiness high in the catalogue of grave sins," Charles and Sebastian also preserve "nursery freshness . . . that fell little short of the joy of innocence" (*BR* 45).

Oxford is beautiful, encouraging drinking and camaraderie, but it also attracts Charles for other reasons. Freedom is intoxicating after the "hard bachelordom of English adolescence, the premature dignity and authority of the school system," and Charles senses

5: Oxford Revisited, 1924 and After

that he "grew younger daily" at Oxford (*BR* 44–45). Charles's reaction derives from Waugh's feeling of liberation at Oxford, where he had been "reborn in full youth" (*ALL* 171). Charles also finds Oxford an agreeable alternative to life with his family. Like Waugh, Charles prefers Oxford to the bourgeois milieu in which he has been raised, and life at home becomes increasingly uncomfortable as he becomes absorbed in the university. Having spent more than his allowance, too poor to go abroad, Charles is forced to spend his vacation at home, where relations with his father "deteriorated sharply" (*BR* 65) and "strife was internecine" (*BR* 72). Oxford is also attractive to Charles, as it was to Waugh, because it requires little study. Charles does no work until he faces preliminary examinations. Like Waugh himself, Charles has to pass in order to remain at Oxford. He succeeds after telling Sebastian not to enter his rooms, sitting up with "iced black coffee and charcoal biscuits, cramming [himself] with the neglected texts" (*BR* 45). Oxford is in every way more attractive in *Brideshead Revisited* than it is in *Decline and Fall,* and each attraction represents one reason Waugh liked the university.

Homosexual affairs were another reason Waugh liked Oxford, at least when he had been there. Though Waugh is not very explicit in *Brideshead Revisited,* there are clear indications that Charles goes through a homosexual phase at Oxford. Charles is obviously in love with Sebastian, whom he finds "magically beautiful" (*BR* 31). Sebastian objects during Eights Week when all of Oxford is "pullulating with women," enjoining Charles to "come away at once, out of danger" (*BR* 23). They leave Oxford in a borrowed car, driving until they can be alone together. Sebastian, "without warning," stops the car, the day having become "hot enough" to make them "seek the shade." They lie down to eat, drink, and smoke, "Sebastian's eyes on the leaves above him," Charles's eyes "on his profile." The "fumes of the sweet, golden wine" seem to lift them a "finger's breadth above the turf and hold [them] suspended" (*BR* 24). Their intimacy is clearly on the verge of homosexuality, and Charles senses the possibility. He feels constrained by his background, but other considerations lead him to experiment. Invited to luncheon by Sebastian, he is conscious of a "tiny, priggish warning voice . . . which in the tones of Collins" says it is "seemly to hold back." Charles is "in search of love," however, and he goes "full of curiosity and the faint, unrecognized apprehension that . . . at last [he] should find that low door in the wall, which others . . . had found before [him]." The door is supposed to open on an "enclosed and enchanted garden, which was somewhere, not overlooked by any window, in the heart of that grey city" (*BR* 31). Charles wants to be alone with Sebastian so that he can express love and at the same time avoid censure for a socially unacceptable act. Charles finally gets his wish when, during vacation, Sebastian invites him to Brideshead. They have a "heavenly time alone" (*BR* 78) but feel threatened by the imminent return of Sebastian's family, as Sebastian decides that soon they "shall have to hide" (*BR* 88).

There are other suggestions of homosexual attraction between Charles and Sebastian, but Waugh never mentions their having sex. Conventions of publishing at the time prevented him from being very explicit. He noted in his diary that he felt "very much the futility of describing sexual emotions without describing the sexual act." Meals in *Brideshead* are rendered in great detail, and Waugh wanted to use comparable detail in descriptions of the "two coitions—with his wife and Julia. It would be no more or less obscene than to leave them to the reader's imagination," bound to be less "acute" than Waugh's own (*DEW* 564–65). Waugh gave no indication that he wanted to do the same for Charles and Sebastian. The characters' apparent chastity prompts Davis's remark that their relationship is "not specifically or primarily homosexual," as Sebastian appears to be in "what Freud would call the pregenital stage."[13] Davis's characterization of the relationship is questionable even if one stays within the novel, and if one chooses to go outside of it, biography strongly suggests a different reading. *Brideshead Revisited* is Waugh's attempt to come to terms with his experience at Oxford, and the novel includes several subtle references to an important part of the experience, homosexuality. Waugh was not willing to share knowledge of his homosexual phase with the public—his autobiography, written near the end of his life, twenty years after *Brideshead,* never mentions it—but he sometimes referred to this phase in the presence of close friends, such as Christopher Sykes and Nancy Mitford. Waugh seems to have talked about his homosexuality only after the novel had been written; composition helped him to articulate feelings still unsettled after twenty years. He was still embarrassed by his homosexual phase and reluctant to deal with it as candidly as he did later. Waugh's impulse to evoke Oxford and all it meant led him to advert to a homosexual affair between Charles and Sebastian, though lingering reservations about his own affairs determined the oblique nature of the references.

Waugh's reservations are part of a larger ambivalence about Oxford in *Brideshead Revisited,* ambivalence stemming from the con-

5: Oxford Revisited, 1924 and After

viction that, however attractive Oxford might be, it is, as in "The Balance," incapable of fulfilling the need for discipline, order, and meaning. Those who seek happiness at Oxford are, like Charles, inevitably disappointed. When Charles and Sebastian return to Oxford for their second year, they find it depressing rather than stimulating. Charles observes that it is "typical of Oxford . . . to start the new year in autumn," remembering that the "autumnal mood possessed" them, "as though the riotous exuberance of June had died with the gillyflowers," replaced by the "damp leaves, smouldering in a corner of the quad" (*BR* 104). The sense of youth associated with Oxford has gone, and Sebastian feels "precisely one hundred years old," while Charles feels "middle-aged" (*BR* 105). The novelty of Oxford has worn off, as Charles tells Sebastian that they have "had all the fun" they can expect there (*BR* 105). Charles sees the change in both of them, as they have "lost the sense of discovery which had infused the anarchy of [their] first year." Charles begins "to settle down" (*BR* 106). Friends are no longer as interesting as they had been. Charles and Sebastian keep to themselves, "each so much bound up in the other" that they do "not look elsewhere for friends." Together they "shed" their old friends and make "no others" (*BR* 107). Even drinking is no longer satisfying: Charles realizes that though they both drink, Sebastian is a "drunkard in quite a different sense." Charles drinks "through an excess of high spirits, in the love of the moment, and the wish to prolong and enhance it;" Sebastian drinks "to escape" (*BR* 129).

Oxford is still an alternative to Charles's bourgeois family, but their influence begins to moderate his behavior. He misses his cousin Jasper, who has finished, because he needs "him to shock." Charles has come back "glutted and a little chastened, with the resolve to go slow." His father's "whimsical persecution" has convinced him of the "folly of living beyond [his] means" (*BR* 106). Charles's acceptance of responsibility is a step toward maturity, incidentally helping him to understand his father. Charles also shows some concern for vocation, starting his second year by joining the Ruskin School of Art (*BR* 106). Oxford offers Charles fewer delights because he perceives both the limitations of pleasure and the necessity of accepting responsibility. Oxford is "not as it had been" in his first year (*BR* 140), and he tells his father that it may be "rather a waste of time going back to Oxford" for a third year (*BR* 146).

Charles's experience reflects Waugh's in many ways. Like Charles, Waugh tried to cut spending, probably after being reprimanded by his father. Charles's relationship with his father in

Brideshead is part of a larger preoccupation with fathers and sons running through Waugh's later writings, beginning in *Work Suspended* and culminating in *A Little Learning*'s sixteen-page chapter entitled "My Father." As his father aged and then died, Waugh began to lament their usually distant relationship, reconciling himself to what his father had been. Over the years, partly through writing, Waugh developed a "growing appreciation . . . of his quality and . . . a growing pleasure in his company" (*ALL* 64). Appreciation is evident even in *Brideshead,* where Charles's father seems somewhat cruel. Cruelty forces Charles to see that he can't go on spending money as irresponsibly as he had in his first year; in a way, it helps him to grow up. Charles's reaction reflects, not resentment Waugh felt toward his father in the 1920s, but sympathy he developed for his father's vexation, once he had recognized that his father had been paying for Oxford and that "money is the root of almost all family differences" (FS HRHRC).

Charles also resembles Waugh in artistic interest and weariness with Oxford, but the most important similarity is love for another man. Alastair Graham appears in *Brideshead Revisited* as Sebastian Flyte. There are several similarities: both found their mothers oppressive, both turned up drunk in Paris, and both eventually crept off into seclusion, Graham in Wales, Sebastian in Morocco. As Heath points out, the "name Alastair even appears instead of Sebastian at several points in the manuscript."[14] Terence Greenidge, among others, thought that Sebastian had been drawn after Hugh Lygon, second son of the seventh Earl Beauchamp. Like Lygon, Sebastian is an aristocrat, and, like Sebastian, Lygon was "rather empty," at least in Greenidge's opinion.[15] Suffice to say that Sebastian is another composite, based primarily on Graham but also influenced by Lygon, who had died in 1936.

The mingling of two old friends in one character is an important indication of Waugh's thinking about Oxford in 1944, when, by writing the novel, he once again came seriously to terms with his experience at the university. Waugh endows his narrator and alter ego with greater perspicacity than he had shown in diaries and letters of the 1920s, though Charles is remembering experiences from twenty years before, just as Waugh was writing about Oxford after twenty years had passed. Charles worries about Sebastian's drinking, Sebastian becomes "listless and morose" (*BR* 107), and the two drift apart as soon as their Oxford days are over. For drama and probably also for personal reasons, Waugh allows Charles to recognize the dangers of Oxford and the limitations of Sebastian rather more quickly than he had recognized the same dangers and

5: Oxford Revisited, 1924 and After

the limitations of Graham and Lygon. The end of the relationship in *Brideshead Revisited* appears to be altogether less painful, due more to rational considerations than the end of Waugh's relationship with Graham had been. Waugh decided to represent his twenty-year-old affair as a matter rather less serious than it had been, dealing with a painful episode by undercutting its importance. Waugh's regret over the end of the affair was real, and the regret pervading *Brideshead* is unmistakable, but by 1944 Waugh had realized the futility of his relationship with Graham and had retrospectively attributed recognition of futility to his narrator. As Heath writes, "There can be no doubt that in describing Ryder's 'outdistancing' of Sebastian, Waugh was trying to lay to rest his affection for Alastair Graham and the debilitating aestheticism he represented. Indeed, Waugh's loss of Graham was tantamount to the loss of his youth, the painful but necessary loss of part of his personality."[16] Again I would add that Graham represented homosexuality as well as aestheticism, and that, as in the novel, Graham was "the forerunner" of Waugh's more mature love of women—and God (*BR* 303). Lygon was also a forerunner, though he and Waugh seem not to have been romantically involved. Waugh had been inclined to admire Hugh, a handsome young aristocrat who had proven to be fragile and insubstantial, like Sebastian in the novel. Waugh had wanted to believe in the inherited grace of the aristocracy, but he had often found it lacking, and he had had to look elsewhere for meaning, finding it in Roman Catholicism in particular. *Brideshead Revisited* is largely about this fundamental change of heart.

Evidence from the text supports this interpretation. At the end of his relationship with Sebastian, after Lady Marchmain has sent him away from Brideshead for giving her son money for drink, Charles says that as he

> turned back in the car to take what promised to be my last view of the house, I felt that I was leaving part of myself behind, and that wherever I went afterwards I should feel the lack of it, and search for it hopelessly, as ghosts are said to do, frequenting spots where they buried material treasures without which they cannot pay their way to the nether world.
> "I shall never go back," I said to myself.
> A door had shut, the low door in the wall I had sought and found in Oxford; open it now and I should find no enchanted garden.
>
> I had left behind me—what? Youth? Adolescence? Romance? . . .
> "I have left behind illusion," I said to myself. (*BR* 169)

In abjuring Alastair Graham and Hugh Lygon, Waugh had left behind all these things, as well as homosexuality, drunkenness, and the life of riot he enjoyed and occasionally revived in later years.

The idea that Waugh was somehow distinguishing between parts of himself is also the best means of coming to terms with Anthony Blanche. Most simply, Blanche is a caricature of acquaintances Waugh had made at Oxford, evoking the atmosphere of the university in the 1920s. Blanche is clearly related to Ambrose Silk, and Waugh himself said that an "aesthetic bugger" appears in his novels "under various names—that was 2/3 Brian [Howard] 1/3 Harold Acton" (*LEW* 505). In *Brideshead* the aesthetic bugger isn't exiled, as Ambrose Silk is in *Put Out More Flags.* Anthony Blanche does disappear for a while in *Brideshead,* but he is missed as Ambrose is not. Charles, dealing with the emptiness of Oxford in his second year, decides that Blanche had "taken something away with him when he went . . . and all his friends, among whom he had always been a stranger, needed him now" (*BR* 107). Blanche turns up at an exhibition of Charles's South American paintings, dismissing them as "simple, creamy English charm, playing tigers." Charles agrees. The paintings remind Blanche of "dear Sebastian when he liked so much to dress up in false whiskers," Blanche having *"warned"* Charles about charm and the Flyte family (*BR* 273).

Several critics have tried to explain this eccentric but perceptive and persistent character. Terry Eagleton decides that "Blanche represents the Sebastian style carried to a tainted and parodic extreme, and so is attractive in his resemblance to Sebastian but distasteful in so far as he displays the admired upper-class manner in its worst light, shorn of its saving moral strengths."[17] Blanche is more outrageous than Sebastian, but Sebastian is not important in the second part of the novel, and there is no reason for Waugh to bring Blanche back to contrast upper-class manners. Blanche also has his own kind of strength, making him more resilient than Sebastian. Davis offers more sophisticated analysis. He notes the contrast between Blanche and Sebastian, but he also compares and contrasts Blanche and Jasper, Blanche and Charles, and Blanche and Charles's father. Davis perceives that Waugh has carefully chosen lines from *The Waste Land* for Blanche to recite, linking him to Tiresias, who lived as a man and as a woman, and making Blanche a "kind of prophet."[18]

Davis's explanation of Blanche's departure and return is less satisfying. He describes Blanche at Oxford as a "stage manager" whose "theater provided Sebastian with a self-contained world of play into which he could escape," Blanche leaving Charles and

5: Oxford Revisited, 1924 and After 165

Sebastian "without scenario or direction."[19] Charles and Sebastian certainly lose the playfulness they had enjoyed with Blanche, but Charles does not lack direction as he begins to settle down, and the intensity of his relationship with Sebastian leaves little room for other friends anyway. Davis goes on to suggest that Blanche is "reintroduced . . . to bury Charles's reputation, not to praise it." Blanche's "criticism serves as a kind of penance and, by destroying the old, leaves Charles free to move in new directions."[20] Charles doesn't suffer from Blanche's criticism, since he knows it is valid. He has already started to move in new, or at least different, directions: he has returned to England and has received at least one commission to do the sort of work he is known for.

Davis also writes that "Blanche's appearance establishes other perspectives of time and value." Blanche has warned Charles against charm, but the "values implied in contrast have brought Anthony to the Blue Grotto, which is condemned more in aesthetic than in moral terms."[21] Charles's own aesthetic efforts have just been condemned, however, and he is hardly able to criticize Blanche's choice of surroundings. The Blue Grotto is just a convenience for Blanche, so he can disorient Charles and distract him from the high society of the gallery. In terms of time, Blanche evokes the memory of Oxford, and "this memory allows Charles to establish a connection with his youth that is rare in book 2 but very important for the novel as a whole."[22] It is hard to see why this memory should be very important, since Julia evokes similar memories several times in book II. Finally, Davis finds that the "mocking ghost of Anthony Blanche is raised and dismissed" in a conversation between Charles and Cordelia.[23] Blanche has blamed the suicide of a governess on Cordelia, but Charles doesn't even mention the charge or the source, and once again Blanche seems remarkable more for persistence than for inaccuracy. Davis understands what Blanche is doing early in *Brideshead,* but his comments on Blanche late in the novel are questionable, marginally relevant to the function of the character.

Again, biographical perspective provides another way of explaining both the novel and the character. More than prophet, contrast or evocation, Blanche is both a reflection of people Waugh had known and an aspect of the author himself. Humphrey Carpenter sees in Blanche Waugh's own "capacity to imagine life in more lurid colours than it really displays,"[24] a reasonable view, but one that nevertheless fails to explain Blanche's persistence. More centrally, Blanche seems to represent Waugh's critical detachment; something, he implies, he lost when he was seduced by the charm of Graham and Lygon, but something that inevitably returns to evaluate both his affairs and his art. Blanche cannot be overcome as easily as Ambrose Silk is deceived by Basil Seal, and his persistence probably reflects the difficulty Waugh had in suppressing homosexual tendencies. Blanche, in his role as critic, also reminds Waugh and his narrator that Oxford wasn't as pleasant as they would like to remember, functioning in the same way as the skull in the bowl of roses on Charles's table, bearing the motto *Et in Arcadia ego*. Such a character is not necessary or even appropriate in *Decline and Fall*, written three years after Waugh had left the university, but twenty years after leaving Oxford Waugh needs Blanche to keep the novel from devolving into pure sentiment. Knowledge that Blanche is right, that Oxford wasn't perfect, makes the situation of both narrator and author that much more poignant.

Characterization of Charles Ryder also says something about Waugh's state of mind in 1944. In many ways, Charles is closer to Waugh's experience than any of his other heroes. There are some important differences, however. Charles is a painter, not a writer, and Davis proposes three reasons for the change. First, in his drawing and painting Charles "successfully unites the image that obsesses him and the active principle that animates him, or, in other words, fuses feeling and form, vision and technique." Second, Davis sees Waugh drawing on the "künstlerroman," with *Brideshead* using "artistic development as a principle of organization." Third, "Waugh makes Charles an artist in order to dramatize his love of human creations and his celebration of them in art as good in themselves."[25] The biographical reason for making Charles an artist is simpler and more plausible. In *Brideshead* Waugh is imagining what life might have been like if, like Charles, he had been allowed to leave Oxford and study art in Paris, as he had wanted to do in 1923. Waugh allows Charles to play the same imaginative game, causing him to "wonder whether, had it not been for Sebastian, [he] might have trodden the same path as Collins round the cultural water-wheel." Charles's father "in his youth sat for All Souls and, in a year of hot competition, failed; . . . that early failure impressed itself on him," and Charles develops an "ill-considered sense that there lay the proper and natural goal of the life of reason." Charles thinks that he too "should doubtless have failed, but, having failed, [he] might perhaps have slipped into a less august academic life elsewhere" (*BR* 44). Waugh is remembering his father's third-class degree at New College, as well as his own less august academic life, teaching at Arnold House, Aston Clinton, and Notting Hill. He is close to imagining himself as the middle-

5: Oxford Revisited, 1924 and After

aged schoolmaster in *Scott-King's Modern Europe,* written a few years after *Brideshead.* As an artist, Charles avoids all that, as fiction gives Waugh the chance to imagine that he could have avoided it, too.

Charles's reference to the role of Sebastian suggests another connection between the novel and the life of the author. Important as Sebastian is, Charles becomes disillusioned with him and Oxford more quickly than Waugh had with Graham, Lygon, and the university. Important also is Charles's decision to leave; he does not do poorly on examinations and lose his scholarship, as Waugh had done, and he is not the victim of selfish dons, as Paul Pennyfeather is. Waugh may have been reluctant to deal with his performance on examinations, but it seems more likely that he is again emphasizing Charles's renunciation of Oxford and all it represents. Charles sees through Oxford more quickly than Waugh had, and the perception of his narrator, improved through hindsight, undercuts Oxford's attractions. Charles sees no reason to stay, deciding that Paris would be better for him. By working out the consequences of Charles's decision in the novel, Waugh suggests that he might have ended his affair with Graham sooner than he had, and that he might have spent 1925 and 1926 more productively than he had, if only he had been allowed to leave the university.

Charles's experience also diverges from Waugh's in his relationship with dons. Dons are still repugnant in *Brideshead,* one of the few similarities between it and *Decline and Fall.* The most prominent is Mr. Samgrass, an "intellectual-on-the-make" (*BR* 110), who gives false evidence in Sebastian's defense in order to gain influence in the family. Charles feels "distaste" for Mr. Samgrass (*BR* 125), who is one of the people dividing him from Sebastian; perhaps Waugh remembered Urquhart's effect on Pares. There are no gratuitous portraits of conniving dons in *Brideshead,* no conflicts between them and Charles at the university, indicating the difference between Waugh's emotions when he wrote *Brideshead* and those he had felt when writing *Decline and Fall.* Waugh's experience at Oxford was much closer to Charles Ryder's than to Paul Pennyfeather's, again reflecting a significant shift in the writer's perspective. Waugh was more curious about conflicts in his past, more willing to explore their complexity, less interested in settling old scores through simplified characterization. *Brideshead Revisited* is more autobiographical than *Decline and Fall,* though this fact becomes important only in biographical terms. *Brideshead* is not autobiography, and it is at best trivial, at worst pointless to equate characters in the novel with people Waugh had known. It is important that by 1944 Waugh had come to terms with his experience at Oxford, representing it more fully, and more fairly, in fiction. A successful novelist, he no longer felt much resentment of Oxford, and he represents the university's dons and undergraduates with much less absurdity. Artistically and personally, he no longer needed Paul Pennyfeather's innocence to attract readers' sympathy in *Brideshead,* describing Charles's drunkenness in detail and suggesting a phase of homosexuality.

Brideshead is not a confession prompted by some psychological need to relieve guilt. Davis considers the novel "less a confession than an apology . . . justifying rather than criticizing past behavior."[26] Biographical reading suggests just the opposite, that Waugh was not justifying, but criticizing his past. *Brideshead*'s theme is memory, contrasting past joy made possible by ignorance and present equanimity informed by knowledge and experience. According to Davis, Waugh "sees memory as connected with artistic inspiration and, by implications realized if not overtly stated in the epilogue, as a sign of God's grace and therefore as an indication of hope for the future."[27] The epilogue is hopeful, but not because the narrator can recover the past through memory. Oxford is clearly an invaluable experience, but it is not enough to form the basis of Charles's, or Waugh's, life and art, since Oxford lacks order and meaning sufficient for their needs. As Charles asks, remembering that he liked his "'bad set and . . . getting drunk at luncheon'; that was enough then. Is more needed now?" (*BR* 45).

The answer is yes, and in Waugh's terms the one thing needful is the Roman Catholic faith. Faith exposes the frivolity of the past and the insignificance of disappointment, enabling Charles, and Waugh himself, to confront the desolation of the present cheerfully, even hopefully. Worldly amusements Waugh had enjoyed, including not only Oxford, alcohol, and sex, but also the aristocracy, marriage, and military service, amounted to vanity and provided at best fleeting satisfaction. Their shallowness is revealed in *Brideshead,* a novel Waugh wrote at age forty, when he had experienced all these things and had failed to find any a lasting diversion. Novel-writing itself may have been somewhat worldly, but it helped Waugh to reach an understanding of his faith much more profound in 1944, when he wrote *Brideshead,* than it had been in 1930, when he had converted. In the early 1920s he had been happy at Oxford, but consciousness of futility made memories painful and tainted them with regret for wasted time. The presence of so many childish things, which occupied Waugh in one way or another from 1921 to 1945, and the author's almost systematic way of demonstrating their emptiness make *Brideshead* crucial to understanding Waugh's life before 1945. *Brideshead* is not the culmination of his vision—that comes later, in the war trilogy—but it is a central statement of his development as a man and an artist. In theme and tone *Brideshead* is more serious than *Decline and Fall,* and aesthetic considerations also contribute to the importance of *Brideshead* in Waugh's career. Such considerations are subordinate to biographical matters, however, partly because Waugh had already tried to give the former expression, without complete success, in *Work Suspended,* partly because *Brideshead* is so obviously autobiographical in Waugh's use of experience.

Brideshead Revisited is Waugh's last novel to show concern about Oxford. The university receives some slight mention here and there, and after 1944 Waugh drew much more material for fiction from postwar travels, problems of the faith, and military experience that had prompted him to write *Brideshead* in the first place. It is as if he had finally resolved lingering discomfort over his experience at the university. Sense of resolution about Oxford, and everything else, is powerful in the novel's final scene, when Charles takes comfort in the endurance of Roman Catholicism despite his disappointment in the university, marriage, art, and the army. Waugh's last uses of Oxford in fiction are of some interest, however. In *The Ordeal of Gilbert Pinfold* (1957), one of the hero's hallucinations claims that Gilbert often sang "ridiculous songs outside men's rooms at Oxford. He made a row outside the Dean's rooms. That's why he got sent down. He accused the Dean of the most disgusting practices. It was all a great joke."[28] As in many of the hallucinations Waugh suffered in 1954, the charge is not completely accurate, since Waugh had not been sent down. If it can be taken as one of Waugh's own, the hallucination seems to stem from lingering guilt over hostility to Cruttwell and failure to take a degree. In *Unconditional Surrender,* Guy Crouchback meets Major Cattermole, the "same age as Guy, tall, stooping, emaciated, totally unsoldierly, a Zurbaran ascetic with a joyous smile." Cattermole mentions Balliol in the early 1920s and Guy realizes that they had been up together, though Cattermole had led a "very quiet life" and had "wasted [his] time as an undergraduate working." He remembers seeing Guy "about with the bloods," later referring to his "academic colleagues," using "precise, donnish phrases" (*US* 208–10). Cattermole is a version of Richard Pares, who had died of muscular sclerosis in 1958, little more than a year before Waugh started writing the novel. The character's name recalls Pares's fascination with the diction of Lewis Carroll. Cattermole has little relevance to the story, his inclusion mostly a gesture of respect for an old friend. In *Basil Seal Rides Again,* his last work of fiction, Waugh is still making excuses for homosexuality at Oxford. Basil supposes that there had been women at Oxford in his day, but he insists that he "never met them." He also says that the "sort of fellow who takes up with undergraduettes has something wrong with him."29

If Waugh began to show less interest in his experience at the university, he remained interested in Oxford itself. Often he insulted undergraduates, faculty, and architecture. Many insults came from Waugh's resentment over his treatment at Oxford and perhaps from his sense of failure as well. In *Rossetti* the Union Debating Hall is described as an "ugly enough building, designed by Woodward, the arch-fiend of Oxford architecture" (*R* 85). In *Labels* even Oxford seems "comparatively vital by contrast" with a Muslim university (*L* 112). These gibes were written about the same time as *Decline and Fall* by an author who held a grudge. Even after Waugh had become successful as a writer, he could not resist poking fun at the university. In *The Tablet* in June 1939, Waugh noted that news of Oxford "in the papers has been disquieting; personal experience has often been worse." He enumerated complaints, including undergraduates who "pass resolutions to exempt themselves from military service" and dons who "think and write like provincial school-mistresses." Waugh approved of Oxford's decision to award an honorary degree to P. G. Wodehouse, the university having "suddenly exerted its failing strength in an action worthy of its tradition" (*ALO* 83–84).

After *Brideshead,* Waugh continued to abuse Oxford, though more often in private papers, less often in print. He found the Union especially disappointing, as in 1946, when he watched the audience "falling off their benches with laughter at the most banal jokes" (*LEW* 229). Waugh objected to a "deplorable development," the practice of having guest speakers at every debate. He explained that in "sturdier days" there had been only "one guest a term," the Union owing "its prestige to the great number of well known politicians who spoke there as undergraduates." Waugh considered it a "come-down for the Union to ape the ways of a broadcast symposium"; only its "inherited high reputation" enabled it to attract "distinguished elderly men who will come without payment, often to be insulted."30 In his autobiography Waugh observed that in the 1930s, perhaps because of radio, the Union had come to rely on "more and more professional entertainers." By the 1960s, it had become "common to have all four speakers . . . drawn from outside the university. The undergraduates merely sprawl back and express their prejudices with jeers." The Union had been better in the 1920s, when Waugh had been an undergraduate, the debates "still essentially an undergraduate activity." He and his friends had wanted "to dispute with one another and demonstrate [their] own powers" (*ALL* 187). Waugh had liked the Union because it had given him opportunities to show off, to tell others what to think and do, and to entertain himself by starting heated arguments or by defending outrageous positions. He could never stand to listen to authorities on anything, and he could not understand undergraduates who chose to listen to people more prominent than themselves.

Waugh's sense of importance was obviously at odds with the new regime at the Union, and he thought that the rest of his generation would also consider it odd. Largely contemptuous toward politicians anyway, he affirmed that his friends had been "much more interested in the performances of Christopher Hollis and Douglas Woodruff than in those of Cabinet Ministers" (*ALL* 187). Dwelling on his generation's virtues gave Waugh a chance to denigrate those who came after them. In 1948 he gave a lecture to "Papist undergraduates," and a "very polite gentle young man . . . said: 'I should like to ask Mr W. whether it is true, as we are always being told, that we are much stupider & less cultured & amusing than undergraduates were in his day.'" Waugh "had to say 'Well yes it is' and he said very sadly 'I thought so' and sat down. Sad" (*LEW* 267). In his contribution to *The Compleat Imbiber*, an "entertainment" compiled by Cyril Ray, Waugh recognized that it is "tedious for the young to be constantly told what much finer fellows their fathers were and what a much more enjoyable time we had. But there you are; we were and we did" (*EAR* 611).

Waugh's belief in his generation's superiority came naturally to a man who saw history as a process of decline. Waugh's sense of decline was so strong that he attributed yet superior grace to the generation before his own. He noted that at the Union in the "golden age of Ronald Knox there were no outsiders at all" (*ALL* 187). Waugh tended to exaggerate the abilities of Knox and those of Knox's generation. Their time at Oxford, before the First World War, is, according to Waugh, "legendary." The "heroic group" had "died young leaving a unique reputation for brilliance, high-spirits and grace, and . . . a rich, determining tradition in English life seems to have withered and died with them" (*EAR* 347). Even when he noticed Oxford's persistent shortcomings, Waugh came back to the unsurpassed excellence of men who had been there before the First World War. In his biography of Knox, Waugh described Balliol College in 1906: "Ignominious in its early history, heterogeneous in composition, inhabiting buildings of the most joyless architecture in the University, with scant cellar and mediocre kitchen, it still professed 'a tranquil consciousness of effortless superiority' which Ronald's generation was the last to justify" (*RK* 81). Waugh and his contemporaries could hardly have equalled such illustrious predecessors. They had tried, since some had been "sharply conscious of those legendary figures" who had been "wiped out in the First World War." Waugh's preconceptions meant that he and his friends had been bound to fall short of the mark, and they had often been "reproachfully reminded . . . of how impoverished and subdued [they] were in comparison with those great men." Waugh's infatuation with effortless superiority and the irrecoverable beauty of the past meant that his generation could never have hoped to duplicate the feats of the one before. Waugh and his friends had followed, as best they could, the example set by their predecessors, and even innocent imitation had made them vulnerable, in Waugh's view, to undeserved reproaches. Waugh noted, with some resentment, that after the Second World War, his contemporaries had come to be "regarded with a mixture of envy and reprobation, as libertines and wastrels" (*ALL* 170).

The superiority of one generation to the next became for Waugh part of the university's general decline through the years. He knew that he was, in a way, fooling himself, recognizing that only a

> small minority . . . of those who pass through the university of Oxford are captivated by her genius. Those few are likely, for good or ill, to remain lifelong votaries of what has always been largely an illusion. It is the illusion of youth suddenly freed from the shackles of school, not yet shackled by the responsibilities of maturity, living for three or four years in isolation in what was once the most beautiful city in the kingdom, and it is the privilege of each enamored generation to look back upon its own brief period as the final flowering of the centuries. All subsequent change seems a deterioration, for one of the prime delusions of that suspended youth is of changelessness.

Waugh also realized that all who "love Oxford have created a fantasy for themselves of an earlier generation." Critically self-conscious as usual, Waugh resisted the temptation to romanticize the past, but still he could not help loathing the "changes of this half-century," including the "overcrowding of the university, the multiplicity of technical tricks taught in the schools, the overpowering presence of the huge industrial connurbation at Cowley, the instrusion of girls into all parts of the celibate life—all deplorable to the elderly." Architecture had not improved, had not even upheld an earlier standard, at the end of a "great continuous process of building which extended from the fourteenth to the middle of the eighteenth century. . . . Nothing erected since deserves artistic consideration" (*DIM* HRHRC). By 1960 Waugh could only "despair of Oxford," and in 1961 he wrote that Cambridge had become the "better place" (*LEW* 552, 558).

Waugh continued to disparage Oxford for many reasons. Certainly his attitude stemmed from his iconoclastic nature, almost incapable of regarding anything as immune from ridicule. Waugh had never enjoyed studying, and he had found a university degree quite unnecessary in an otherwise productive and fulfilling life. He was likely to demean those who worked hard to obtain what he had been unable to earn. In his day, there had been "no feverish competition for admittance" (*ALL* 167), though his effort to win a scholarship had been nothing if not feverish. At the same time, Waugh treasured the privilege of association with Oxford. By denigrating the university, Waugh seemed to be discarding an enviable opportunity, arguing for his own effortless superiority. If Waugh's disparagement of Oxford seems largely a personal matter, there may have been at least one public reason for it, related to his conception of the university's seductive appeal. He knew that many people were drawn, and would continue to be drawn to Oxford, viewing it, as he had, as an end in itself and thus missing what, in Waugh's terms, were more important issues. He delighted in exposing Oxford's faults because he wanted others to see them as well, and to turn from Oxford to the more crucial consideration of the welfare of one's soul.

Waugh's criticism of Oxford probably also rose from his sense that some undergraduates had been ungrateful to him. In 1935 he had published *Edmund Campion,* dedicating all royalties to rebuilding Oxford's Campion Hall. Identifying himself more publicly with his religion, Waugh in 1936 agreed to speak to the Newman Society on the war in Abyssinia. Waugh offered a Roman Catholic, pro-Italian perspective, and *Cherwell,* leaning toward Marxism, dismissed his account as "frivolous and inaccurate," seeing Waugh as an "oppressive agent of the Establishment."[31] Later that year Waugh went to Campion Hall and was disappointed in Father Martin D'Arcy's "latest *bric-a-brac*," finding "a lot of trash including watercolours by undergraduates and reproductions cut from books" (*DEW* 412). Despite the bric-a-brac, Waugh returned annually to celebrate the rebuilding of the hall. In 1946 he published

"The Hospitality of Campion Hall," indulging in his usual extravagant praise of other Roman Catholics (*EAR* 316-19). By 1955 Waugh's patience was wearing thin. He went back to Oxford, but the priest did not arrange to meet him at the station, nor did Waugh feel "welcome at Campion." He resolved to "break the habit of going up for what each year becomes a less cordial celebration" (*DEW* 747). Waugh was always well-disposed toward those who shared his religion, but he did not readily forgive those who seemed to have forgotten his importance and generosity. He refrained from public criticism of other Roman Catholics, perhaps directing resentment instead against undergraduates in general.

Waugh's enduring affection for Oxford is, however, obvious in *Brideshead Revisited* and *A Little Learning*. In 1963, a few years before his death, affection also drew him to the fortieth anniversary of the Oxford Railway Club. The club was an "original way . . . to spend a jovial evening" (*ALL* 195). Waugh and his friends had boarded a train for Leicester or Brighton and had usually returned to Oxford the same night. Credit for the idea went to John Sutro, who attended the fortieth anniversary along with Waugh, Harold Acton, Terence Greenidge, Bob Boothby, the Marquess of Bath, Roy Harrod, Christopher Sykes, Cyril Connolly, Ran Antrim, and several "junior guests," including Waugh's son Auberon and son-in-law Giles FitzHerbert. Whatever complaints he had about Oxford, Waugh was seldom reluctant to reaffirm association with the university and friends he had met there, or to introduce his children to its charms. Despite the reunion, the anniversary was disappointing, like so many of Waugh's experiences at Oxford. He saw that the "sexagenarians were really not up to it all. . . . The general verdict: 'Anyway John is enjoying it'" (*DEW* 788).

In the letter describing the anniversary, addressed to Alfred Duggan, another Oxford contemporary, Waugh mentioned his "reminiscences of their youth" and asked Duggan for details concerning the car he had kept at Oxford (*LEW* 615–16). Waugh was at work on his autobiography, about a fifth of it dealing with Oxford years. He decided that his university had been close to that of his father, equally close to that of his great-grandfather, but not so close to that of his children. The town had been

> still isolated among streams and meadows. Its buildings proudly displayed their grey and gold, crumbling ashlar, now condemned by the pundits as 'leprous' and renovated at prodigious cost. Its only suburb comprised the Ruskinian villas and well-kept gardens round the Woodstock and Banbury Roads. The motor works at Cowley existed, but

were far from sight or sound of the university. During term tourists were few. The surrounding woods and hills were those the Scholar Gypsy haunted and could be reached on foot in the middle of the road. (*ALL* 167–68)

It seems fitting that Waugh, at the end of his life, devastated by decisions of the Second Vatican Council and alienated from the Church he had loved for more than thirty years, turned in his last book once more to consider Oxford and the life he had led there. In forty years he had found much that was wrong with Oxford, but in his short time there he had been happy, for one of the few times in his life. He remembered that experience, and dwelt upon it fondly, as long as he lived.

6
Spirals of Self-Discovery

IN 1924, after he had left Oxford, Waugh sensed that a phase of life had ended. He turned twenty-one that fall, and though he couldn't have known it, one-third of his life was over. He had had a good education, but he considered it "preparation for one trade only; that of an English prose writer" (*ALL* 140). Waugh kept writing after Oxford, but he also tried teaching, printing, reporting, and cabinet making before writing his first book, *Rossetti,* and starting *Decline and Fall* in 1927. He had to research *Rossetti,* but *Decline and Fall* stemmed largely from his life at Oxford and in public schools. He depended more on imagination to depict what he was less familiar with—the aristocracy, prisons, and heterosexuality. *Decline and Fall* ridiculed the vocation of the "Modern Churchman" and pointless innovations of modern architecture. Waugh also sketched the Bright Young People, symbol of his generation. Obviously he was developing new interests, partly because he had severed himself from his former life, partly because he was writing more than he ever had.

Waugh's association with the Bright Young People was more important than any other he maintained in the mid 1920s. They supplied material and offered a sense of belonging when he felt alienated from family and Oxford friends. Waugh admired the insouciance of the Bright Young People, but he doubted that their influence could do him any good, just as he had doubted the benefits of Oxford. Waugh rendered their "cumulative futility" in *Vile Bodies* (*LEW* 39), and their notoriety helped to make the novel a best-seller in 1930. Newspapers began to ask Waugh for columns, and socialites began to invite him to parties. Before he had written *Vile Bodies,* Waugh had married Evelyn Gardner. Her infidelity in 1929 and their divorce embittered Waugh, affecting, apparently, his representation of love in *A Handful of Dust* and other novels. Divorce seems to have hastened conversion to Roman Catholicism in 1930, problems of the faith emerging as a theme in *Brideshead*

6: Spirals of Self-Discovery

Revisited and later fiction. Divorce also propelled him on worldwide travels, used in *Black Mischief, A Handful of Dust,* and *Scoop*. Military service did not start until 1939, but it became important in turn, generating *Brideshead* and presenting problems in *Put Out More Flags* and *Sword of Honour*.

All these associations influenced his fiction, but Waugh was not just storing experiences he could reshape in novels. He was looking for something to affirm in a confusing, chaotic world. Oxford had seemed worth working for, but once Waugh was there, he wanted to escape. From other perspectives, twenty and forty years later, Oxford seemed to acquire some value. Waugh had turned to the Bright Young People, who fled from purpose and morality, but again he felt lost and looked elsewhere. Marriage seemed to offer more commitment than homosexuality had, but She-Evelyn shattered Waugh's illusions. His second marriage lasted thirty years with little effect on marriage in his fiction, almost always leading to betrayal. Disappointed in people, Waugh turned to God and joined the Roman Catholic Church, its principles constant through centuries. Still restless, he started to travel, looking for better places but never finding them. He met more and more aristocrats, impressed by their freedom from constraint, discouraged when they proved venal, bogus, or shallow. World war seemed to offer aging Bright Young People a chance for redemption if Communism and Fascism could be kept on the same side, but Britain betrayed Waugh by trying to befriend the Soviet Union. At the end even the Church astonished him by abandoning its liturgy, spoiling the only association Waugh had affirmed consistently in fiction. Waugh is known for his impulse to scorn, but an even more basic impulse was to embrace, serving some end regarded as moral or at least righteous, excusing his distaste for the misguided. Waugh embraced and then scorned many people and causes, and changes of heart are the very bases of his fiction. The novels can be read as records of change, more subtle and more revealing than the opinions in diaries, letters, and journalism.

Waugh's novels are more than just expressions of disenchantment with the passing show. Novels enabled Waugh to represent himself in any way he pleased, alternately as victim and trouble-maker. He manipulated his self-image to correspond with his representation of others, innocent heroes suffering from knaves, corrupt heroes taking advantage of fools. Fluidity of self suggested that there was no need to despair, since life itself could be regarded as a kind of game, presenting one with more and more trying situations, calling for more and more selective exposure of self. As Waugh aged, he manipulated his self-image not only in writing, but also in public. He assumed and discarded roles with ease, often appearing outrageous and impatient, sometimes genial, or envious, or sorry for himself, consistent only in that he was unpredictable. As Waugh grew disenchanted with more and more causes he had once embraced, gamesmanship probably became more and more important. Paul Fussell notes that "the objective comic vision" helped Waugh to transform "anger and violence into verbal art and verbal play."[1] Writing showed Waugh that he need not always be shocked by stupidity or malice, that he could depend on them to engender dynamics of hope and disillusion in his fiction. Waugh's novels are not really satires, in that he never expected anyone to recognize folly and change. Instead, they are celebrations of human perseverance, whether wicked or noble. Rogues like Captain Grimes never change, but neither do the idealistic heroes, who find new causes when old ones have been discredited. Conflict between two types of characters reflected Waugh's own oscillation between hope and despair. He often felt frustrated, but imagining other points of view led to appreciation of them. Experience had shaped his personality, as Waugh realized that other experiences produced other types, often indifferent to the crusades he considered indispensable.

Writing was also a way to detach himself from conflict. Waugh as novelist orchestrated struggles between varied impulses, homosexual and heterosexual, social and individual, spiritual and iconoclastic. He divided himself between characters in some novels, such as *Put Out More Flags* and *Brideshead Revisited,* but by then he had learned that characters could be more than one side of a conflict. They could also represent potential selves, such as John Plant and Charles Ryder, who have been born into circumstances similar to Waugh's own, but who make different choices and develop in different ways. If character and author could start from the same point and move in different directions, they could also start from different points and approach identity later. Tony Last and Guy Crouchback are born aristocrats, but Waugh suggests identity by subjecting them to experiences like his own in love and war. Imagining alternate selves helped Waugh to overcome anger, frustration, and resentment that seem to have consumed much creativity when he was young. He saw that privilege was insignificant, fleeting in time of trials awaiting everyone. He also saw that life had value apart from associations he often depended on, apart from the writing for which he is remembered. Waugh claimed that God created individuals to do one thing no one else could do,

6: Spirals of Self-Discovery

indicating that novel writing was not his calling, only another trade, the equivalent of carpentry. Waugh was trying to be humble, but few people have written so many interesting, enjoyable books. Waugh was also disingenuous, affirming association with divinity, dismissing novels as mere artifacts, denying that they could be engaged in anything as worldly as analysis of himself. Separating himself from novels was obviously a means of self-protection, discouraging those seeking revelations about the author in his fiction. Few have listened, ignoring Waugh when he was most clear and emphatic, one more example of an apparently earnest protagonist in conflict with what he liked to regard as a deluded but persistent chorus.

Waugh's early works are his first ventures into the almost unfathomable depth of his own being, and though they never achieve the complexity of later works, they do make the latter possible, developing several methods of investigation, turning into some blind alleys, but also initiating spirals of self-discovery. These spirals extended back and forth through time, inviting Waugh to review his past, to imagine other presents, and to anticipate the future in the many books needed to understand all of his life.

Notes

Chapter 1. Not at Home in Hampstead, 1903–1916

1. Evelyn Waugh, *A Little Learning* (Boston: Little, Brown, 1964), 48.
2. Martin Stannard, *Evelyn Waugh: The Early Years 1903–1939* (New York: Norton, 1987), 6–7.
3. Ibid., 32.
4. Alec Waugh, *My Brother Evelyn and Other Portraits* (New York: Farrar, Straus and Giroux, 1967), 164.
5. Evelyn Waugh, "Father and Son," MS, Evelyn Waugh Manuscript Collection, the Harry Ransom Humanities Research Center, the University of Texas at Austin (hereafter referred to as HRHRC). Waugh changed his mind in *A Little Learning,* which contains the final version of "Father and Son," also published as "My Father" in the *Sunday Telegraph* for 2 December 1962. His "earliest memories" of Arthur "are of his gasping and choking," caused by "asthma and bronchitis" (*ALL* 64).
6. Evelyn Waugh, *The Diaries of Evelyn Waugh,* ed. Michael Davie (Boston: Little, Brown, 1976), 5.
7. Evelyn Waugh, *The Letters of Evelyn Waugh,* ed. Mark Amory (1980; reprint, New York: Penguin, 1982), 190.
8. Claud Cockburn, "Evelyn Waugh's Lost Rabbit," *The Atlantic,* December 1973, 58.
9. Evelyn Waugh, "Fidon's Confetion," MS, Evelyn Waugh Manuscript Collection, HRHRC.
10. Stannard, *Early Years,* 37–38.
11. Evelyn Waugh, diary, September 1911-June 1912, Manuscript Collection, HRHRC.
12. Stannard, *Early Years,* 39–40.
13. Cecil Beaton, *Self-Portrait with Friends: The Selected Diaries of Cecil Beaton 1926–1974,* ed. Richard Buckle (London: Weidenfeld and Nicolson, 1979), 227.
14. Humphrey Carpenter, *The Brideshead Generation: Evelyn Waugh and his Friends* (Boston: Houghton Mifflin, 1990), 49.
15. Selina Hastings, *Evelyn Waugh: A Biography* (Boston: Houghton Mifflin, 1994), 17.
16. Cockburn, "Lost Rabbit," 58–59.
17. Stannard, *Early Years,* 40.
18. Robert J. Kloss, "The Origins of Waugh's 'Victim as Hero,'" *Journal of Evolutionary Psychology* 7 (1986): 288.
19. Ibid., 285.
20. Ibid., 295, 288–89.

21. Evelyn Waugh, *Evelyn Waugh, Apprentice: The Early Writings, 1910–1927*, ed. Robert Murray Davis (Norman, Okla.: Pilgrim, 1985), 21.
22. Evelyn Waugh, "The Sheriff's Daughter or In Parker's Ranch," MS, Evelyn Waugh Manuscript Collection, HRHRC.
23. Evelyn Waugh, "A Woman's Curse," "The Slaves of Hurre Len. A Revised Rajah Shoo," and "In Quest of Thomas Lee," MSS, Evelyn Waugh Manuscript Collection, HRHRC.
24. Evelyn Waugh, "Why Britain is at War," MS, Evelyn Waugh Manuscript Collection, HRHRC.
25. Evelyn Waugh, "Told by the Refuggee," MS, Evelyn Waugh Manuscript Collection, HRHRC.
26. Evelyn Waugh, *Work Suspended* (1942); reprinted in *Work Suspended and Other Stories Written Before the Second World War* (Harmondsworth: Penguin, 1967), 170–71.
27. Evelyn Waugh, *A Handful of Dust* (1934; reprint, Boston: Little, Brown, 1962), 16.
28. Robert Murray Davis, et al., eds., *A Bibliography of Evelyn Waugh* (Troy, N.Y.: Whitston, 1986), 27.
29. Carpenter, *Brideshead Generation*, 54.
30. Alec Waugh, *My Brother Evelyn*, 167.

Chapter 2. A Less Important Place than Eton, 1917–1920

1. David Pryce-Jones, ed., *Evelyn Waugh and his World* (Boston: Little, Brown, 1973), 17.
2. Hastings, *Evelyn Waugh*, 52.
3. Pryce-Jones, *Waugh and his World*, 17.
4. Ibid., 16.
5. Ibid.
6. Stannard, *Early Years*, 47.
7. Evelyn Waugh, *The Essays, Articles and Reviews of Evelyn Waugh*, ed. Donat Gallagher (Boston: Little, Brown, 1983), 7–8.
8. Pryce-Jones, *Waugh and his World*, 18.
9. Ibid.
10. Cockburn, "Lost Rabbit," 58.
11. Alec Waugh, "Memories," *The Atlantic*, April 1974, 36.
12. Tom Driberg, "The Evelyn Waugh I Knew," *The Observer*, 20 May 1973, 30.
13. Neither essay appears to be with the rest of Waugh's juvenilia at the Harry Ransom Humanities Research Center, the University of Texas at Austin. Presumably he destroyed both of them.
14. Stannard, *Early Years*, 51.
15. Pryce-Jones, *Waugh and his World*, 19.
16. Dudley Carew, *A Fragment of Friendship: A Memory of Evelyn Waugh when Young* (London: Everest, 1974), 42.
17. Jeffrey Heath, "The Lush Places," *Evelyn Waugh Newsletter* 13, no. 2 (1979): 5.
18. Alec Waugh, *My Brother Evelyn*, 165.
19. Ibid., 166.

20. Pryce-Jones, *Waugh and his World,* 19.
21. Michael Davie, editor of the diaries, deleted the names of the two boys.

Chapter 3. Limited Bolshevist, 1920–1921 and After

1. Robert Murray Davis, *Evelyn Waugh and the Forms of his Time* (Washington: Catholic University Press of America, 1989), 180.
2. Ibid., 180–81.
3. Ibid., 181.
4. Ibid., 182.
5. Pryce-Jones, *Waugh and his World,* 20.
6. Ibid.
7. Ibid.
8. Carew, *Fragment of Friendship,* 30.
9. Tom Driberg, *Ruling Passions* (London: Jonathan Cape, 1977), 49.
10. Carew, *Fragment of Friendship,* 19.
11. Ibid., 25.
12. Ibid., 37.
13. Davis, *Bibliography,* 32–33.
14. Stannard, *Early Years,* 58.
15. Ibid., 64.
16. Evelyn Waugh, *Decline and Fall* (1928; reprint, Boston: Little, Brown, 1956), 45.
17. Evelyn Waugh, *Scott-King's Modern Europe* (London: Chapman and Hall, 1947), 9.
18. Evelyn Waugh, *Officers and Gentlemen* (Boston: Little, Brown, 1955), 22.
19. Evelyn Waugh, *Men at Arms* (Boston: Little, Brown, 1952), 115.
20. Evelyn Waugh, *Charles Ryder's Schooldays and Other Stories* (Boston: Little, Brown, 1982), 247.
21. Davis, *Forms of his Time,* 186.
22. Ibid.
23. Ibid., 186–87.
24. Ibid., 187.
25. Evelyn Waugh, *Unconditional Surrender* (London: Chapman and Hall, 1961), 300.

Chapter 4. *Et in Arcadia Ego,* 1922–1924

1. Evelyn Waugh, *A Little Order: A Selection from his Journalism,* ed. Donat Gallagher (Boston: Little, Brown, 1977), 16–17.
2. Pryce-Jones, *Waugh and his World,* 11.
3. Michael Davie, ed., *The Diaries of Evelyn Waugh,* 158.
4. Christopher Sykes, *Evelyn Waugh: A Biography* (1975; reprint, New York: Penguin, 1977), 79.
5. Alec Waugh, *My Brother Evelyn,* 172.
6. Ibid.
7. Christopher Hollis, *Oxford in the Twenties: Recollections of Five Friends* (London: Heinemann, 1976), 86.
8. Ibid.

9. Cockburn, "Lost Rabbit," 54.
10. Stannard, *Early Years*, 78.
11. Alec Waugh, *My Brother Evelyn*, 173.
12. Stannard, *Early Years*, 412.
13. Hollis, *Oxford*, 86.
14. Alec Waugh, *My Brother Evelyn*, 173–74.
15. I am grateful to Paul A. Doyle for having pointed this out.
16. Stannard, *Early Years*, 486.
17. Pryce-Jones, *Waugh and his World*, 230.
18. Evelyn Waugh, *Labels: A Mediterranean Journal* (London: Duckworth, 1930), 170.
19. Hollis, *Oxford*, 86.
20. Alec Waugh, *My Brother Evelyn*, 183.
21. Evelyn Waugh, diary, 11 November 1921, Manuscript Collection, HRHRC.
22. John W. Osborne quotes the assertion of A. L. Rowse that as an undergraduate "Evelyn had three satisfying homo affairs." If there really were three, Waugh has managed to obscure the identity of the third man. See Osborne, "The Relationship of Charles and Sebastian," *Evelyn Waugh Newsletter and Studies* 25, no. 1 (1991): 4–5, and Rowse, *Glimpses of the Great* (Lanham, Md.: University Press of America, 1985), 196.
23. Carew, *Fragment of Friendship*, 61.
24. Evelyn Waugh, letter to Dudley Carew, Manuscript Collection, HRHRC.
25. Hollis, *Oxford*, 74.
26. Carpenter, *Brideshead Generation*, 74.
27. Driberg, *Ruling Passions*, 55.
28. "Luned" is Luned Jacobs; "Alastair" is Alastair Graham.
29. Stannard, *Early Years*, 82–83.
30. Hollis, *Oxford*, 78.
31. Carpenter, *Brideshead Generation*, 113.
32. Ibid., 127.
33. Cockburn, "Lost Rabbit," 54.
34. Ibid., 55–56.
35. Alec Waugh, "Memories," *The Atlantic*, April 1974, 36.
36. Anthony Powell, Harold Acton, and John Sutro, "Three Evocations of Evelyn Waugh," *Adam International Review*, nos. 301–3 (1966): 8.
37. Hollis, *Oxford*, 88.
38. Cockburn, "Lost Rabbit," 57.
39. Hollis, *Oxford*, 85.
40. Carpenter, *Brideshead Generation*, 90.
41. Pryce-Jones, *Waugh and his World*, 37.
42. Carpenter, *Brideshead Generation*, 92.
43. Hollis, *Oxford*, 85.
44. Charles E. Linck, Jr., "The Development of Evelyn Waugh's Career: 1903–1939" (Ph.D. diss., University of Kansas, 1962), 104–5. HRHRC.
45. Evelyn Waugh, *The Life of the Right Reverend Ronald Knox* (London: Chapman and Hall, 1959), 86.
46. Evelyn Waugh, *Rossetti: His Life and Works* (New York: Dodd, Mead, 1928), 79.
47. Evelyn Waugh, "A Little Hope," MS, Evelyn Waugh Manuscript Collection, HRHRC.
48. Davis, *Bibliography*, 34.

49. Carpenter, *Brideshead Generation*, 66.
50. Davis, *Bibliography*, 36.
51. Ibid., 35–36.
52. Stannard, *Early Years*, 76.
53. Davis, *Bibliography*, 38–40.
54. Terence Greenidge, *Evelyn Waugh in Letters*, ed. Charles Linck (Commerce, Tex.: Cow Hill Press, 1994), 172. The film seems to have been lost, but *666* may have been an early version of "Out of Depth," a story Waugh would write in 1933. The hero wakes up in the twenty-fifth century, able to understand little more than the Latin words of a black priest.
55. Evelyn Waugh, letter to Dudley Carew, 1922, Manuscript Collection, HRHRC.
56. Pryce-Jones, *Waugh and his World*, 37.
57. Alec Waugh, *My Brother Evelyn*, 172.
58. Evelyn Waugh, letter to Dudley Carew, 1923, Manuscript Collection, HRHRC.
59. Anthony Powell, *Infants of the Spring*, vol. 1 of *To Keep the Ball Rolling: The Memoirs of Anthony Powell* (London: Heinemann, 1976), 166. Waugh seems to have done no more than illustrate programs for the Oxford University Dramatic Society.
60. Ibid., 154.
61. Evelyn Waugh, letter to Dudley Carew, 1924, Manuscript Collection, HRHRC.
62. Jeffrey Heath, *The Picturesque Prison: Evelyn Waugh and his Writing* (Kingston, Ont.: McGill-Queen's University Press, 1982), 3–4.
63. Carpenter, *Brideshead Generation*, 124.
64. Evelyn Waugh, letter to Dudley Carew, 1924, Manuscript Collection, HRHRC.
65. Stannard, *Early Years*, 94–95.

Chapter 5. Oxford Revisited, 1924 and After

1. Stannard, *Early Years*, 95.
2. Carew, *Fragment of Friendship*, 45.
3. Martin Stannard thinks the account of the brothel "grossly exaggerated," refers to Waugh's "false worldliness . . . which probably disguises a fastidious distaste for such exoticism," and suggests that Waugh was "pretending to himself that the price was 'prohibitive.'" See *Early Years*, 122. Waugh often grossly exaggerated in his diary, and Stannard perceives that the Louvre interested him more than brothels, but it is hard to believe that Waugh wrote "attractive" if he meant "distasteful." It seems plausible that Waugh could not afford 300 francs for a prostitute, since he was earning fewer than £200 a year as a schoolmaster. Stannard seems once again to be minimizing Waugh's homosexuality.
4. Evelyn Waugh, "The Balance," in *Georgian Stories 1926* (New York: Putnam, 1927), 301.
5. Driberg, *Ruling Passions*, 56.
6. Julian Jebb, "Evelyn Waugh," in *Writers at Work:* The Paris Review *Interviews*, Third Series (New York: Viking, 1967), 108.
7. Heath, *Picturesque Prison*, 9.
8. Evelyn Waugh, *Black Mischief* (New York: Farrar and Rinehart, 1932), 147.

9. Evelyn Waugh, *Put Out More Flags* (Boston: Little, Brown, 1942), 37.
10. Heath, *Picturesque Prison,* 153, 155.
11. Evelyn Waugh, *Brideshead Revisited* (Boston: Little, Brown, 1945), 21.
12. Robert Murray Davis, Brideshead Revisited: *The Past Redeemed* (Boston: Twayne, 1990), 72.
13. Ibid., 51.
14. Heath, *Picturesque Prison,* 178.
15. Greenidge, *Waugh in Letters,* 4.
16. Heath, *Picturesque Prison,* 178.
17. Terry Eagleton, *Exiles and Emigres: Studies in Modern Literature* (London: Chatto and Windus, 1970), 60.
18. Davis, Brideshead, 68–78.
19. Ibid., 86.
20. Ibid., 112.
21. Ibid.
22. Ibid., 113.
23. Ibid., 122.
24. Carpenter, *Brideshead Generation,* 357.
25. Davis, Brideshead, 53–54.
26. Ibid., 73.
27. Ibid., 107.
28. Evelyn Waugh, *The Ordeal of Gilbert Pinfold* (London: Chapman and Hall, 1957), 75.
29. Evelyn Waugh, *Basil Seal Rides Again* (Boston: Little, Brown, 1963), 10. HRHRC.
30. Evelyn Waugh, "*Dominus Illuminatio Mea,*" MS, Evelyn Waugh Manuscript Collection, HRHRC.
31. Stannard, *Early Years,* 422.

Chapter 6. Spirals of Self-Discovery

1. Paul Fussell, "Waugh in his Letters," in *The Boy Scout Handbook and Other Observations* (New York: Oxford University Press, 1982), 193.

Bibliography

There are many other sources by and about Evelyn Waugh. The following are those I have found most useful, especially for Waugh's youth and writing related to youth.

Beaton, Cecil. *Self-Portrait with Friends: The Selected Diaries of Cecil Beaton 1926–1974.* Edited by Richard Buckle. London: Weidenfeld and Nicolson, 1979.

Beaty, Frederick L. *The Ironic World of Evelyn Waugh: A Study of Eight Novels.* DeKalb: Northern Illinois University Press, 1992.

Blayac, Alain, ed. *Evelyn Waugh: New Directions.* New York: St. Martin's, 1992.

Bradbury, Malcolm. *Evelyn Waugh.* London: Oliver and Boyd, 1964.

Carens, James F., ed. *Critical Essays on Evelyn Waugh.* Boston: G. K. Hall, 1987.

———. *The Satiric Art of Evelyn Waugh.* Seattle: University of Washington Press, 1966.

Carew, Dudley. *A Fragment of Friendship: A Memory of Evelyn Waugh when Young.* London: Everest, 1974.

Carpenter, Humphrey. *The Brideshead Generation: Evelyn Waugh and his Friends.* Boston: Houghton Mifflin, 1990.

Cockburn, Claud. "Evelyn Waugh's Lost Rabbit." *The Atlantic,* December 1973, 53–59.

Cook, William J., Jr. *Masks, Modes, and Morals: The Art of Evelyn Waugh.* Rutherford, N.J.: Fairleigh Dickinson University Press, 1971.

Cooper, Artemis, ed. *The Letters of Evelyn Waugh and Diana Cooper.* New York: Ticknor and Fields, 1992.

Davis, Robert Murray, Paul A. Doyle, Donat Gallagher, Charles E. Linck, and Winnifred M. Bogaards, eds. *A Bibliography of Evelyn Waugh.* Troy, N.Y.: Whitston, 1986.

Davis, Robert Murray. Brideshead Revisited: *The Past Redeemed.* Boston: Twayne, 1990.

———. *Evelyn Waugh and the Forms of his Time.* Washington: Catholic University of America Press, 1989.

———. *Evelyn Waugh, Writer.* Norman, Okla.: Pilgrim, 1981.

Doyle, Paul A. *A Reader's Companion to the Novels and Short Stories of Evelyn Waugh.* Norman, Okla.: Pilgrim, 1989.

Driberg, Tom. "The Evelyn Waugh I Knew." *The Observer,* 20 May 1973, 30–34.

———. *Ruling Passions.* London: Jonathan Cape, 1977.

Eagleton, Terry. *Exiles and Emigres: Studies in Modern Literature.* London: Chatto and Windus, 1970.

Fussell, Paul. "Waugh in his Letters." In *The Boy Scout Handbook and Other Observations*. New York: Oxford University Press, 1982.

Garnett, Robert R. *From Grimes to Brideshead: The Early Novels of Evelyn Waugh*. Lewisburg, Pa.: Bucknell University Press, 1990.

Green, Martin. *Children of the Sun: A Narrative of 'Decadence' in England after 1918*. New York: Basic Books, 1976.

Greene, Donald. "A Partiality for Lords: Evelyn Waugh and Snobbery." *American Scholar* 58 (1989): 444–59.

Greenidge, Terence. *Degenerate Oxford?: A Critical Study of Modern University Life*. London: Chapman and Hall, 1930.

———. *Evelyn Waugh in Letters*. Edited by Charles Linck. Commerce, Tex.: Cow Hill Press, 1994.

Hastings, Selina. *Evelyn Waugh: A Biography*. Boston: Houghton Mifflin, 1994.

Heath, Jeffrey. "The Lush Places." *Evelyn Waugh Newsletter* 13, no. 2 (1979): 5–8.

———. *The Picturesque Prison: Evelyn Waugh and his Writing*. Kingston, Ont.: McGill-Queen's University Press, 1982.

Hollis, Christopher. *Evelyn Waugh*. London: Longmans, 1954.

———. *Oxford in the Twenties: Recollections of Five Friends*. London: Heinemann, 1976.

Jebb, Julian. "Evelyn Waugh." In *Writers at Work: The Paris Review Interviews*. Third Series. New York: Viking, 1967.

Kloss, Robert J. "The Origins of Waugh's 'Victim as Hero.'" *Journal of Evolutionary Psychology* 7 (1986): 285–97.

Linck, Charles E., Jr. "The Development of Evelyn Waugh's Career: 1903–1939." Ph.D. diss., University of Kansas, 1962. The Harry Ransom Humanities Research Center, The University of Texas at Austin.

Littlewood, Ian. *The Writings of Evelyn Waugh*. Oxford: Basil Blackwell, 1983.

Lodge, David. *Evelyn Waugh*. New York: Columbia University Press, 1971.

McCartney, George. *Confused Roaring: Evelyn Waugh and the Modernist Tradition*. Bloomington: Indiana University Press, 1987.

Osborne, John W. "The Relationship of Charles and Sebastian." *Evelyn Waugh Newsletter and Studies* 25, no. 1 (1991): 4–5.

Powell, Anthony. *Infants of the Spring*. Vol. 1 of *To Keep the Ball Rolling: The Memoirs of Anthony Powell*. London: Heinemann, 1976.

Pryce-Jones, David, ed. *Evelyn Waugh and his World*. Boston: Little, Brown, 1973.

Rowse, A. L. *Glimpses of the Great*. Lanham, Md.: University Press of America, 1985.

Stannard, Martin, ed. *Evelyn Waugh: The Critical Heritage*. Boston: Routledge, 1984.

———. *Evelyn Waugh: The Early Years 1903–1939*. New York: Norton, 1987.

———. *Evelyn Waugh: The Later Years 1939–1966*. New York: Norton, 1992.

Stopp, Frederick J. *Evelyn Waugh: Portrait of an Artist*. London: Chapman and Hall, 1958.

Sykes, Christopher. *Evelyn Waugh: A Biography*. 1975. Reprint, New York: Penguin, 1977.

Waugh, Alec. *The Early Years of Alec Waugh.* London: Cassell, 1962.

———. *The Loom of Youth.* London: Richards, 1917.

———. "Memories." *The Atlantic,* April 1974, 36.

———. *My Brother Evelyn and Other Portraits.* New York: Farrar, Straus and Giroux, 1967.

Waugh, Arthur. *One Man's Road.* London: Chapman and Hall, 1931.

Waugh, Evelyn. "The Balance: A Yarn of the Good Old Days of Broad Trousers and High Necked Jumpers." In *Georgian Stories 1926.* New York: Putnam, 1927.

———. *Basil Seal Rides Again or The Rake's Regress.* Boston: Little, Brown, 1963. The Harry Ransom Humanities Research Center, The University of Texas at Austin.

———. *Black Mischief.* New York: Farrar and Rinehart, 1932.

———. *Brideshead Revisited: The Sacred and Profane Memories of Captain Charles Ryder.* Boston: Little, Brown, 1945.

———. *Charles Ryder's Schooldays and Other Stories.* Boston: Little, Brown, 1982.

———. *Decline and Fall.* 1928. Reprint, Boston: Little, Brown, 1956.

———. *The Diaries of Evelyn Waugh.* Edited by Michael Davie. Boston: Little, Brown, 1976.

———. Diaries and Stories, 1910–1916; Diaries, 1919–1921; and Diaries and Letters, 1922–1926. MSS. Evelyn Waugh Manuscript Collection. The Harry Ransom Humanities Research Center, The University of Texas at Austin.

———. "*Dominus Illuminatio Mea.*" MS. Evelyn Waugh Manuscript Collection. The Harry Ransom Humanities Research Center, The University of Texas at Austin.

———. *Edmund Campion.* New York: Sheed and Ward, 1935.

———. *The End of the Battle* [*Unconditional Surrender*]. Boston: Little, Brown, 1961.

———. *The Essays, Articles and Reviews of Evelyn Waugh.* Edited by Donat Gallagher. Boston: Little, Brown, 1983.

———. *Evelyn Waugh, Apprentice: The Early Writings, 1910–1927.* Edited by Robert Murray Davis. Norman, Okla.: Pilgrim, 1985.

———. "Father and Son." MS. Evelyn Waugh Manuscript Collection. The Harry Ransom Humanities Research Center, The University of Texas at Austin.

———. *A Handful of Dust.* 1934. Reprint, Boston: Little, Brown, 1962.

———. *Helena.* 1950. Reprint, New York: Penguin, 1963.

———. *Labels: A Mediterranean Journal.* London: Duckworth, 1930.

———. *The Letters of Evelyn Waugh.* Edited by Mark Amory. 1980. Reprint, New York: Penguin, 1982.

———. *The Life of the Right Reverend Ronald Knox, Fellow of Trinity College, Oxford and Pronotary Apostolic to his Holiness Pope Pius XII.* London: Chapman and Hall, 1959.

———. "A Little Hope." MS. Evelyn Waugh Manuscript Collection. The Harry Ransom Humanities Research Center, The University of Texas at Austin.

———. *A Little Learning: The First Volume of an Autobiography.* Boston: Little, Brown, 1964.

———. *A Little Order: A Selection from his Journalism.* Edited by Donat Gallagher. Boston: Little, Brown, 1977.

———. *Love Among the Ruins: A Romance of the Near Future.* London: Chapman and Hall, 1953.

———. *The Loved One: An Anglo-American Tragedy.* Boston: Little, Brown, 1948.

———. *Men at Arms.* Boston: Little, Brown, 1952.

———. *Officers and Gentlemen.* Boston: Little, Brown, 1955.

———. *The Ordeal of Gilbert Pinfold: A Conversation Piece.* London: Chapman and Hall, 1957.

———. *P.R.B.: An Essay on the Pre-Raphaelite Brotherhood, 1847–1854.* N.p.: Alastair Graham, 1926. The Harry Ransom Humanities Research Center, The University of Texas at Austin.

———. *Put Out More Flags.* Boston: Little, Brown, 1942.

———. *Rossetti: His Life and Works.* New York: Dodd, Mead, 1928.

———. *The Scarlet Woman: An Ecclesiastical Melodrama.* 1924. Reprint, *Evelyn Waugh Newsletter* 3, no. 2 (1969): 2–7.

———. Videocassette. *The Scarlet Woman: An Ecclesiastical Melodrama.* Little Rock: Video Duplicating Services, 1993.

———. *Scoop.* Boston: Little, Brown, 1938.

———. *Scott-King's Modern Europe.* London: Chapman and Hall, 1947.

———. *Sword of Honour. A Final Version of the Novels: Men at Arms (1952), Officers and Gentlemen (1955), and Unconditional Surrender (1961).* London: Chapman and Hall, 1965.

———. *Unconditional Surrender.* London: Chapman and Hall, 1961.

———. *Vile Bodies.* 1930. Reprint, Boston: Little, Brown, 1958.

———. *When the Going was Good.* 1946. Reprint, Boston: Little, Brown, 1984.

———. *Work Suspended.* 1942. Reprint, in *Work Suspended and Other Stories Written Before the Second World War.* Harmondsworth: Penguin, 1967.

Wölk, Gerhard. "Evelyn Waugh: A Supplementary Checklist of Criticism." *Evelyn Waugh Newsletter* 23, no. 2 (1989): 6–7; *Evelyn Waugh Newsletter and Studies* 24, no. 2 (1990): 6–7; 25, no. 2 (1991): 7–8; 26, no. 2 (1992): 5–6; 27, no. 2 (1993): 6–7.

Index

Abyssinia, 112, 173
Actium, Battle of, 31
Acton, Harold, 114, 119, 120, 123, 141, 145, 146, 164, 174
Ada (character), 149–50
aestheticism, 78, 120–23, 128, 134, 136, 147, 157, 163
Amazon, 33
Anglican Church, 27, 39–40, 43, 91
Annan, Noel, 69
anti-Semitism, 31–32, 54
"Antony, Who Sought Things That Were Lost," 133
Apthorpe (character), 98
architecture, 39, 72, 97, 103, 105, 106, 170, 172, 173, 176
aristocracy, 28–29, 40–41, 74, 91, 95, 121, 163, 168, 176, 177, 178
"*Ars Amoris* for _____," 68–69
Ascension Day, 44–45
Athens, 144
athletics, 62, 63–64, 79, 123
Atlantic, The, 122
Author-Biography (Hunt), 112
Azania (setting), 156

Babcock, Sister (nurse), 47
"Balance, The," 146–50, 153, 155, 157, 161
Balfour, Patrick, 139
Balliol College (Oxford), 50, 108, 117, 118, 119, 124, 125, 126, 139, 169, 172
Barnell, Tom (character), 33
Barnes (boy at Lancing), 53
Barnsley (boy at Lancing), 67
Basil Seal Rides Again, 103, 170
Basingstoke, Lord (character), 147
Bates, Frank (character), 98, 99
Baycraw (character), 23–24
Beaton, Cecil, 26
Beauchamp, seventh Earl, 162
Bedivere (character), 78

Beerbohm, Max, 88
Beggar's Opera, The (Gay), 92
Belgium, 33
"Bells of Heaven, The" (Hodgson), 100
Bergson, Henri, 84
Berkhamsted School, 49
Beste-Chetwynde, Margot (character), 134, 153
Bevan (boy at Lancing), 82, 98
Bible in Art, The, 46
Black Mischief, 155–56, 177
blacks, 134
Blanche, Anthony (character), 78, 164–66
Bleak House (Dickens), 19
Blue Grotto (setting), 165
Boase, T. S. R., 115, 134
Bollinger Club (*Decline and Fall*), 150–51, 152, 154, 155
bolshevism, 53, 55, 62–63, 69, 71, 72, 79–80, 81, 82, 90, 93, 126
Boot, William (hero of *Scoop*), 74, 154
Borrowington, Lord (character), 127
Bors (character), 78
Bottomley, Horatio, 72, 74
Bourchier, Basil, 39, 40
Bowlby, Mrs. Henry, 67
Bowlby, Rev. Henry, 49, 52–53, 58, 107
Bowra, Maurice, 129
Brains Trust, 128
Brideshead Revisited, 33, 41, 78, 97–98, 99, 102, 170, 176–77, 178; and Oxford, 101, 157–69, 174
Bright Young People, 176, 177
Bulfrey (setting), 73–74
Bulfrey Combe (setting), 73–74, 75
Bullingdon Club, 116, 154
Burghclere, Lady, 114
"Buttocks" (boy at Lancing), 53
Byron, Lord, 83–85

Cambridge University, 149, 173
Campion Hall (Oxford), 173–74

Canterbury, 91, 92
Cantonville Chase (setting), 24
Carew, Dudley, 64, 83, 87, 88, 89, 117, 132, 136, 137, 138, 139, 144
Carmichael, A. A. (character), 99
Carpenter, Humphrey, 27, 39, 165
Carroll, Lewis, 169
Cattermole, Major (character), 169–70
Celia (character), 33
Chagford, 21
Chapman and Hall, 19, 113, 116, 136
"Charles Ryder's Schooldays," 97–102
Chatham (club), 130
Cherwell, 105, 123, 126, 131, 133, 134, 173
Cholmondley, Sebastien (character), 134
Christ Church (Oxford), 128, 129, 154
Christianity, 40–41, 47–48, 69, 71, 84, 85, 86–87, 94
Clonmore, Billy, 142
Cockburn, Claud, 22, 28, 49, 54, 111, 121–22, 124–25
Coetz (master at Heath Mount), 34
Collins (character), 158, 159, 166
"Come to the Coach-house Door, Boys," 37
Common Entrance examination, 44, 46
"Community Spirit, The," 93
Compleat Imbiber, The (Ray), 171
Connolly, Cyril, 108, 125, 133, 174
"Conspiracy to Murder," 135
"Convention," 72
Conversion, 82–83, 85, 100
Cooper, Mr. (master at Heath Mount), 24
Cordelia (character), 165
Corinthians, First, 72
Corpse Club, 93
Crease, Francis, 64, 65–67, 69–70, 71, 86, 100
cricket, 18, 34, 50, 81, 84, 121, 123
"Cristopher" (character), 33
Crouchback, Guy (hero of war trilogy), 41, 74, 76, 77, 96, 104, 178
Cruttwell, C. R. M. F., 109–15, 125, 127, 129, 134, 140, 153, 169
cubism, 50–51
"Curse of the Horse Race, The," 23, 32
Curtis, Mr. (character), 134–35

Curtis-Dunne (character), 100
Cynic, The, 38–39, 51

Daily Mail, 105, 106
Daily Telegraph, 35
D'Arcy, Father Martin, 173
Davie, Michael, 25, 107, 182 n. 21
Davis, Robert Murray, 73, 74, 75, 98, 99, 101, 158, 160, 164–65, 166, 168
Dawkins, R. M., 129–30
"Death Wish, The," 77, 104
Decline and Fall, 23, 62, 78, 96, 103, 104, 105, 169; and Oxford, 113, 124, 134, 150–55, 157, 159, 166, 167, 170, 176
diaries (Evelyn Waugh), 145, 160, 177, 184 n. 3; in childhood, 23, 24–25, 28–29, 32, 36, 37, 38; at Lancing, 55–56, 58, 62, 67, 78, 81, 85, 93, 97, 100, 102, 182 n. 21; and Oxford, 107, 118, 138, 162
Die-Hards, 130–31
Digby-Vaine-Trumpington, Alastair (character), 155, 157
Dilettanti, 56–57, 63
Doure, Adam (hero of "The Balance"), 147–50, 153
Doyle, Paul A., 183 n. 15
Drawing and Design, 50–51
Dream of Gerontius (Newman), 41
Driberg, Tom, 61, 64, 85, 86, 108, 115, 117–18, 132, 141, 154
Duggan, Alfred, 174
"Dumpy" (master at Heath Mount), 25
"Dungy" (boy at Lancing), 53, 98

Eagleton, Terry, 164
Early Years of Alec Waugh, The, 94
Edmund Campion, 173
"Edward of Unique Achievement," 134–35, 153
Egerton-Verschoyle, Mr. (character), 147
El Maduff (character), 33
Elmley, Viscount (eighth Earl Beauchamp), 126
"Englishman's Home, An," 113
Erasmus, 110
Eton College, 26, 49, 50, 60, 61, 117, 120
Euripides, 146

INDEX

"Father and Son," 180 n. 5
Fernden (school), 25, 43
Fidon (character), 23–24
"Fidon's Confetion," 23–24, 32, 33, 76
First World War, 33–37, 39, 41, 43, 45, 46, 47, 49, 52, 61, 65, 73–75, 76, 96, 97–98, 110, 171–72
FitzHerbert, Giles, 174
Flashfire Dick (character), 33
Fletcher (boy at Heath Mount), 27
Flyte, Sebastian (character), 158, 159–60, 161, 162–65, 166, 167
Flytes (family in *Brideshead Revisited*), 41, 164
"Fragments: They Dine with the Past," 135
France, 36, 143
Freeman, Mrs. (acquaintance), 28
Freud, Sigmund, 160
Fulford, Roger, 44, 45, 47, 48, 49, 50, 53, 54, 64, 68, 79, 81
Furness, Mr. (character), 147
Fussell, Paul, 178

Gardner, Evelyn (first wife), 56, 76, 114, 144, 145, 149, 176, 177
Geogan (boy at Heath Mount), 27
Germans, 31–32, 34, 36, 54, 74
Gielgud, Tasha, 145
Gladys (character), 149
God, 65, 85–86, 89, 91, 102, 163, 177, 178
"God Moves in a Mysterious Way" (hymn), 69
Gods (at Lancing), 80–81
Golders Green, 32, 54, 107, 108, 126–27, 134
Gordon, E. B. (master at Lancing), 58, 59, 63, 64, 98, 100
Gordon, George (Lord Byron), 83–85
Gosse, Edmund, 19
Graham, Alastair, 118, 120, 140, 141, 143–44, 145, 146, 149, 157, 158, 162, 163, 164, 166, 167, 183 n. 28
Graves (character), 98–100
Greene, Graham, 49
Greenidge, Terence, 111, 114, 117, 126, 127, 162, 174
"Groves, The" (latrines), 45–46, 68
Guthrie, James, 142

Hale, G. V., 88–89, 90
Hamlet (Shakespeare), 72, 121
Hampstead, 18, 22, 31–32, 36, 46, 54, 73–74, 104, 107, 119
Hampstead Garden Suburb, 39
Hampstead Heath, 54, 126
Handful of Dust, A, 33, 37, 113, 156, 176, 177
Hansard, Mrs. (friend of Alec), 144
Harper's Bazaar, 113
Harris, Dick (master at Lancing), 44, 45, 46, 47, 58, 98, 100
Hastings, Selina, 46
Hay, Mrs. (character), 147
Head's House (Lancing), 58, 63, 64, 79, 80, 81, 82
Heath, Jeffrey, 64, 138, 154, 157, 162, 163
Heatherley's Art School, 141, 142
Heath Mount School, 25–26, 27–28, 34, 35, 38, 41, 43, 44, 46, 47, 54, 57, 114
Hertford College (Oxford), 50, 95, 107, 111, 113, 115, 116, 117, 124, 136, 140, 154
heterosexuality, 92, 119, 133, 134, 145, 156, 176, 178
Hiawatha (Longfellow), 41
"History Previous," 132
Hodgson, Ralph, 100
Hollis, Christopher, 111, 112, 114, 117, 119, 123–24, 125–26, 131, 143, 146, 171
homosexuality, 43, 61, 68, 94–95, 106, 117–20, 124, 125, 127, 133, 137, 142, 145–46, 157, 159–60, 163, 164, 166, 168, 170, 177, 178, 183 n. 22, 184 n. 3
"House: An Anti-climax, The," 82
House Shield (Lancing), 79–80
Howard, Brian, 145, 164
Howitt (master at Lancing), 47
Hunt, Cecil, 112
Hurre Len (character), 33
Hynchcliffe, Mr. (master at Heath Mount), 26, 38
Hypocrites' Club, 117–18, 125, 126, 129, 138, 141, 142

immortality, 41, 56, 65, 77, 85, 87
"In Defence of Cubism," 50–51
India, 19, 131
"In Quest of Thomas Lee," 33
Ireland, 140, 143

Isis, 105, 111–12, 120, 126, 130, 131, 132, 136, 139
"I Suppose That When I Leave," 88–89
Italian Renaissance, 109
Italy, 146
Ivy House (Hampstead), 21

Jack (character), 32–33
Jacobs, Barbara, 51–52, 75
Jacobs, Luned, 52, 55, 75, 118, 183 n. 28
Jasper (character), 158, 161, 164
Jeremy (character), 132–33
Jews, 31–32, 54, 77–78, 134
Joad, C. E. M., 128–29
John Bull, 72
Jolliffe, John, 113
Julia (character), 160, 165
juvenilia (Evelyn Waugh), 17, 23–25, 28–29, 32–34, 37, 38–39, 41, 103

Kaiser Wilhelm II, 34
Kanyi, Madame (character), 104
Kenya, 141
King James Version, 46
Kloss, Robert J., 30
Knox, Ronald, 127–28, 171–72
Kut-al-Imara House (setting), 96

Labels, 113–14, 128, 170
Lanchester, Elsa, 126
"Lancing Chapel," 64–65, 69
Lancing College, 25, 26, 27, 41, 51, 53, 54, 55, 66, 67, 68, 75, 76, 77, 78, 89, 95, 106, 107, 108, 109, 115, 116, 117, 118, 119, 126, 137; athletics at, 62, 63–64, 79, 123; code of conduct, 44; debates at, 56–58, 69, 131; during First World War, 45–47, 49, 52; founding of, 43, 97; houses at, 58, 64; magazine, 80, 90, 91, 92–93; masters at, 58–60, 65, 90, 93, 114; Officers' Training Corps, 47, 60–62, 70, 72, 79–81; rank among public schools, 49–50, 60; religious beliefs at, 47–48, 86; in Waugh's fiction, 96–102, 104, 131–32
Lancing College Debating Society, 24, 90, 91, 92, 105
Landor, Walter Savage, 71
Last, Tony (hero of *A Handful of Dust*), 33, 37, 74, 154, 178

Launcelot (character), 78
Lebouge, Monsieur (character), 34
Lee, Thomas (character), 33
"Legend: A Sequel to Twelve Years On," 131–32
Legge, Guy (character), 135
"Lenard" (character), 33
Limits (society), 38
"Little Hope, A," 130
Little Learning, A (autobiography), 54, 146, 162, 180 n. 5; on childhood, 17, 22, 25, 26, 27, 32; on Lancing, 46, 48, 51, 55, 60, 64, 65, 69, 78, 80, 102–3; on Oxford, 108, 109–10, 115, 117, 118, 125, 128, 139, 154, 160, 170, 174–75
Lloyd George, David, 57, 124
London, 18, 25, 36, 43, 44, 46, 48, 51, 52, 54, 107, 122, 139, 142
Longe, John, 81, 85, 88–89, 90, 93, 94
Longfellow, Henry Wadsworth, 41
Loom of Youth, The (Alec Waugh), 43–44, 52, 73, 79, 82, 84
Lord Randal (ballad), 20
Lucas (master at Lancing), 59, 60
Lucy (nurse), 18, 23
Ludendorff offensive, 52
Lundy Island, 143
Lurnstein (character), 77–78
Lygon, Hugh, 146, 162, 163, 164, 166, 167
Lyne, Cedric (character), 157

Macassor, Mr. (character), 146–47
magic, 21, 135, 141
Malory, Sir Thomas, 78
"Maps," 72
Marchmain, Lady (character), 163
Master of Scone (character), 151, 153
Mayne, Rachel, 144
Men at Arms, 96, 98
Midsomer Norton (site of aunts' house), 17, 20, 21, 23, 30, 33, 39, 42, 46, 107, 141
mid-Victorian ethos, 17, 20, 42
military service, 21, 25, 61–62, 95, 96, 102, 168, 169, 170, 177
Mill, John Stuart, 132
"Mr. Loveday's Little Outing," 113
Mitford, Nancy, 118, 160
Moira (character), 75

Molson, Hugh (Lord), 55, 56, 57, 61, 64, 90, 91–92, 107
Moon, Wilfred, 155
Morris, William, 128
Morte D'Arthur (Malory), 78
"Multa Pecunia," 32, 33
"Muriel" (therapist's daughter), 30
Murray, Basil, 124, 156
Mussolini, Benito, 113
"My Father," 162, 180 n. 5
"My History," 24–25

Nash's Pall Mall Magazine, 113
"National Game, The," 123
New College (Oxford), 107, 166
Newman, John Henry Cardinal, 41, 158
Newman Society (Oxford), 173
"new men" (Lancing), 44
New Reform Club, 124–25, 130
New Statesman, 129
North End (village), 18, 20, 54

"Ode on the Intimations of Immaturity," 83–85
Officers and Gentlemen, 96
Officers' Training Corps, 47, 60–62, 70, 72, 73, 74, 79–81, 82, 86
O'Malley (character), 98–99
"On His Seventy-fifth Birthday" (Landor), 71
Ordeal of Gilbert Pinfold, The, 169
Osborne, John W., 183 n. 22
"Out of Depth," 184 n. 54
Oxford Broom, 105, 133
Oxford Carlton Club, 130, 134
Oxford Magazine, 130
Oxford Movement, 97
Oxford Railway Club, 174
Oxford Union, 24, 105, 106, 115–16, 130–31, 135, 138, 156, 170–71
Oxford University, 28, 50, 56, 60, 76, 86–87, 91, 93, 96; clubs, 117–18, 123, 124, 125, 126, 129, 130, 141; dons at, 25, 109–15, 116, 125–30; examinations, 110, 117, 132, 134; homosexuality at, 68, 95, 117–20, 124, 127, 142, 145, 183 n. 22; politics at 124, 130–31; value of, 105–6, 107, 118; Waugh's first terms, 108–10, 115–17, 120; in Waugh's nonfiction, 113–14, 127–30, 139, 154, 160, 170–75; in Waugh's novels, 101, 106, 109, 124, 125, 150–70, 176, 177; in Waugh's stories, 113, 131–35, 146–50 184 n. 54; Waugh's studies at, 105–6, 108–10, 115, 118, 132, 138–39; Waugh visits, 106–7, 141–43, 155
Oxford University Dramatic Society (O.U.D.S.), 116, 121, 138, 184 n. 59

pantheism, 84
Pappenheimer (boy at Heath Mount), 27, 34
Pares, Richard, 118–19, 120, 125, 129, 130, 133, 158, 167, 169–70
Paris, 95, 116, 137, 145, 162, 166, 167
Parliament, 112
Pastmaster, Peter (character), 155, 157
Pennyfeather, Paul (hero of *Decline and Fall*), 77, 96, 150–52, 153–55, 156, 157, 167, 168
Peter (hero of unfinished novel), 73, 74–75
Philbrick (undergraduate/character), 123–24
"Philosopher, The," 77, 78
Pistol Troop, 31–32, 38, 54
Plant, John (hero of *Work Suspended*), 35, 178
Plunket Greene, Olivia, 143, 144–45, 149
Ponsonby, Elizabeth, 145
"Portrait of Young Man with Career," 132–33
Port Said, 144
Postlethwaite, Mr. (character), 151, 153
Potts, Arthur (character), 152, 153
Powell, Anthony, 119, 123
Poxe, Lord (character), 135
Praed, Winthrop Mackworth, 67
P.R.B.: An Essay on the Pre-Raphaelite Brotherhood, 1847–1854, 143
Prendergast (undergraduate/character), 124
prisons, 96, 138, 176
Proust, Marcel, 146
Pryce-Jones, Alan, 107
Punch, 36
Put Out More Flags, 78, 113, 156–57, 164, 177, 178
Puttock (master at Lancing), 59

Quennell, Peter, 119, 124, 125, 136
Quest, Imogen (character), 147

"Rajah Shoo" (story), 33
Ralf (character in unfinished novel), 73, 74, 75
Ralfe (character in "Fidon's Confetion"), 23-24
Ray, Cyril, 171
"Reconsiderations: an Oxford book of Wild Oats," 93
Red Cross, 34, 35
refugees, 35
reincarnation, 56
representative government, 109
"Return of Launcelot after the Siege of Joyous Gard," 78
Rhine River, 110
Rodd, Peter, 156
Roman Catholic Church, 17, 31, 40-41, 69, 95, 102, 106, 112, 114, 126-27, 141, 149, 163, 168-69, 175, 176, 177
Romantic period, 83, 84
Ronald Knox, 127-28, 172
Ross (character), 82
Rossetti, 128, 155, 170, 176
Rousseau, Jean Jacques, 132
Roxburgh, J. F., 60, 64, 67-68, 69-70, 96, 99, 112, 115
Roxburgh of Stowe (Annan), 69
Ruskin School of Art, 137, 161
Russian Revolution, 53
Ryder, Charles (hero of *Brideshead Revisited* and "Charles Ryder's Schooldays"), 97, 98-102, 158-68, 169, 178

St. Jude's (Hampstead), 39, 48
St. Simon, Comte de, 132
Samgrass, Mr. (character), 167
Sandhurst, 36
Scarlet Woman, The, 126-27, 142
Scone College (*Decline and Fall*), 151, 152, 154
Scoop, 156, 177
Scotland Yard, 32
Scott-King's Modern Europe, 96, 167
Scott-Moncrieff, C. K., 146
Scoundrel, the (nurse), 29
Seal, Basil (character), 37, 74, 103-4, 124, 155-56, 157, 166, 170
Second World War, 21, 49, 55, 62, 104, 128, 172, 177

Seth (character), 156
"Seven Deadly Sins, The," 133-34
Shakespeare Society, 79
Shaw, George Bernard, 72, 87, 156
Sherborne (school), 43, 94
"Sheriff's Daughter or In Parker's Ranch, The," 32-33
Silk, Ambrose (character), 78, 156, 164, 166
"Sir Thomas More and the English Lay Recusants" (Trevor-Roper), 129
666 (film), 134, 184n. 54
"Slaves of Hurre Len, The," 33
Sniggs, Mr. (character), 150-51, 153
Soviet Union, 177
Spectator, 26
Spenser (boy at Heath Mount), 26
Spierpoint (setting), 97, 98, 100, 101
Stannard, Martin, 18, 25, 64, 119, 133, 144, 184n. 3
Stewart (character), 82
Story of Rome, The (gift), 31
Stowe (school), 60
strikes, 55, 76-77
Stubbs (character), 152, 153
suicide, 89-90, 129, 135, 146, 147-48
Sutro, John, 146, 174
Sword of Honour, 177. See also war trilogy
Sykes, Christopher, 146, 160, 174

Tablet, The, 170
Temple at Thatch, The, 141, 146
Texas, University of, 25, 37, 181n. 13
Thames River, 30
Theodosia (great-grandmother), 40
Thirty-Four Decorative Designs (Crease), 66
Tiresias, 164
"Told by the Refuggee," 34, 36
Tom (hero of "Fidon's Confetion"), 23-24
Tonbridge (school), 50
Townsend (hero of *Conversion*), 82-83
Treble (master at Lancing), 59
Trevor-Roper, Hugh (Lord Dacre), 129
Tse Fing (character), 33
Tulkinghorn, Mr. (character), 19
"Twilight of Language, The," 57

INDEX

"Unacademic Exercise," 135
Unconditional Surrender, 103–4, 169–70
Underhill (house), 18, 21, 24, 65
"University Sermon to Idealists Who Are Serious Minded and Intelligent, A" 132
Urquhart, Sligger, 125–28, 129, 133, 153, 167

Vaughan, Ernest (character), 147
Vernon, Mr. (master at Heath Mount), 25, 34
Victorian age, 17, 120
Vile Bodies, 105, 155, 176

Wales, 129–30, 143, 152, 162
Walpole, Horace, 147
war gap, 81, 93
War Office, 35
war trilogy (*Sword of Honour*), 41, 76, 77, 98, 101, 104, 169, 177
"Was Oxford Worth While?" 105, 156
Waste Land, The (Eliot), 164
"Water Rat" (master at Heath Mount), 25
Waugh, Alec (brother), 18, 25, 30, 38, 51, 54–55, 66, 94, 105, 106, 119, 144, 146; in Evelyn's writing, 23–24, 73–76, 83–85; during First World War, 34, 36, 37, 52; *The Loom of Youth*, 43–44, 52, 73, 79, 82, 84; and Oxford, 107, 110–11, 112, 113, 114, 121–23, 126, 136–37
Waugh, Arthur (father), 20, 23, 24, 27, 44, 46, 47, 55, 63, 68, 70, 71, 89, 96, 180n. 5; chooses schools, 26, 38, 41–42, 43, 97; in Evelyn's fiction, 76, 97, 162; house in North End, 18, 20, 24, 54; and Oxford, 105–7, 116, 120–21, 126, 131, 133, 137, 138, 140, 141, 174; prefers Alec, 18, 119; as publisher, 19, 25, 28, 35, 116; relations with Evelyn, 18, 19, 25, 28–29, 30, 31, 33–34, 35–37, 40–41, 65–66, 67, 80, 88, 94–95 121, 146
Waugh, Auberon (son), 174
Waugh, Catherine nee Raban (mother), 18, 23, 27, 28, 35, 39, 40, 45, 66, 71, 76, 89, 96, 97–98, 138, 141; and schools, 25, 38, 43, 46, 47
Waugh, Connie (aunt), 20, 39, 82–83

Waugh, Elsie (aunt), 20, 21, 39, 82–83
Waugh, Evelyn: aggression at Oxford, 107, 122; and alcohol, 105–6, 108, 120, 137, 139 141–42; and Alastair Graham, 118, 120, 140, 141, 143–44, 145, 146, 149, 157, 158, 162, 163, 164, 166, 167, 183 n. 28; alienation, 17, 41, 46, 77, 78, 90–91, 134, 139, 154,.176; and aristocracy, 28–29, 40–41, 55, 74, 91, 163, 176, 177, 178; in athletics, 62, 63–64, 79, 123; and aunts' house 17, 20, 21, 23, 30, 33, 39, 42, 46, 103, 141; and authority, 25, 35, 38, 58–60, 61 63–64, 79–83, 86, 90, 92–93, 99–101, 137, 171; as bolshevist, 53, 55, 62–63, 69, 71, 72, 79–80, 81, 82, 90, 93, 126; childhood and later writing, 17, 19, 20, 21, 22, 23, 24 25, 26, 27, 30–31, 33, 35, 37, 40–41, 103–4, 179; clubs at Oxford, 117–18, 123, 124, 125, 126, 129, 130, 138, 141; different selves, 76, 82, 102, 104, 127, 148, 164, 178; distaste for Lancing, 49–50, 60, 61, 90–91, 93, 96, 97, 102; and dons, 109–15 125–30, 135, 152–53, 155, 167–68, 170; dynamics of hope and despair, 22, 178; early interests, 19, 23; and effortless superiority, 90, 172, 173; emphasizes own innocence, 77, 83, 103, 115, 154; enters Lancing College, 43–47; expenses at Oxford, 105–6, 120–21, 136–37; faith, loss of, 69, 70, 85–87, 88–89; family life, 18, 27 29–32, 47; and fictional characters, 76, 113, 124, 133, 134–35, 162, 164–68; and fictional heroes, 74, 77, 98, 99–102, 103–4, 141, 150, 153–55, 156, 157, 158–59, 161–62, 166–69, 177–78; final examinations at Oxford, 110, 112, 126, 138–39, 140 167; during First World War, 33–37, 39, 43, 45–47, 49, 52; forms groups, 31–32, 37–38, 56–57, 93, 117; friendship with Crease, 64, 65–67, 69–70; friendship with Roxburgh, 67–68, 69–70; goes to school, 25–26; and Golders Green, 31–32, 54–55, 107, 108, 126–27, 134; as iconoclast, 56–58, 64, 65, 173; imaginative habits, 94, 95, 97, 103–4; inner conflicts, 12, 48, 101, 102, 178;

Lancing and later writing, 73, 77, 78, 82, 83, 92, 94, 96–103; life and fiction after 1924, 146–70, 176–79; as martyr, 20, 48–49, 89, 104, 157; museums, 21, 37; Oxford's value to, 105–6, 107, 118, 150; and Oxford Union, 105, 106, 115–16, 130–31, 170–71; phase of piety, 39–41, 43, 47–48, 57, 97; as Roman Catholic, 31, 40, 69, 86, 95, 100, 112, 114, 127, 135, 149, 163, 168–69, 173–74, 175, 176–77; as schoolmaster, 96, 130, 143, 146, 149, 166–67, 176, 184 n. 3; self-image of 177–78; sense of importance, 22, 38–39, 41, 86–87, 88, 142–43, 171; sexuality, 71, 92 93–95, 106, 111, 117–20, 122, 124–25, 127, 137, 144–46, 160, 166, 183 n. 22, 184 n. 3; social climbing, 20, 28–29, 74; studies at Oxford, 105–6, 108–10, 115, 118, 132, 138–39; studies for scholarship, 60, 86, 91, 93, 95, 173; and suicide, 89–90, 129, 135, 146, 147–48; and women, 24, 51–52, 118, 144–45, 163; writing and drawing, 23–24, 33, 34, 39, 87, 106, 133, 135, 137; writing in 1920–1921, 57, 64–65, 71–76, 77–78, 82–85, 88–89, 92–93; writing at Oxford, 105, 106, 120, 123, 126–27, 131–36, 138, 139

Waugh, Evelyn. Works: "Antony, Who Sought Things That Were Lost," 133; "*Ars Amoris* for ———," 68–69; "The Balance," 146–50, 153, 155, 157, 161; *Basil Seal Rides Again*, 103, 170; *Black Mischief*, 155–56, 177; *Brideshead Revisited*, 33, 41, 78, 97–98, 99, 101, 102, 157–69, 170, 174, 176–77, 178; "Charles Ryder's Schooldays," 97–102; "Come to the Coach-house Door, Boys," 37; "The Community Spirit," 93; "Conspiracy to Murder," 135; "Convention," 72; *Conversion*, 82–83, 85, 100; "The Curse of the Horse Race," 23, 32; *The Cynic*, 38–39, 51; *Decline and Fall*, 23, 62, 78, 96, 103, 104, 105, 113, 124, 134, 150–55, 157, 159, 166, 167, 169, 170, 176; diaries, 23, 24–25, 28–29, 32, 36, 37, 38, 55–56, 58, 62, 67, 78, 81, 85, 93, 97, 100, 102, 107, 118, 138, 145, 160, 162, 177, 182 n. 21, 184 n. 3; *Edmund Campion*, 173; "Edward of Unique Achievement," 134–35, 153; "An Englishman's Home," 113; "Father and Son," 180 n. 5; "Fidon's Confetion," 23–24, 32, 33, 76; "Fragments," 135; *A Handful of Dust*, 33, 37, 113, 156, 176, 177; "History Previous," 132; "The House: An Anti-climax," 82; "In Defence of Cubism," 50–51; "In Quest of Thomas Lee," 33; "I Suppose That When I Leave," 88–89; juvenilia, 17, 23–25, 28–29, 32–34, 37, 38–39, 41, 103; *Labels*, 113–14, 128, 170; "Lancing Chapel," 64–65, 69; "Legend," 131–32; "A Little Hope," 130; *A Little Learning*, 17, 22, 25, 26, 27, 32, 46, 48, 51, 54, 55, 60, 64, 65, 69, 78, 80, 102–3 108, 109–10, 115, 117, 118, 125, 128, 139, 146, 154, 160, 162, 170, 174–75, 180 n. 5; "Maps," 72; *Men at Arms*, 96, 98; "Mr. Loveday's Little Outing," 113; "Multa Pecunia," 32, 33; "My Father," 162, 180 n. 5; "The National Game," 123; "Ode on the Intimations of Immaturity," 83–85; *Officers and Gentlemen*, 96; *The Ordeal of Gilbert Pinfold*, 169; "Out of Depth," 184 n. 54; parody of Landor, 71; "The Philosopher," 77, 78; "Portrait of Young Man with Career," 132–33; *P.R.B.*, 143; *Put Out More Flags*, 78, 113, 156–57, 164, 177, 178; "Return of Launcelot," 78; *Ronald Knox*, 127–28, 172; *Rossetti*, 128, 155, 170, 176; *The Scarlet Woman*, 126–27, 142; *Scoop*, 156, 177; *Scott-King's Modern Europe*, 96, 169; "The Seven Deadly Sins," 133–34; "The Sheriff's Daughter," 32–33; "The Slaves of Hurre Len," 33; *The Temple at Thatch*, 141, 146; "Told by the Refuggee," 34, 36; "The Twilight of Language," 57; "Unacademic Exercise," 135; *Unconditional Surrender*, 103–4, 169–70; unfinished novel, 73–76, 96; "A University Sermon," 132; *Vile Bodies*, 105, 155, 176; war trilogy (*Sword of Honour*), 41, 76, 77, 98, 101, 104, 169 177

"Was Oxford Worth While?" 105, 156; *When the Going was Good,* 84; "Why Britain is at War," 33; "Winner Takes All," 76; "A Woman's Curse," 33; *Work Suspended,* 35, 156, 162, 169; *The World to Come,* 41, 65; "The Youngest Generation," 93
West Hampstead, 18
Wheatley (character), 98
When the Going was Good, 84
White Rose (club), 124
"Why Britain is at War," 33
Winchester College and Wykehamists, 26, 50, 117
"Winner Takes All," 76
Wodehouse, P. G., 170
"Woman's Curse, A," 33

Wood, Field-Marshal Sir Evelyn, 27
Woodard, Rev. F. A., 58–59, 80, 81–82, 83, 90
Woodard, Nathaniel, 43
Woodruff, Douglas, 171
Worcester College (Oxford), 50
Wordsworth, William, 84
Work Suspended, 35, 156, 162, 169
World to Come, The, 41, 65
"Wuffles" (nickname), 27
Wuffles and Company, 38

"Youngest Generation, The," 93
Yugoslavia, 21

Zeppelins, 35, 36, 37
Zurbaran, Francisco de, 169